HIGHER
EDUCATION SUPPLEMENT

the
effective
academic

a handbook for enhanced academic practice

STEVE KETTERIDGE   STEPHANIE MARSHALL   HEATHER FRY

KOGAN
PAGE

ACKNOWLEDGEMENTS

The editors are deeply indebted to all those who have contributed to this book. We are particularly grateful to authors of chapters, and to those who have provided the personal perspectives and case studies that have further enriched the text.

We wish to record out thanks to Professor Gus Pennington for his enduring interest and invaluable discussions, which helped to firm up our ideas on the development of this book.

Finally we are grateful to Jonathan Simpson at Kogan Page who has advised us throughout writing and publication.

Steve Ketteridge
Stephanie Marshall
Heather Fry

First published 2002

Kogan Page Limited
120 Pentonville Road
London N1 9JN
UK

Stylus Publishing Inc.
22883 Quicksilver Drive
Sterling VA 20166–2012
USA

The views expressed in this book are those of the authors and are not necessarily the same as those of *The Times Higher Education Supplement*.

British Library Cataloguing in Publication Data

A CIP record for this book is available from the British Library

ISBN 0 7494 3570 4

Typeset by YHT Ltd, London
Printed and bound in Great Britain by Biddles Ltd, Guildford and King's Lynn
www.biddles.co.uk

Contents

List of Contributors

THE EDITORS

Steve Ketteridge is Director of Educational and Staff Development at Queen Mary, University of London. He has extensive experience working on the development of academic practice in research-led universities and research councils, gained with academic staff, researchers and graduate students, especially in science, technology and engineering. He has a particular interest in research supervision and management. Previously he was a lecturer in microbiology in the University of London and has taught students across a wide range of disciplines from life sciences to civil engineering. With Heather Fry and Stephanie Marshall, he co-edited the highly successful *A Handbook for Teaching and Learning in Higher Education: Enhancing academic practice*, first published by Kogan Page in 1999.

Stephanie Marshall is Director of Staff Development and Provost of Goodricke College at the University of York. After teaching and managing in secondary schools, she took up a post as a lecturer in educational studies, where she lectured on, primarily, models of teaching and learning and the management of education. She was subsequently seconded to become the university's first part-time adviser in academic staff development. In her present role, she has had extensive experience working on projects firstly to promote and develop academic practice, and secondly (more recently) management development. With Steve Ketteridge and Heather Fry, she edited *A Handbook for Teaching and Learning in Higher Education: Enhancing academic practice*.

Heather Fry is Head of the Imperial College Centre for Educational Development, London. After teaching and lecturing in Nigeria she returned to Britain, subsequently working at the Institute of Education and at St Bartholomew's and the Royal London School of Medicine and Dentistry, also parts of the University of London. She teaches, publishes and researches in a range of areas, notably teaching, learning and assessment, especially in medical and dental education, curriculum change and course design, and policy in higher and professional education. She is joint editor with Steve Ketteridge and Stephanie Marshall of *A Handbook for Teaching and Learning in Higher Education: Enhancing academic practice*.

THE AUTHORS

David Allen is Registrar and Secretary of the University of Birmingham.

Rob Cuthbert is Deputy Vice-Chancellor (Academic Development) at the University of the West of England, Bristol. He has worked as an academic, manager and consultant in universities, colleges and government agencies in the UK, North America, Africa and China, and publishes widely on higher education.

Leela Damodaran is Professor and Head of the Human Sciences and Advanced Technology (HUSAT) Research Institute, Loughborough University. Her expertise, particularly in strategic management of change and of knowledge, is in demand by organizations seeking successful exploitation of emerging technologies.

Martyn Davies is Head of the Pharmacy School (a leading international centre for biomedical research) at the University of Nottingham. His research interests lie in biophysics and surface analysis.

Hugh Davis is a Senior Lecturer in Computer Science at the University of Southampton. He is Director of Learning and Teaching in the Faculty of Engineering and Applied Science. He researches in learning technologies and has been involved in the implementation of communications and information technology since the early 1980s.

Ewan Ferlie is currently Professor of Public Services Management at Imperial College Management School and was previously Deputy Director at the Centre for Corporate Strategy and Change, Warwick Business School.

Anne Gold is a Senior Lecturer in Education Management at the Institute of Education, University of London. She is Head of the Management Development Centre and course leader for an MA on Women and Management in Higher Education. She also works with the Association of Commonwealth Universities in their Management Development for Women in Higher Education programme.

George Gordon is Director of the Centre for Academic Practice, University of Strathclyde. He served as an academic auditor with the Committee of Vice-Chancellors and Principals, and has written widely on matters relating to quality assurance in higher education.

Catherine Haines is Assistant Director of Educational and Staff Development at Queen Mary, University of London. She has wide-ranging experience in the development of academic practice, working with academic staff and graduate students across UK universities and Research Councils.

Janet Harvey was previously Senior Fellow at the Centre for Corporate Strategy and Change, Warwick Business School.

Alan Hurst is Professor of Education at the University of Central Lancashire. A member of Skill: National Bureau for Students with Disabilities, he has worked with the funding councils and the Quality Assurance Agency to develop policy and provision for disabled students.

Tom Kennie is Director of the Ranmore Consulting Group where he specializes in the development of leaders in higher education. He is also a part-time professor at Sheffield Hallam University, and co-directs the Top Management Programme for Higher Education.

Mervyn King is Deputy Governor of the Bank of England, responsible for monetary policy. Prior to this post he was the Bank of England's Chief Economist and Executive Director, further to being Professor at the London School of Economics.

Johanna Laybourn-Parry set up the Institute of Environmental Sciences at the University of Nottingham in 1998, where she is currently Professor of Environmental Biology. Addressing problems facing industrialized societies and the developing world, she has drawn together a wide spectrum of expertise to enhance problem solving and research capabilities.

Robin Middlehurst is Professor and Director of Development in the School of Educational Studies at the University of Surrey. She also leads a research and development group on policy and change in higher education. Within higher education, she has led or participated in major national research projects on leadership in universities, quality and standards in higher education and on the policy implications of developments in 'borderless education'.

Gus Pennington is Chief Executive of the Higher Education Staff Development Agency (HESDA), the UK's National Training Organization for higher education concerned with promoting professional development for all categories of staff. Professor Pennington is a council member of the Institute for Learning and Teaching.

Andrew Pettigrew was the founder and first Director of the Centre for Corporate Strategy and Change, Warwick Business School.

Rob Shorrock was the National Development Officer for the NUS between 1989 and 1997, involved in assisting student unions in organizational development. He was the key author of the *Union Officers Manual*, a definitive text for running student unions.

Brenda Smith is Head of the UK's Learning and Teaching Support Network, Generic Centre. Professor Smith has acted as a consultant and facilitated seminars in many countries across the world.

Stan Taylor is Director of Quality and Standards at Newcastle University, and is responsible for academic staff development. His background is as an academic and then as a staff developer, delivering workshops on various aspects of research supervision.

Keith Trigwell is a Principal Research Fellow at the University of Oxford's Institute for the Advancement of University Learning. From a background in university science teaching, he has developed an international reputation through his studies of qualitative differences in university teaching and learning.

Sir David Watson is an historian, and Director of the University of Brighton. His academic interests are in the history of ideas and in higher education policy, on which he writes extensively. He was a member of the Dearing Committee, is a member of the Higher Education Funding Council's (England) Learning and Teaching Committee, and chairs the Steering Committee for the Economic and Social Research Council's research programme into teaching and learning and the Universities UK's Longer Term Strategy Group. He is one of the five elected council members of the Institute for Learning and Teaching.

Su White is Learning and Teaching Co-ordinator in the Faculty of Engineering and Applied Science at the University of Southampton, and an institutional reviewer for the Quality Assurance Agency. She researches in learning technologies and has been involved in the implementation of communications and information technology since the early 1980s.

Ken Young is Professor of Politics at Queen Mary, University of London, where he was Vice-Principal with responsibility for research from 1992–98. He was Senior Research Fellow at the Policy Studies Institute before moving to a chair at the University of Birmingham in 1987.

INDIVIDUALS WHO HAVE CONTRIBUTED CASE STUDIES AND COMMENTARIES

Liz Allen, National Association of Teachers in Further and Higher Education
David Andrew, University of North London
Claire Barnes, Queen Mary, University of London
Susanne Byrne, Queen Mary, University of London
John Brennan, Centre for Higher Education Research and Information, Open University
Roger Brown, Southampton Institute
Larry Bunt, University of Westminster
Jamie Darwen, Education and Development Adviser, University of Warwick Student Union
Rosemary Deem, Professor of Education, Graduate School of Education, University of Bristol (project director)
John Doidge, University of Leicester
Ellen Goldstein, Associate Director, Center for Teaching and Learning, City College of New York
Pamela Hampshire, Educational Competences Consortium Ltd
Philip Harvey, University of Exeter
Mick Healey, National Teaching Fellow, Cheltenham and Gloucester College of Higher Education
Mary Henkel, Associate Reader, Centre for the Evaluation of Public Policy and Practice, Brunel University
Alan Jenkins, Oxford Brookes University
Peter Mertens, Institute for Animal Health, BBSRC
Sarah Moore, Student Member of the Philosophy SSLC, University of Warwick
Marie Morehen, University of Nottingham
Maggie Nicol, National Teaching Fellow, St Bartholomew School of Nursing and Midwifery, City University, London
Robert Partridge, Director, York Award, University of York
Steve Pashley, Leeds Metropolitan University
John Ratcliffe, Director of the Faculty of the Built Environment, Dublin Institute of Technology
Vicki Roth, Assistant Dean, University of Rochester, New York
Anne Sibbald, Senior Adviser, Higher Education Staff Development Agency
Andrew Snowden, University of Wolverhampton
Chris Ward, Ranmore Consulting

List of Abbreviations and Acronyms

ACAS	Advisory, Conciliation and Arbitration Service
AUT	Association of University Teachers
BBSRC	Biotechnology and Biological Sciences Research Council
BSL	British Sign Language
CPD	continuing professional development
CVCP	Committee of Vice-Chancellors and Principals, now UUK
DfEE	Department for Education and Employment, since June 2001 Department for Education and Skills
DfES	Department for Education and Skills, prior to June 2001 DfEE
DSA	Disabled Student Allowance
EFQM	European Foundation for Quality Management
ESRC	Economic and Social Research Council
GCE	General Certificate of Education
GLTC	Generic Learning and Teaching Centre
GMB	General and municipal workers union
GMC	General Medical Council
HE	higher education
HEFCE	Higher Education Funding Council for England
HEQC	Higher Education Quality Council, now defunct
HERA	Higher Education Role Analysis
HESA	Higher Education Statistics Agency
HESDA	Higher Education Staff Development Agency (the NTO for Higher Education), previously known as UCoSDA, Universities' and Colleges' Staff Development Agency
HR	human resources
HRD	human resource development
HRM	human resources manager
IiP	Investors in People
ILT	Institute for Learning and Teaching
IPD	Institute of Personnel and Development
LTSN	Learning and Teaching Support Network
NATFHE	National Association of Teachers in Further and Higher Education
NDT	National Disability Team
NHS	National Health Service
NSF	National Science Foundation

NTO	National Training Organization
NUS	National Union of Students
PBL	problem-based learning
PI	performance indicator
PLTL	peer-led team learning
PRP	performance-related pay
QAA	Quality Assurance Agency (for higher education)
RAE	Research Assessment Exercise
R&D	research and development
SHEFC	Scottish Higher Education Funding Council
SMART	specific, measurable, action oriented, resources, time
SRHE	Society for Research into Higher Education
SSLC	staff–student liaison committee
STAIR	simplistic, tactical, active resistance, impractical, risk
STEPE	social, technological, economic, political and environmental
SWOT	strengths, weaknesses, opportunities and threats
TAPPS	Training and Accreditation Programme for Postgraduate Supervisors
TQEF	Teaching Quality Enhancement Fund
TQM	total quality management
UCAS	Universities and Colleges Admissions Service
UCEA	Universities and Colleges Employers Association
UUK	Universities UK, until 30 November 2000 CVCP, Committee of Vice-Chancellors and Principals

Introduction

Steve Ketteridge, Stephanie Marshall and Heather Fry

What makes three academics, some might say ex-academics, decide to write and edit a book such as this? Some might suggest it was for the royalties, for the pleasure of working together, for the intellectual challenge, or to advance our own careers. All these suggestions have elements of the ludicrous as well as the truth, but the overriding motivation was a perception that there was an interesting area that is little written about, or at least not in a satisfactory manner, and which as a consequence left many academics short-changed. We thought there were interesting things to be said in new ways, and by different people. This feeling was reinforced by the perception that some of the directions of change in higher education which had taken place in late 20th century Britain were being consolidated (for example, expansion of higher education), and consequent changes were under way which higher education would need to address. We have in mind matters such as increasing direction of policy by means of earmarked government funding, the increasing 'market' in intellectual property and the impact of new technologies.

The idea that academics might wish, or at least feel the need, to engage in planned development and consideration of their various roles is a relatively new one, but it is an idea espoused by this book and increasingly by the higher education community as a whole.

POTENTIAL READERSHIP

The Effective Academic is written with the early to mid-career academic in mind. It considers selected aspects of academic life and work from the perspective of those with, or aspiring to, leadership and management responsibilities, perhaps of a course team or large research project, a head of group, leader of departmental teaching or research, an aspiring head of department, or those who have greatness thrust upon them. For this reason it does not include mention of, for example, the basics of teaching or getting published, or the rudiments of applying for research grants. The former are considered in the highly successful *A Handbook for Teaching and Learning*:

Enhancing academic practice, by the same editors (Fry, Ketteridge and Marshall, 1999). *The Effective Academic* broadens the agenda from the specific learning and teaching perspective of our earlier book.

The main frame of reference is the UK, especially England, Wales and Northern Ireland, but some aspects of effective academic practice are readily transferable, and need to be so, in an increasingly global and mobile world. The book may also be of interest to members of academic staff from outside the UK, or those entering academe from industry or public service, whatever their level, who wish to acquaint themselves with elements of higher education in the UK in the 21st century.

The subtitle of the book, *A handbook for enhanced academic practice*, indicates its thrust. The focus is on the practical, on 'what might I need to consider and know to do this part of my job, and how might I do it better', rather than abstract or philosophical. Nonetheless the authors, largely being academics themselves and bearing in mind the audience they are writing for, have attempted to avoid prescription while creating a practitioner-friendly approach. The emphasis on the practical is tempered by appropriate reference to the research base and theory where they are available and appropriate, and occasionally by the speculative. Established best practice is also offered. The book attempts to include in a short compass five areas of academic activity, each of which is a field of study in its own right. Any shortcomings it might suffer on this account are entirely the responsibility of the editors. The subject matter is selective and directed rather than all-encompassing and discursive.

DISTINCTIVE FEATURES

The authors of each chapter are experts, often writing about their chosen area of research and/or work, and endeavouring to work through and lay bare its implications for effective practice. The book draws on expertise from many parts of higher education and from many different perspectives and disciplines, with some 50 contributors. It makes use of personal perspectives, case studies and expert views to enrich the overall mix.

The chapters can be read in any order, according to interest or need. Each section is introduced by the editors and by one or more 'personal perspectives' which give personal insight into the subject matter of the chapter. The expert views and case studies which seek to exemplify one or more themes of each chapter add interest. Most chapters also feature 'enhancing practice'. The purpose of this feature is to assist readers to develop understanding of the subject matter in the context of their own work environment; it is also hoped the feature will help readers to engage fully with the topic, to obviate the risk of mere superficial processing of information.

SCOPE

The Effective Academic is divided into five parts. 'The turbulent environment' considers three essential elements of the context within which UK higher education is located, namely the international environment for higher education, the national policy context and its impact on institutions, and the student perspective on these arenas. The editors believe that UK higher education will increasingly have to take a strategic approach to all it does, and that understanding the policy context is key. 'Running the business' reflects another fact of academic life and survival: amateur administration and management will no longer suffice, nor will neglect of people and their satisfaction and development (whether considered from the perspective of personal survival of the 'manager' or that of the department or institution). Hence the three chapters of this part focus on planning and people management. 'Creating intellectual wealth' tackles elements in leading, managing and growing the research function of universities, including the process of research supervision, support for research staff, and engendering a strategic approach to research development. 'At the digital chalk-face' concerns teaching and learning, and is predicated on the shift in emphasis from the former to the latter which has occurred. The selective approach highlights issues for those taking on the management of courses and teaching, including matters relating to curriculum design, introducing more information technology into learning and teaching, learning from the British quality assurance experience and teaching students with disabilities. The final section, 'The harsh reality', steps back to consider how individual academics might attempt, in an increasingly intensive and demanding world, to control and direct their own careers and development.

REFERENCES

Fry, H, Ketteridge, S and Marshall, S (1999) *A Handbook for Teaching and Learning: Enhancing academic practice*, Kogan Page, London

Part 1
The Turbulent
Environment

Introduction

The Editors with David Watson

This part of the book sets out some of the wider perspectives within which academics carry out their work and conduct their careers. It concerns itself with matters beyond the lecture theatre, library or lab bench. It focuses on international and national higher education policy and contexts, and the student perspective on higher education. The section forms a backdrop to subsequent sections, insofar as these broad contexts influence and impinge upon the work of academics in higher education.

In Chapter 1 Robin Middlehurst introduces global and international trends and developments in higher education and considers their impact within the United Kingdom. Her chapter is followed by Rob Cuthbert's, which sets out the main elements of contemporary higher education policy in England.

Chapter 3, by Rob Shorrock, traces the development of student union services and presents a student perspective on contemporary higher education in the United Kingdom. All these authors point to the implications of policy and the student perspective for the practising academic: as manager, researcher and teacher working in a turbulent environment.

Sir David Watson, Director of the University of Brighton, draws upon his disciplinary background in history from the perspective of over a quarter of a century spent in higher education to open the section, by indicating how he makes sense of change in higher education, of the turbulent environment.

Reinventing the University – A Personal Perspective
by David Watson

The premise of this introductory essay is that universities have constantly invented and reinvented themselves. Change is, to a large extent, the status quo of university life; only the pace of change may have varied during the long history of universities as institutions and as communities.

As a teacher in higher education over the past quarter of a century, as a commentator on higher education, and most recently as the head of an institution, I have developed ways of thinking about and analysing contemporary higher education which derive from both observation and practical experience. My primary perspective comes from my disciplinary training and academic practice, and is historical. As a university manager, however, I also have to consider strategic questions such as how an institution places and markets itself against a range of opportunities and threats. In this personal contribution I offer a summary of these two approaches, hoping that they will prove useful for others wishing to make sense of the contemporary higher education context, of their own place within it, and of the wider context for their work.

It has been one of the real strengths of the university system over the centuries that it has proved capable of periodically reinventing itself, as well as of managing the necessary balance between continuity and change. Each phase of reinvention has carried forward some elements of the previous regime into a new and changed context. There are various dimensions of this process.

Patterns of *participation* have changed. Thus, for example, the late medieval university produced rhetoricians and mathematicians, the early modern university served theologians and natural scientists, the 19th century university trained civil servants, and the modern university supports a range of professionals from engineers to teachers and health workers. The *technological environment* has changed. Thus, for example, the march of modern science and that of the university have gone almost hand in hand. Both have experienced rapid expansion, with no clear end in sight and, partly as a consequence, both have struggled to maintain what they regard as appropriate levels of resource. *Social expectations* have changed. Thus, for example, universities have been successively refuges for the poor and devout, finishing schools for the elite, and engine-rooms of modern technocracy and democracy. In this latter process, as state investment has increased, so too has the political anticipation of policy-related returns.

Universities have always wanted to be somewhat apart from the worlds of social, economic and technical life, and to maintain both a critical and a disinterested standpoint. Such a Faustian bargain with the state is reflected in the UK by the so-called 'Dearing compact', emerging from the National Committee of Inquiry into Higher Education (NCIHE, 1997: 283). In summary, it represents an ideal whereby institutions retain their independence and gain increased security in return for clearer accountability and greater responsiveness to a wide range of legitimate stakeholders (Watson and Taylor, 1998). The ideal has, of course, always had its internal critics.

There are epistemological as well as policy currents at play here. For other critics, 20th century developments in particular meant the steady erosion of a Newmanesque vision of the university as the repository of liberal, non-technical knowledge. For some, the decline has been almost apocalyptic in its effect.

Advocates of a new, a fashionable, or simply a timely preoccupation (like knowledge management or investing in people) can claim that institutions should turn themselves upside down to accommodate the compact as they view it. Proponents of the status quo counter that this is just another way of describing what they have always been doing anyway. Steering the pragmatic and the progressive middle course is always a challenge.

Table 1.0.1   Inventing the university

A   Domains of activity
A1 Teaching and professional formation
A2 Research and scholarship
A3 Service to business and the community
B   Student outcomes
B1 Employability
B2 Further study
B3 Modern citizenship
C   Patterns of influence
C1 Subjects and disciplines
C2 Level and purpose
C3 Sponsors and stakeholders
D   Reputational positioning
D1 Promotion and marketing
D2 Local, regional, national and international scales
D3 Competition, collaboration and complementarity
E   Resources
E1 Core funding
E2 Competitive funding
E3 Contracts
F   Cultures
F1 Institutional history
F2 Decision making
F3 Loyalty and identification

Note: earlier versions of this analysis were discussed at the Organization of Economic Cooperation and Development Forum on Knowledge Management (Ottawa, September 2000) and the University of Brighton EdD Distinguished Lecture Series (Brighton, December 2000). The author is grateful to participants on both occasions for their comments and advice.

Optimizing the performance of the college or university requires overcoming such tensions by the overlay of a shared sense of institutional purpose and progress, just as major corporations are increasingly sensitive to the positive or negative effects of their internal culture and dynamics.

In Table 1.0.1, I offer some conceptual and practical options for describing such strategic choices. In the framework in the Table, dimension A is about how the institution balances its activity across its core functions. Contemporary discussions centre intensively on the research–teaching–service axis (the notion of the teaching-only university has gone out of fashion) and on the extent to which the modern university can tap (or can afford to forgo) the market for professional services other than teaching and research.

Dimension B is about what happens to students as the prime (but, of course, not the exclusive) clients of the university. As higher education systems expand, the instrumental concerns about both the personal and social rates of return on investment achieve greater prominence. 'Employability' is a politically acceptable shorthand here, but in a world of lifelong learning, professional and personal career progress may soon become at least as important. Simultaneously, the university has a role in producing the scholars and the scientists of the future, and hence in reproducing itself. Meanwhile, we should be thinking hard about the implications for civil society of a participation rate which in due course will regularly see between a third and a half of the young population (towards the top of the class and occupational hierarchy) having been exposed to higher education.

Dimension C is chiefly about extrinsic influences. The culture and dynamics of subject disciplines impose their own constraints. (In some disciplines, like for example the humanities, the teaching and research agenda are inextricably entwined; in others, like the natural sciences, they can be more easily separated.) Level and purpose will also, for example, differentiate the university structured around professional formation from that with more exclusively scholarly commitments. Meanwhile the external sponsors and stakeholders (that is, those who regard themselves as the prime paymasters) have an increasingly formal (and legitimated) role in both the curricular conversation and the research agenda.

Dimension D is about institutional ambition and image. The focus on distinctive selling points of individual institutions leads into questions about which contributions they see as geared to which geographical spheres (from the local to the global environment). This can lead to some peculiar distortions (like the exclusive association of excellence in the UK research assessment exercise (RAE) with international impact). The '3 Cs' in D3 point to another set of dilemmas, concerned with the dynamics of partnership. Potential errors here include an approach to collaboration solely designed to maximize perceived institutional advantage or to overcome perceived institutional weakness. Issues of sector organization (including stratification by level or function) are also relevant.

Dimension E is about who pays for what (and how, and for what in return). The balance between these elements raises questions about institutional autonomy (as in freedom to make strategic decisions), about isomorphic behaviour (as large-scale purchasers like governments and national agencies pursue their own policy goals through higher education), and about cross-subsidy (the UK system has, for example, been in the throes of a large-scale transparency review designed to establish the extent to which public funding has been applied for the purposes intended). Among the key sources of management controversy in higher education institutions are contractual terms and overheads of various kinds.

Finally, Dimension F is where most of these issues come together. In seeking to rationalize and improve the processes of institutional management there are some unavoidable influences which can operate for good or ill. Institutions cannot escape their history, nor in the vast majority of cases would they wish to do so. Given this history, most vital decisions are made through influential proposition by individuals or groups followed by the securing of at least partial consensus. As a result, and as I have tried to argue elsewhere, the best higher education leadership is often by stealth (Watson, 2000: 94–98).

Each of the lines in Table 1.0.1 can be opened out into an array of possibilities. From such arrays individual universities make choices, explicitly and implicitly, about their own pattern of activities and ambitions. Market and other pressures (notably state-supported expansion of higher education, which is now a global phenomenon) drive both whole systems and individual institutions into making such choices more disciplined and explicit. Departments and individuals within institutions can understand much about institutional behaviour by examining these dimensions.

REFERENCES

National Committee of Inquiry into Higher Education (NCIHE) (1997) *Higher Education in the Learning Society* (*Dearing Report*), HMSO, London

Watson, D and Taylor, R (1998) *Lifelong Learning and the University: A post-Dearing agenda*, Falmer, London

Watson, D (2000) *Managing Strategy*, Society for Research into Higher Education/Open University Press, Buckingham

1	# The International Context for UK Higher Education

Robin Middlehurst

INTRODUCTION

Universities and colleges have been international institutions for hundreds of years. In recent times, as more universities have been created in the UK, greater differentiation of mission is occurring. This means that some institutions are focusing predominantly on local and regional markets and others on international or global markets. However, all universities and colleges need to take account of international developments since many of these developments will have a direct or indirect impact on national policies and institutional practice. This chapter concentrates on this international context, illustrating, wherever relevant, the actual or potential impact of developments on the UK higher education sector as a whole or on particular types of institution. It draws on a variety of international research.

The chapter is organized into sections that cover:

- internationalization and globalization;
- European and wider international policy themes and trends in higher education;
- 'borderless education' and international markets.

INTERNATIONALIZATION AND GLOBALIZATION

Internationalization

Universities around the world share a number of common features that give them a particular role in society. This role is recognizable internationally.

Universities are public or private 'institutions of learning' with missions that embrace both education for life and work, and knowledge creation, preservation and dissemination for the economic, social and cultural benefit of society. Within this institutional role, many universities carry out a range of activities that are specifically international. These include teaching (importing students to the UK or exporting programmes overseas), research (engaging in international research collaborations or undertaking research that is peer-referenced internationally), knowledge sharing (international conferences and networks) and cultural exchanges. In professional areas, standards of practice may be set internationally, and in an era of multinational projects and companies, universities play a key part in ensuring the mobility of professionals across national boundaries.

While the international role and the international activities of universities are not new, a more recent concept is the internationalization of universities. 'Internationalization' involves developing an international focus for many, if not all, university activities so that the curriculum for all subjects includes international dimensions, the student experience includes international opportunities, research is recognizably international and the wider public service role of the university involves international outreach. Jane Knight (1999: 15) has captured the variety of approaches to internationalization that she has observed across institutions:

- The activity approach: involves student/faculty exchanges, technical assistance, international students or collaborative programmes.
- The competency approach: development of new skills, knowledge, attitudes and values in students and staff. This includes curriculum development and learning outcomes which might be described as 'international competences'.
- The ethos approach: emphasizing the creation of a climate in which international and intercultural values and initiatives are fostered.
- The process approach: integrating international or intercultural dimensions into teaching, research and public service through a combination of activities, policies and procedures.

Enhancing Practice

- What approach to 'internationalization' is most prevalent in your institution?
- In what ways might you enhance the educational experience of students and the quality of your academic activities through an approach to internationalization at the unit level (ie department, programme or project levels)?

In many respects, Knight's four approaches above capture different stages in the evolution towards a distinctively 'international' university.

Globalization

The differences between globalization and internationalization are subtle and there is considerable overlap between the two terms. The historical roots of internationalization lie largely in political, social and cultural domains: international education, for example, has often been seen by governments as a useful foreign policy tool, ensuring peace and security among nations through cross-cultural communication and understanding. Globalization, on the other hand, is more closely associated with modern economic and technological trends. Knight defines globalization in a higher education context as 'the flow of technology, economy, knowledge, people, values, ideas... across borders. Globalization affects each country in a different way due to a nation's individual history, traditions, culture and priorities' (1999: 14).

Peter Scott (1998: 122) offers a wider perspective on globalization, beyond the purely economic. He points to the impact of global environmental changes, the threat of social and political conflicts and the growth of hybrid world cultures created by the mingling of global-brand culture and indigenous traditions (what some describe as the spread of the 'McDonald's' culture). Both definitions highlight an important feature of globalization: that of 'worldwide interconnectedness' leading to particular kinds of impact. It is largely because of this feature that globalization is significant for all higher education institutions, whether they see themselves predominantly as local and regional in focus or as international and global. The 'free flows' of technology, finance, ideas, as well as conflicts and environmental change across nations and continents mean that globalization affects everyone. However, the precise impact of globalization will vary, as Knight suggests. It is for each institution or academic unit as much as for each country to identify how it will respond to the opportunities and threats posed by globalization.

One of the most insightful definitions of globalization is provided by two Dutch researchers, writing for the OECD (Lubbers and Koorevaar, 2000). In their definition they capture both the objective and the subjective aspects of this phenomenon as well as its dynamic:

> Globalization is a process in which geographic distance becomes a factor of diminishing importance in the establishment and maintenance of cross-border economic, political and socio-cultural relations. This process reaches such intensity that relations change fundamentally, and people become aware of that change. The potential internationalization of relations and dependencies creates opportunities, but also causes fear, resistance, actions and reactions.

(Lubbers and Koorevaar, 2000: 173)

At a practical level, there are several ways in which globalization can have an impact on academic life. Some issues and trends to watch out for include:

- moves towards more standardized (or internationally acceptable) curricula and modes of delivery;
- calls for greater coordination and harmonization of regulatory procedures across countries to facilitate the transfer of credit and qualifications and to ensure comparable quality in educational outcomes;
- the development of global 'brands' in higher education (some are already well-developed, for example Oxford, Cambridge, Harvard and Yale, but new consortia of institutions, such as Universitas 21, a consortium of 18 research-intensive universities, are also emerging);
- the opportunities and threats of cultural imperialism in terms of the export of Western curricula in the English language: the dangers are potentially acute in Africa and parts of Central and Eastern Europe;
- opportunities for the development of new skills (international competences) and the refinement, through continuing professional development, of existing ones (IT training, professional updating);
- opportunities to change existing educational paradigms in terms of the structure of programmes and curricula, the media used for teaching and learning, and the quality and range of the educational experience for students; globalization of e-learning presents one such opportunity.

The potential impact of globalization on academic practice can perhaps be summed up in terms of a dilemma: will the direction of change be towards greater cultural homogeneity or continuing (and greater) diversity in higher education? Several factors suggest a trend towards homogeneity of provision, offered by a smaller number of international providers. Factors include the strength of the English language and of Western economies, the search for mass markets and economies of scale in the delivery of education (particularly distance or virtual education) and economic competition between countries for trade in goods and services. However, there are also pointers towards greater diversity. Individuals and companies are seeking customized educational opportunities, different countries offer the potential for niche markets in particular fields, and technological connections provide the potential for educational content tailored to cultural preferences and political sensitivities. For the moment, institutions and academic units would be wise to back both horses. However, in due course technology will offer possibilities for 'mass customization', enabling universities and colleges to provide individualized learning opportunities for mass markets.

> ### Enhancing Practice
>
> - What threats and opportunities can you identify for your academic practice from globalization?
> - How might you prepare your academic unit/institution for the impact of globalization? Consider three practical steps that you might implement in the forthcoming year.

EUROPEAN AND WIDER INTERNATIONAL POLICY THEMES AND TRENDS IN HIGHER EDUCATION

In this section, a number of policy themes and general trends will be explored. As background to this discussion, it is worth thinking about international policy themes in relation to a number of different geographical groupings of countries. These groupings exert particular influence on institutional and academic practice in the UK for a variety of historical and economic reasons. The most obvious groupings are:

- the European Union and the wider European continent;
- Western industrialized competitors: the United States, Canada, Australia and New Zealand, countries which operate in an economic and technological context that has much in common with the UK;
- the Commonwealth countries, with whom the UK has many social, political and economic ties;
- other parts of the world (such as the Middle East or South America) where the UK, and particular institutions in the UK, have both historical and recent connections, but which are more distant from the UK in terms of common policy themes affecting higher education systems.

This list refers particularly to the areas of the world where policy themes exert influence or have much in common with policy directions in the UK. It should not be confused with the list of countries that the then Department for Education and Employment (DfEE) and Department of Trade and Industry (DTI) in the UK designated 'priority countries' for British educational exports. The countries on the DfEE/DTI list (from 1998) include China, Malaysia, Singapore, Hong Kong, Japan, India, Brazil and Russia. Some of these countries overlap with those with whom the English Funding Council (HEFCE) is building collaborative relationships (China, Brazil, South Africa, India, United States, Japan, Thailand, Indonesia, France and Ireland). Institutions and academic units would be wise to take note of both lists. These countries will benefit from increased British Council marketing (with a larger marketing budget over the next few years), thus enabling universities and colleges to get help to launch programmes overseas, draw international students to the UK or build international collaborative ventures.

The international policy themes that are explored in this section include knowledge-based economies, lifelong learning and social cohesion; mobility and transnational education; regionalism; and the commercialization of universities. These themes are not exhaustive, but they present a flavour of current policies. There is often considerable overlap between the themes, both conceptually and operationally, and also some potential conflicts.

Knowledge-based economies, lifelong learning and social cohesion

Knowledge-based economies

As we settle into the 21st century, there are few economies around the world that are not promoting the idea that knowledge or 'intellectual capital' is a key driver of economic and social development. The concept of a knowledge-based or knowledge-driven economy has emerged in parallel with technological advances in a number of areas, for example in information and communications technologies, brain technologies and robotics, and biotechnologies. In Europe, in the UK's competitor countries and in other industrialized nations, the particular impact of the communications and information revolution has highlighted the importance of knowledge, skill and the ability to learn. The consequences of this emphasis for higher (and further) education are already significant: both national governments and European-level institutions are increasingly viewing tertiary education sectors and institutions as instruments for the delivery of public policy. (See Chapter 2.) For the historically autonomous universities in the UK, this emphasis is perhaps felt even more strongly than by many of the state-supported continental universities.

The UK's Department of Trade and Industry sets out the vision and the challenges of a knowledge-based economy in a white paper (DTI, 1998). The foreword by the Labour prime minister, Tony Blair, expresses the context and policy direction quite clearly:

> The modern world is swept by change. New technologies emerge constantly, new markets are opening up. There are new competitors but also great new opportunities. Our success depends on how well we exploit our most valuable assets: our knowledge, skills and creativity. These are the key to designing high-value goods and services and advanced business practices. They are at the heart of a modern, knowledge driven economy... We must invest in British capabilities... in education, in science and in the creation of a culture of enterprise.

> *(DTI, 1998: 5)*

The policy directions outlined in the DTI's white paper are clearly visible in other international contexts, as can be seen from examining recent OECD publications (OECD, 1996 and 2000, for example).

Lifelong learning and social cohesion

Closely connected to the idea of knowledge-based economies driven by technological change and global competition is the concept of learning as 'lifelong'. Seen from this perspective, lifelong learning is necessary because knowledge changes fast and individuals therefore constantly need to update their knowledge and skills. However, viewed from a different perspective, the need to continue learning throughout life is desirable for individual fulfilment, the enhancement of life chances and as an aspect of healthy and constructive citizenship, enabling people to keep up with a changing world and to live a full, long and creative life.

As a policy theme, both aspects of lifelong learning are visible, often linked to visions of a 'learning society' in which higher education plays an important role. Lifelong learning as an aspect of 'upskilling' for economic prosperity has been described as 'the skill growth model' of a learning society in contrast to 'the personal development model' that emphasizes self-fulfilment (Rees and Bartlett, 1999). Recent national reports on higher education in several countries have adopted the theme of a learning society, for example the UK's National Committee of Inquiry report, *Higher Education in the Learning Society* (NCIHE, 1997); the Australian report of the West Committee, *Learning for Life*: *Review of higher education financing and policy* (DEETYA, 1998), and the white paper of the European Union, Education and Training, *Teaching and Learning*: *Towards the learning society* (European Commission, 1995). In the UK, the notion of what a learning society might mean in practice has also been examined in a major Economic and Social Research Council (ESRC) research programme. This programme has added considerably to our knowledge of how (across Europe, in particular) the idea of lifelong learning in a learning society is being enacted. The final products of the research provide valuable insights for institutions, academics and policy makers. (See, for example, the two volumes of research findings on *Differing Visions of a Learning Society* (Coffield, 2000).

A further dimension of the 'personal development model' of individual fulfilment and active citizenship highlights lifelong learning as an instrument for achieving social cohesion. A major concern in industrialized countries is the still-widening gap between rich and poor at home (as well as in the developing world). Castells has produced extensive evidence to show how new forms of capitalism are creating 'a sharp divide between valuable and non-valuable people and locales' (1998: 161). He paints a bleak picture of a 'fundamental split In societies all over the world: on the one hand, active, culturally self-defined elites... on the other hand, increasingly uncertain, insecure social groups, deprived of information, resources and power, digging their trenches of resistance' (1998: 340). With the expansion in usage of information and communication technologies (ICT), the potential for creating a 'digital divide' between those who have access to such technologies and those who do not is also an important policy concern.

Enhancing Practice

The public, social and economic role of universities is a major policy theme. As a reflective practitioner you might consider:

- how your institution is engaging with these policy themes;
- what educational services, in the broadest sense, your academic unit might offer to meet (or challenge) these policy themes;
- what kind of partnerships you might need to establish/develop further in order to make a contribution to these policy themes.

Mobility: professionals, academics and students and transnational education

The idea of the European Community (EC) involves an open area for trade in goods and services and a common framework for development in many social and political fields. As part of the economic dimension, trade requires the mobility of professionals across national boundaries. While the EC has no powers to force convergence of educational systems, curricula or programmes, education and training clearly have a key part to play in facilitating the mobility of professionals. As a result, mobility issues and regulations have a wash-back effect on educational policy, particularly, for example, in the field of credit transfer (see also Chapter 2) and mutual recognition of qualifications. Several European countries have moved towards a common European Credit Transfer System (ECTS), particularly to facilitate student study abroad.

ECTS is built around 'learning agreements' between home and host institutions and standardized numbers of study points (eg one year of full-time study is given 60 study points). A transcript record lists courses and study results for a mobile student and a 'conversion table of national grading scales' has been developed to allow for a foreign evaluation of a student on specific courses to be translated into the usual grading system of the home university.

Other European mechanisms also facilitate mobility and exchanges. The European National Information Centre (ENIC) linked to National Academic

Recognition Information Centres (NARICs) offers advice on the recognition of foreign diplomas and degrees. A variety of national and EU level formalities including declarations, conventions and agreements about 'mutual recognition' of qualifications underpins this advice. In future, these centres and their electronic databases may develop a more significant role in relation to credit recognition. An important instrument for this purpose will be the 'diploma supplement' (jointly developed by the European Commission, Council of Europe and UNESCO/CEPES) which will provide a standardized format for describing the type, level, content and status of a given award.

The European Union has established a range of initiatives in education and training, distance learning and research that serve to assist mobility and to develop networks and links to enhance the 'European dimension' in learning, skills development and knowledge creation. These initiatives offer useful sources of income for developmental activities (although with clear strings attached) and opportunities for international collaboration for institutions and academic units.

Under the banner of 'Growth, Competitiveness, Employment: The challenges and ways forward into the 21st Century' (1993), the EU portfolio of initiatives includes SOCRATES (education programmes); LEONARDO (training); PROMETEUS (multimedia access to education and training); ATLAS (education and multimedia); and GRUNDTVIG (transnational education). The TEMPUS-PHARE portfolio is specifically geared to Central and Eastern Europe in the same domains as those above. In parallel, research initiatives are centred on the Fourth (1994–98) and Fifth (1998–2002) Framework Programmes, with a Sixth under negotiation and development. Access and mobility, skills updating, new methods of working and learning, multimedia technology, tools and infrastructure, links between higher education and industry, and systems and services for the citizen are all part of the focus of these initiatives.

Sometimes stimulated by these initiatives, sometimes independent of them, a variety of transnational educational arrangements has emerged. A research project for the European Commission (2000–01) has attempted to create a typology of patterns of transnational education. These include:

- franchised education (institutions and/or programmes);
- virtual universities (online learning);
- distance learning;
- branch campus operations;
- international corporate education/training;
- for-profit education providers;
- international consortia;
- joint degrees;

- dual (or multiple) awards;
- twinning and articulation arrangements.

Each of these arrangements has important quality assurance implications of which institutions and academic units need to be aware. The UK's Quality Assurance Agency (QAA) provides useful sources of initial guidance in their *Guidelines on the Quality Assurance of Distance Learning*, March 1999 (QAA, 1999a) and their *Code of Practice for the Assurance of Academic Quality and Standards in Higher Education: Section 2: Collaborative provision*, July 1999 (QAA, 1999b). Both of these guidance documents will be updated regularly with reference to the UK context; however, it is also worth looking out for guidance documents that may be produced at a European level by the European Network of Quality Assurance Agencies (ENQAA) or the International Network of Quality Assurance Agencies in Higher Education (INQAAHE).

An enhanced European dimension in quality assurance is consistent with the general policy direction indicated in the Sorbonne (1998) and Bologna (1999) Declarations. These two ministerial agreements propose a common qualification structure in Europe, based on a sub-degree level (of one to two years of ECTS credits); a first degree level (three to four years of credits); a Master's degree level (five years, including at least one year of Master's level credits); and doctoral level (variable, but equivalent to seven to eight years' credits). This structure is similar enough to the qualification structure in the UK to not pose insurmountable problems for this country. In other countries, significant change is needed to conform to this structure, but movement in these directions is already happening. The consequences of convergence will mean the potential for both greater collaboration and greater competition on a global scale.

Regionalism

A further policy driver in Europe is the emphasis on regional development and growth. Universities have been encouraged to play a full part in such development, through stimulating research, enterprise, skills development and economic and social regeneration (Goddard and Chatterton, 1999; Davies, 1998). The recent Confederation of European Rectors (CRE) project, *The Dialogue of Universities with their Stakeholders: Comparisons between different regions of Europe* (Davies, 1998), demarcates three categories of European region – peripheral regions, regions of economic renewal, regions of high economic concentration – and assesses the role of universities in regional development. Inter-institutional cooperation is often a key mechanism for achieving such development and a number of regional consortia have developed in different parts of Europe, for example the Umea Regional Group in the north of Sweden. Other examples include the Oresund Science Region between Malmo in Sweden and Copenhagen in Denmark which links universities, local government and companies in four industry sectors, and the University of the Arctic which links universities from North America, Russia and Scandinavia.

In the UK, the impact of regional policies can be seen clearly. It is evident in the newly devolved administrations (in Scotland and Wales) and in the creation of regional development agencies, in economic regeneration initiatives and in the regional dimensions of the newly formed learning and skills councils. Universities and colleges are helping to shape regional agendas in a number of ways, and it is likely that regionalism will continue to be a strong driver of institutional development.

Enhancing Practice

- What kinds of regional initiatives is your university/college promoting?
- How might your academic unit develop or enhance regional partnerships?

Commercialization of higher education

A policy theme that is strong in the UK, Australia and Canada – and that has been evident for much longer in the United States (see Davies, 1987, for a discussion of 'entrepreneurial universities') – is that of 'commercialization' of higher education. On the research side, this theme is manifested under the banners of technology transfer and links between higher education and business. More recently, as the unit of resource for universities provided by the state has declined, the emphasis on entrepreneurial activity and the generating of income from non-state sources has extended to a wider range of university activities, including teaching and learning. Higher education has been urged to become more businesslike in its management processes and to act more like a business in key areas, for example in the marketing of postgraduate programmes, continuing professional development or conference arrangements. In these commercial aspects, UK universities have more in common with their North American and Australian counterparts than with their continental European sisters, although the advent of 'e-learning' and the widespread squeeze on the public resources available to higher education in Europe may change this picture.

Higher education in the UK has for some time been encouraged to be 'entrepreneurial'. (The DfEE's Enterprise in Higher Education (EHE) Initiative in the early 1990s illustrates this well.) More recently, Burton Clark undertook a valuable analysis of entrepreneurialism in a sample of European universities, producing a useful set of case studies of how five European universities have been successful in creating a culture of enterprise across the institution (Clark, 1998). Current trends in higher education appear, however, to be going further than the creation of a culture of enterprise. There seems to be widespread movement towards the commercialization of higher education, where the language and modes of thinking are those of business and the market. For some universities, the discussion includes changing their status from public to private institutions, or as some would argue, recapturing the independence which was originally granted by charters and statutes. The pressures for movement come partly from inside the sector and partly from outside. Within the sector, the drivers include:

- less dependence on state funding, prompting a search for diversified income sources (see also Chapter 2);
- exploitation of commercial opportunities (eg residences, catering, IPR, continuing education);
- adoption of business methodologies in many parts of university operations (see Chapter 4);
- creation of spin-off companies of various kinds, many linked to science parks.

Outside higher education, the interacting forces of globalization, developments in technology and the growth of knowledge-based economies have made 'education and training' a major business sector in the West. Estimates of the size of the sector vary greatly, and a number of analysts such as Merrill Lynch in the United States and Capital Strategies in the UK track developments in this market. Cunningham *et al* (2000) in their study of *The Business of Borderless Education* comment that 'definitive figures on the size and growth of the industry are not available' (2000: 76), but note that the contemporary imperative of further education and training and the learning and development needs of adults have stimulated a new education and training market during the last 15 years. This market, the 'business of education', now extends well beyond traditional educational institutions to include a range of new providers of education, training and educational services.

Enhancing Practice

- What kinds of entrepreneurial or commercial activity has your academic unit developed, or might it develop in the future? What kinds of benefit (or danger) can you identify from such developments?
- You might consider undertaking a cost-benefit and risk analysis associated with enterprise and commercial initiatives; which departments or units in the university could assist you with this exercise?

'BORDERLESS EDUCATION' AND INTERNATIONAL MARKETS

The notion that higher education is now a business (both inside and outside traditional institutions) is closely associated with another concept that has emerged in higher education, that of borderless education. The term refers to educational developments that cut across (or have the potential to cross) traditional conceptual or geographic boundaries. It describes various forms of convergence in higher education, including the blurring of public/private boundaries, boundaries between further and higher education or education and training, and the crossing of national boundaries and boundaries of time and space made possible by developments in communications and information technology.

Three recent reports use the term 'borderless education' to encompass a variety of new developments that are having – and will continue to have – a profound impact on the size, shape and substance of higher education into the future. Two of these reports are Australian (see Cunningham *et al*, 1998 and 2000, in which the term 'borderless education' is first used). The third is British, published by the then Committee of Vice Chancellors and Principals (now Universities UK) with the title *The Business of Borderless Education: UK perspectives* (2000). The three reports cover developments (and the policy implications arising) in relation to:

- corporate universities;
- private and for-profit higher education;
- media and publishing companies;
- professional associations;
- educational service companies and brokers;
- virtual universities;
- university responses including consortia and partnerships of various kinds.

The UK report includes case studies drawn from four parts of the world: the UK, the United States, major parts of the Commonwealth and continental Europe. The most recent Australian study (Cunningham *et al*, 2000) offers in-depth case studies of nine corporate universities or related organizations. Together these reports provide a detailed summary of the trends and policy themes outlined above, with many examples of how these themes are being played out in practice. Only key examples from the full range of developments are given here.

Corporate universities

There has been significant growth in the number of corporate universities. One US estimate suggests a 400 per cent increase in the last ten years (Corporate Universities Xchange, 1999). Many are in global companies, although US-based (eg McDonald's Hamburger University and Arthur Andersen Performance and Learning) but UK examples include Lloyds TSB, UnipartU and British Aerospace Virtual University. Continental Europe and Australia also have examples of corporate universities (Deutsche Bank's Global Learning Services and Qantas College Online). These 'universities' take different forms ranging from a reorganizing of internal education and training activities to a more substantive restructuring of research, education and knowledge-management services. Only a small proportion of the education and training provision is open to outsiders for a fee; most is targeted at employees, customers or others in the corporate supply chain. Many corporate universities are involved in partnerships with existing universities for the creation of tailored educational programmes. (For example, Ford Motor Company has had university links in the UK for 25 years and it now has extensive relations with universities around the world to meet the educational needs of its employees in 200 different countries.) Only one corporate university (the Arthur D Little School of Management in the United States) currently has independent degree-granting rights (originating in 1976). The existence of corporate universities creates many new opportunities for traditional universities in the realms of research, continuing professional development and work-based learning, as well as in existing areas of undergraduate and postgraduate education.

Private and for-profit education

Several developments are worth noting. First, there has been a growth in private universities, with new ones being set up in Canada, Malaysia, South Africa and Germany in the last two years. However, in parallel there has also been growth among less reputable 'diploma mills', causing concern in some parts of the world and calls for increased regulation of private providers.

Second, public universities are setting up private arms, for example, Melbourne University Private, Deakin Global or New York University OnLine, to target new markets in more flexible ways. Third, there has also been expansion among 'for-profit educational businesses', particularly focusing on the needs of the working adult market, 'the earner-learner' students.

The University of Phoenix is probably the most well known of the 'for profits', not least because it is now the largest private accredited university in the United States (receiving accreditation first in 1978) with 75,000 students registered in 2000. Included in this figure is its fast-growing online division with 14,000 students (from 25 countries) registered in 2000, an increase from approximately 8,000 in 1998. Phoenix has more than 80 learning centres in the United States and has recently expanded its operations into the Netherlands, Germany, and Ireland, with plans for Canada. Classes are small, 14–15 students face-to-face or eight in online classes. Students take one module at a time, each lasting five to six weeks, and they remain together as a cohort. Phoenix is highly professional in its approach to teaching, using many experienced practitioners in its professional and vocational courses in business and management, counselling and healthcare, and IT.

Media/publishing businesses

Media/publishing businesses are increasingly looking to exploit their existing educational content and materials to develop new markets, usually in partnership with universities, but sometimes in competition with them. The big players in this market include Thompson Learning, McGraw Hill and Pearsons. Pearsons' subsidiary, FT Knowledge, is particularly active in the business and management education market, where the company has established partnerships with Wharton Business School in the United States and the Judge Institute, Cambridge in the UK to exploit the executive MBA market (on a global scale). All three companies (Pearsons and Thompson in particular) are also investing strategically in educational testing companies and in Web tools and courseware companies such as Blackboard.com and WebCT. As e-learning develops, the structure of the higher education landscape looks set to change dramatically. (See Chapters 2 and 13.)

Television and telecommunications companies are also involved in borderless education, either in partnerships with existing universities, or through engagement in parallel activities (such as the BBC's new *Learning Journeys*). The possibilities of digital and WAP technologies have enormous potential for multimedia learning, including flexible forms of delivery. Universities and colleges are being encouraged to form 'smart alliances' with these companies, partly to offset investment costs and partly to extend their global reach into new international markets.

Virtual universities and projects: e-learning, educational services and educational brokers

Readers need to beware of the considerable hype and volatility that surrounds borderless developments. This is particularly true in the territory of 'virtual universities'. There are as yet very few truly virtual universities, in terms of providing all current functions, from registration to teaching, assessment and learning support completely online. One current example is Jones International University, accredited in 1999; in 2000 it only had 74 undergraduate and Masters students registered. Several distance learning institutions, including the UK's Open University, the Universitat Oberta de Catalunya and the Fern Universitat Hagen in Germany are making significant moves from traditional distance education to online provision, and a number of countries including France, Finland and the UK (see Chapter 2) have national virtual university programmes and projects.

The growth of corporate and virtual universities is being supported by significant expansion among educational service companies. Their services extend from the provision of information technology and language training to educational testing, educational counselling and guidance, the conversion of educational content to e-learning formats and the building of 'managed learning environments'. Companies like PowerEd promise to build your corporate university for you in six to eight weeks! These companies offer opportunities for universities to outsource some of their functions (for example, assessment or registration) and they are contributing to the potential 'unbundling' of educational processes. Rather than the continuum of the educational service now provided by existing universities, the future may see different organizations creating curriculum content, delivering teaching, undertaking assessment, running learning support centres or awarding a degree. Such possibilities have profound implications for current quality assurance arrangements.

Information and communications technology (ICT) developments including the growth of e-learning are also giving rise to the role of 'educational broker'. Brokers offer services to individuals, for example, learndirect's guidance service (learndirect is the name under which the University for Industry (UFI) trades) or services to institutions and companies. UFI Ltd in the UK and Western Governors' University in the United States act as brokers to the provision of a wide range of education and training opportunities, while Scottish Knowledge markets the provision of Scottish universities worldwide and assists in creating alliances between companies and universities for the development of new programmes. Given the explosion of educational possibilities and potential partners, the role of brokers and navigators may remain important for the foreseeable future.

University responses

In response to the borderless world, universities and colleges are developing national, regional and international alliances. Some of these alliances include higher education institutions alone, others include further education, while others extend to companies and other organizations. A few developments between 1998 and 2000 illustrate the international range:

- University of the Highlands and Islands, a Scottish network of further education colleges with higher education links is growing connections with Canadian, Icelandic and Norwegian universities.
- Global University Alliance includes nine universities on four continents (Europe, North America, Australasia and Asia) to offer graduate and professional online courses in Asia in business subjects. GUA will be set up as a company in Hong Kong in alliance with NextEd.
- World University Network includes four UK and four US universities and will offer a range of collaborative programmes in environmental technology, systems engineering, knowledge management, bioinformatics and public policy.
- Telefonica, IBM and CISCO have established a joint project to develop an online business school, 'Educavia', to offer management and IT subjects up to Master's level for Spanish and Portuguese speakers;
- UNext.com, a private Internet education company, coordinates a US-based consortium involving the Universities of Chicago, Stanford, Columbia and Carnegie Mellon in the United States and the London School of Economics (LSE) and Heriot-Watt in the UK. Accreditation has been granted in the United States and degrees will be awarded under the name 'Cardean'.
- Fathom.com is an online resource that will provide courses and access to reference books, museum exhibits and artistic performances. Much of the site will be accessible at no charge. Partners include the University of Columbia, the New York Public Library, the British Library, Cambridge University Press, FT Knowledge and LSE. Negotiations continue with the Smithsonian National Museum of Natural History.

Enhancing Practice

The territory of 'borderless education' illustrates the interplay between globalization and international policy themes. As the world appears to shrink, the international domain will increase in significance for UK higher education. Competition is truly international, but there are also many opportunities for collaboration. Academics need to keep up to date with developments and constantly to review their own practice in the light of the dynamic international scene.

- In what ways are you ensuring that you are up to date with international developments?
- How does this extend to your academic unit?
- What are the likely implications of borderless developments for your institution/academic unit?
- What action might you take to ensure that your unit is prepared to take advantage of developments in e-learning, including links to the UK's e-university?

OVERVIEW

This chapter has presented some of the international aspects currently having an impact on the policies and behaviour of universities in the United Kingdom. It has sought to describe, in summary form, aspects of the current policy context, thereby highlighting these developments for individuals who are starting to be involved in strategic and policy-making roles.

REFERENCES

Castells, M (1998) *End of the Millennium, vol III*, Blackwell, Oxford

Clark, B (1998) *Creating Entrepreneurial Universities: Organizational pathways of transformation,* International Association of Universities and Elsevier Science, Oxford

Coffield, F (2000) *Differing Visions of a Learning Society, vols I and II*, Policy Press, Bristol

Committee of Vice Chancellors and Principals (now UUK) (2000) *The Business of Borderless Education: UK perspectives*, CVCP, London

Corporate University Xchange (CUX) (1999) *Survey of Corporate Universities Future Directions*, CUX, New York

Cunningham, S *et al* (1998) *New Media and Borderless Education: A review of the convergence between global media networks and higher education provision*, EIP 97/22, Higher Education Division, DEETYA, Canberra

Cunningham, S *et al* (2000) *The Business of Borderless Education*, EIP 00/3, Higher Education Division, DEETYA, Canberra

Davies, J (1987) The entrepreneurial and adaptive university: report of the second US study visit, *International Journal of Institutional Management in Higher Education*, 11(1), pp 12–104

Davies, J (1998) *The Dialogue of Universities with their Stakeholders: Comparisons between different regions of Europe*, Confederation of European Rectors, Geneva

DEETYA (1998) *Learning for Life: Review of higher education financing and policy*, final report of the Committee chaired by Roderick West, DEETYA, Canberra

Department of Trade and Industry (DTI) (1998) *Our Competitive Future: Building the knowledge driven economy*, Cm4176, DTI, London

European Commission (1995) *Education and Training, Teaching and Learning: Towards the learning society*, European Union White Paper (com)(95)(590), Office for Official Publications of the European Commission, Luxemburg

Goddard, J and Chatterton, P (1999) *The Response of Higher Education Institutions to Regional Needs*, Organisation of Economic Cooperation and Development, Paris

Knight, J (1999) Internationalization of higher education, *Quality and Internationalization in Higher Education*, OECD, Paris

Lubbers, R and Koorevaar, J (2000) Primary globalization, secondary globalization and the sustainable development paradigm – opposing forces in the 21st century, *The Creative Society of the 21st Century*, Future Studies, OECD, Paris

National Committee of Inquiry into Higher Education (NCIHE) (1997) *Higher Education in the Learning Society*, report of the National Committee chaired by Sir Ron Dearing, NCIHE/97/850, HMSO, London

OECD (1996) *Measuring What People Know – Human capital accounting for the knowledge economy*, OECD, Paris

OECD (2000) *Knowledge Management in the Learning Society, Education and Skills*, OECD, Paris

Quality Assurance Agency for Higher Education (QAA) (1999a) *Guidelines on the Quality Assurance of Distance Learning*, QAA, Gloucester

QAA (1999b) *Code of Practice for the Assurance of Academic Quality and Standards in Higher Education: Section 2: Collaborative provision*, QAA, Gloucester

Rees, T and Bartlett, J (1999) Models of guidance services in the learning society: the case of the Netherlands, in *Why's the Beer up North Always Stronger? Studies of lifelong learning in Europe*, ed F Coffield, Policy Press, Bristol

Scott, P (ed) (1998) *Globalization of Higher Education*, Society for Research into Higher Education/Open University Press, Buckingham

2 The Impact of National Developments on Institutional Practice

Rob Cuthbert

INTRODUCTION

This chapter considers how national developments (in England and to a lesser degree the United Kingdom) affect institutions of higher education. Its scope is huge, but contestable, because government policies vary in their effectiveness, national agencies vary in the esteem and support they enjoy from the higher education sector, and institutions vary in the extent to which they recognize the applicability of national developments.

A satisfactory account of the interplay of national agencies and institutions, the policy arenas and discourses, would require a book in itself. This chapter is an outline map of the territory, which recognizes that other perspectives are possible and valid. It aims to convey complexity and turbulence without lapsing into bewilderment. Ways are suggested of making sense of national developments, and how they affect institutions and academic practice. This is not a top-down one-way process: the chapter also considers how institutional developments and responses affect national policies and initiatives. Inevitably some strands of the chapter will be out of date in detail, if nothing more, even by the time of publication, but much of the broad thrust will still hold true.

What follows is not a checklist of national agencies and initiatives. Institutions and departments confront that 'checklist' daily, making their own sense of it. This chapter is structured around key entities in the sense-making process: government, auditors, subjects, courses, staff, students and institutions.

The chapter emphasizes developments since the mid-1990s, except where a longer view is instructive, and largely comprises factual information, policy analysis and consideration of institutional options. Institutional managers, leaders and readers must develop their own interpretation of what is happening at national level, and what difference it makes.

GOVERNMENT

'Government' here denotes government departments, agencies and quangos that fulfil governmental functions, notably the higher education funding councils (HEFCs) for England, Scotland and Wales. (Arrangements differ in Northern Ireland.)

In England the Department for Education and Skills (DFES) (formerly DfEE, Department for Education and Employment) is the lead department for most aspects of higher education policy. The Treasury is ever-present. The Department of Trade and Industry (DTI) has a role in research policy and higher education–industry relationships, in particular through the Office for Science and Technology and the Foresight exercise (which provides an appreciation of long-term futures to steer public investment in research, science and technology). Other departments also commission research and oversee some education and training, for example for health professionals. There are also occasional special national inquiries, for example by the Parliamentary Select Committee for Education, on specific issues such as access to higher education, and the general inquiries into higher education chaired by Lord Dearing (NCIHE, 1997) in England and the parallel Scottish (Garrick) Committee report. Wales, Scotland and Northern Ireland have increasingly separate administrations and approaches, although there are usually simultaneous parallel higher education policy initiatives across the UK.

Government policy for higher education can be characterized as concerned with access, funding, control, quality and purpose (Cuthbert, 1988). At any time there will be what Maurice Kogan (1971) has called 'low frequency' and 'high frequency' waves of policy effort. The high frequency emphasis on funding and control which characterized policy in the 1980s and early 1990s perhaps gave way under a Labour government to a greater emphasis on access, quality, lifelong learning and the knowledge economy.

Policymaking: widening participation

In particular there has been a strong push on access to higher education to promote social inclusion. The low frequency approach to widening participation by HEFCs has used 'special initiative' and 'additional student numbers' funds which institutions bid for, and 'formula funding'. 'Special initiatives' fund projects that meet certain policy objectives, and invite competitive bids, while also encouraging collaboration between higher education institutions and others such as further education colleges. 'Additional student numbers' funds are available annually, also subject to bids against specified criteria, which in the late 1990s emphasized widening participation. 'Formula funding' supplements funds for teaching, with a per-student premium for registering students from certain groups, such as those from socio-economically deprived neighbourhoods. To qualify for formula funding, institutions must submit an approved strategy on widening participation.

The funds involved are usually no more than 1–2 per cent of total HEFC funds for teaching. However, hard-pressed institutions find it difficult to resist bidding for income to increase their room for manoeuvre, leading to 'bidding fatigue' in which disproportionate amounts of time and energy are committed to fruitless bids. The HEFCs' stated preference is to move towards strategy-related formula funding, but this still buys a lot of strategic control for a little funding. For example, in 2000–01, English institutions were required to submit to the HEFC not only their annual plans but also a range of strategy statements (on widening participation, learning and teaching, students with disabilities, estates and finance).

The above illustrates many of the common HEFC devices for control and influence – and illuminates for leaders and managers in departments the source or starting point of much responsive activity.

Over time, mutual adjustment between the HEFC and institutions provides some stability and predictability in the relationship. However, the balance can be changed by high-frequency interventions, especially when these come direct from the Department. One signal example was the foundation degree initiative in 2000, part of Secretary of State for Education and Employment David Blunkett's 'Excellence Challenge' to higher education.

Foundation degrees (FDs) were proposed as two-year courses leading to a new qualification. The lack of articulation between the FD and other activities to widen participation was breathtaking. The FD appeared to supplant the higher national diploma, an effective part of higher and further education offerings. It pre-empted forthcoming 'additional student numbers' but there was no evidence of market research, or belief among practitioners that it was needed. After Blunkett's announcement civil servants and HEFCs cobbled together a rationale, but the foundation degree timescale slipped as institutional realities took hold. By 2001 the foundation degree was already looking more like a relatively small-scale enrichment of the widening participation mix than the spearhead originally proclaimed. Clearly national developments do not always transform institutional practice – or perhaps 'you can't buck the market'.

Enhancing Practice

What 'high frequency' interventions are currently having most impact on your institution? Do you consider your institution is taking a sufficiently long view of their significance?

Policymaking: funding higher education

Previous funding methods were markedly different from those in place at the start of the new century; a brief indication of earlier methods is, however, instructive for the contemporary situation. Until 1989 the University Grants Committee (UGC) (for universities) provided undifferentiated quinquennial block grants covering teaching or research. In 1981 it famously decided to maintain the 'unit of resource' (funding per student) by restricting student numbers in response to government expenditure cuts. Demand simply switched to the polytechnics. In the 1970s in the local-authority funded polytechnics and colleges, government tried to influence institutions by setting targets for student–staff ratios. By the mid-1980s a National Advisory Body had developed a funding method for colleges and polytechnics based on payment per student. The 1988 Education Reform Act created independent corporations funded by the Polytechnics and Colleges Funding Council (PCFC), which continued funding per student, resulting in accelerated growth. The Further and Higher Education Act 1992 granted the polytechnics university titles and dissolved the UFC and PCFC, to create three national HEFCs in England, Scotland and Wales, leaving arrangements under the Department of Education in Northern Ireland relatively unchanged.

The unification of the funding councils was not achieved without acknowledging 'diversity of mission' among institutions and corresponding diversity of funding levels. Higher funding levels in UFC institutions were due to the 'dual floor' of funding for research. Research activity was funded partly by this general grant and partly by grants won in competition from the research councils. UFC–PCFC comparisons of the 'unit of resource' and the convergence of funding councils led to the formal separation of funding for teaching from funding for research. The HEFCs now deliver most of their funds to institutions through two streams: teaching (T) and research (R). T funds are distributed by formula, with a set amount per student in each subject. When UFC funding was first disaggregated to create the R stream it was on such a basis that costs per student in UFC institutions appeared on average to be slightly less than those in the PCFC sector. The R funds (once created) were subjected to a national research assessment exercise (RAE) in 1989 involving only UFC institutions. All higher education institutions were eligible to enter subsequent exercises in 1992, 1996 and 2001. The HEFCs' review of research funding in 2000 reaffirmed the post-2001 future of the RAE as the central mechanism in research funding. Through the RAE, research activity is peer-rated for quality on a 7-point scale, and R funds are subsequently distributed according to quality rating and volume of activity as measured by numbers of research-active staff. These national funding changes have had profound effects on teaching, learning and research. (See also Sections 3 and 4 of this book.)

Institutions may spend their total HEFC funds as they wish, but T and R amounts for each institution are published, and the Transparency Review (see below) will increase pressures to use funding more precisely for its ostensible purpose.

The RAE has significantly changed the behaviour of institutions, faculties, schools, departments and individual academics (McNay, 1997; see also Chapter 9). Teaching and research may be inseparable but the tension between them in practice is apparent at every level. Academics divide their time, departments and faculties determine their priorities, and institutions decide their mission and strategies, by reference to the mix of R and T activities and funds. As the funding regime fine-tunes resource allocation to match short-term performance in terms of teaching outcomes and research productivity, institutions struggle to preserve medium-term stability and the long-term perspective on which both good teaching and good research depend.

The lower-frequency work of the Treasury comes in annual spending rounds, and intermittent exercises such as the Comprehensive Spending Review (CSR) during 1998–2000. One significant offshoot of the CSR originated in Treasury dissatisfaction with accountability for research spending. The Treasury's price for providing new research funds was the Transparency Review, which developed a method of apportioning costs into five categories: publicly-supported teaching, publicly-supported research, privately-supported teaching, privately-supported research and 'other'. The method was piloted during 2000–01, for introduction from 2001–02 onwards; undoubtedly it will significantly affect subsequent debates about teaching and research funding.

Policymaking: learning and teaching

The widening participation example shows the limited effectiveness of institutional-level solutions invented or imposed from the top down. Although this lesson has been learnt painfully by HEFCs, they have nevertheless made a series of strategic interventions in learning and teaching, notably the Teaching Quality Enhancement Fund (TQEF) which sought to improve quality and strengthen management of learning and teaching at national and institutional levels. Thus HEFCs invited institutional learning and teaching strategy statements, issued a national report and guidance, and conducted seminars for institutional strategy-writers. Some institutions debated whether the notion of an institutional learning and teaching strategy was meaningful, but all constructed statements qualifying for the associated funding.

In addition, HEFCs jointly established a Learning and Teaching Support Network (LTSN) in 2000. The Network comprises 22 Subject Centres and a Generic Learning and Teaching and Information Technology Centre, established by consortia of subject experts as a national resource for learning and teaching in each subject. The Subject Centres have developed with a lower profile than the parallel QAA exercise in 'subject benchmarking', discussed below, but might be expected to make a bigger long-term difference to practice.

The final strand in the TQEF initiative offers grants to National Teaching Fellows, selected from among competing nominees to celebrate and disseminate outstanding practice. (Two fellows have case studies in Chapter 10.)

In a linked initiative, the government established the Institute for Learning and Teaching (ILT) in 1999, to license academics as the 'profession' that many had always assumed they were (Clark, 1987). Claims to professionalism had previously been rooted in the 'invisible college' of the discipline, which was held to regulate access, discipline and progression within the 'academic profession'. The formation of the ILT can be seen as a national initiative to raise and guarantee 'standards' in HE, but its success depends on willing acceptance by academics of its rationale. Can a 'professional body' regulate access without any claims to formal competence in disciplines, and with little reference to research? The ILT purports to be the objective assessor of disembodied professional expertise in the promotion of learning. Its fate may be a litmus test of whether the transformation from elite to mass higher education was socially inclusive or recreated academic and institutional stratification. In formally professionalizing teaching, a successful ILT will either democratize the academy by enhancing its professional autonomy, or stratify it, by creating one group of institutions where ILT membership counts for something, and another where it does not.

AUDITORS

'Auditors' for this purpose embraces official academic and financial auditors in the National Audit Office, HEFCs, Quality Assurance Agency (QAA) and others, along with the media and other unofficial public scrutineers, such as the creators of 'league tables'. Most prominent in terms of impact on practice has been the QAA (see Chapter 11).

Academic quality assurance and audit

The QAA was created after protracted dialogue between institutions and governments in the 1990s about the most appropriate form of accountability and regulation of teaching in higher education. A lack of public or politicians' confidence in standards fuelled the replacement of separate regulatory mechanisms for the 'old' and 'new' university sectors. The QAA, owned collectively by the institutions in the sector, retained the principle of higher education self-regulation but was an unsatisfactory compromise between barely-reconcilable factions. These ranged from the standard-bearers of the Council for Academic Awards tradition, to the high priests of world-class university impatience with irrelevant bureaucratic control. It might thus have been said of QAA that the institutions were in office but not necessarily in power, and the appointment of the QAA chief executive was a crucial signal of the agency's expected direction. The appointee was John Randall, once National Union of Students President and previously a senior officer at the Law Society, who led a series of developments that caused widespread turbulence in the sector until his resignation in 2001.

Audit has involved successive phases of scrutiny at institutional level (audit and continuation audit) and at subject level. Institutional audits assessed institutions' quality assurance processes; subject review teams assessed and reported on the quality of teaching and learning. The long timescales involved in national programmes have meant permanent revolution in the subject-level assessments in the 1990s and 2000s. 'Teaching quality assessments' (TQAs) gave way to 'subject and programme reviews' (SPRs). The TQA/SPR process rated six dimensions of learning and teaching on a four-point scale. Unofficial 'scores' out of 24 were widely publicized, with only 22 or more generally deemed 'excellent'. The public relations impact prompted institutions to divert increasing resources into managing every aspect of the SPR 'visit'. This expense caused government concern. The Russell Group of elite institutions, some of whom threatened to break away from the QAA regime (Baty, 2001), voiced exasperation. With the opening of the new century, the QAA mapped out a regulatory approach using codes of practice, 42 'subject benchmarks' and 'programme specifications'. Benchmarks set out the content and/or outcomes expected of any degree programme in that subject; programme specifications are course summaries for public and professional consumption. SPRs are expected to give way in 2001 to the 'new method', using codes, benchmarking and programme specifications, with continuous engagement of assessors with subjects rather than one-week visits. Although the approaches have been widely criticized, the academic community has participated in constructing benchmarks and continues to date to supply staff for QAA activities.

In March 2001 David Blunkett proposed a five-year moratorium on subject visits for all departments which had scored 22 or more in the previous TQA or SPR. HEFCE publicly cooperated with this high-frequency intervention, to the undisguised fury of QAA's John Randall. These developments have had and continue to have a major impact on everyday working life for staff, and on the student experience.

'Auditors' also include professional and statutory bodies (PSBs), often criticized for alleged inflexibility or dogmatism. Certainly it has proved difficult, often impossible, to combine QAA audit and review processes with PSB inspections in the way generally proposed as each new QAA approach emerges. Nevertheless the interpenetration of academic and professional spheres somehow seems to enable most professional body regulation to work even in the most unpromising circumstances.

Institutional confidence in QAA was also shaken by the agency's publication in 2000 of proposals for a National Qualifications Framework with four rather than three levels of qualification to honours degree. This accommodated the foundation degree as a separate level, but created a sharp discontinuity in policy development that had started with the Harris Report in 1996 and continued with the Dearing Report. The QAA was rapidly forced to revise its proposals to restore a three-level structure.

Perhaps most damaging but least remarked in QAA's development of the 'new method' was the treatment of inter- and multi-disciplinary courses. The identification of 42 subjects for benchmarking was accompanied by the creation of a working group to examine multi-subject courses. These accounted for a large proportion, on some estimates more than half, of all full-time enrolments. However, the QAA could not accommodate a fundamental challenge to its subject-based philosophy, and the working group was disbanded after producing only an interim report. For institutions with large modular schemes and broad-based faculties and schools, dividing the world for quality purposes into 42 subject categories often called for creative interpretations of QAA intentions. Auditors risked addressing artificial constructs rather than educational realities.

The growth of league tables

Newspaper league tables ran a similar risk. University ranking systems were common in North America long before *The Times* decided to create a UK league table in 1993, with other newspapers rapidly following suit. Academic critiques of league tables did not inhibit their growing popularity. Arguably league tables were an inevitable consequence of the massification of higher education and declining public confidence in standards. In any case their creation and growth is a significant factor conditioning the behaviour of higher education institutions. Belatedly, the sector made an effort to raise the level of public understanding and debate about institutional performance, through the development and publication of performance indicators based on data gathered by HEFCs and the Higher Education Statistics Agency.

Enhancing Practice

What is your view, and that of your institution, of the impact of QAA and RAE scores and league tables on staff morale and taught student recruitment?

SUBJECTS AND DISCIPLINES

The epistemological foundations of higher education are shifting constantly, a truth usually ignored by national bodies and government, even though it must be accommodated by institutions. New disciplines have emerged at the rate of one a year or more over the last 50 years. Old disciplines tend not to die, but fade away, at least in terms of undergraduate popularity. Institutional adaptation to such global changes in markets, fashions or the structure of knowledge can be controversial, particularly if courses and departments close.

Debates about subjects and 'academic shape' influence organization structures. Resistance to change is built in where disciplines and departments are coterminous. Any decline in a subject poses a challenge to the department that is resisted where it cannot be ignored. As changes in subject popularity and discipline boundaries accelerated after 1970, many institutions – especially the polytechnics and colleges sharply exposed to the vagaries of the undergraduate market – created more flexible structures to cope more easily with change. The 1970s saw a vogue for 'matrix structures' in which subject groups and courses formed the two axes of an institutional structure that, in theory at least, could more easily manage to add and subtract from either axis. By the 1990s matrix structures had become just another part of the toolkit for managers, and modular course structures had become the device which could help institutions adjust to changing markets.

Modularization

In modular schemes academic staff are grouped in subject- or discipline-based schools, and courses are broken into discrete modules allowing student choice and creating a range of different named degree awards. It is relatively simple to create new awards, or delete old ones, without major structural consequences. With more difficulty, but less than in a traditional departmental structure, new schools can emerge, and old ones may close or merge.

Modular structures became the norm in the 1990s. Every institution made its own choices in terms of designating subject/discipline groups. In many pre-1992 universities more traditional subject-based department structures persisted, reflecting both their greater emphasis on research, developed within or from a clear discipline base, and their greater insulation from market volatility. Long-term trends led many institutions to withdraw from unpopular subjects such as chemistry and physics, sometimes with adverse publicity about redundancies and/or 'dumbing down' because supposedly 'easier' subjects were becoming more popular. National changes in demand forced institutional and departmental adaptations.

Enhancing Practice

How would you account for the academic shape of your institution?

What counts as a subject

The RAE has 68 units of assessment. To assess teaching, QAA identifies 42 subjects. The national Learning and Teaching Support Network recognizes only 22 subjects. Each categorization might be justified by the purposes to which it is applied, but this poses difficult problems for institutions required to demonstrate the integrity of learning and teaching in a 'subject' whose boundaries differ from the research unit of assessment where coherence is equally highly prized and scrutinized. There are also subject associations of academics, professional bodies and others which suggest other boundaries for academic structures. Any institution trying to be 'responsive' will simply be pulled in all directions.

Views diverge about epistemological territory even within defined subjects. This was exemplified by the first 'subject benchmarks' published by QAA: some were oriented to specifications of essential topics, while others emphasized the skills and qualities developed in students, most eschewing specification of content (Jackson, 2000). Amidst such diversity, fears of the 'nationalization' of the HE curriculum through benchmarking are perhaps exaggerated.

> ### Enhancing Practice
>
> How should your subject develop in your institution, within this national context? Do teaching and research both point in the same direction?

COURSES

From linearity through modularization to credit transfer

The widespread modularization of the undergraduate (and increasingly, of the postgraduate) curriculum is perhaps the most remarkable change in UK higher education teaching and course design in the 20th century. No explicit national initiative promoted modular curricula. No funding method penalized their absence. Modularization was an institutionally-driven initiative with widely varying outcomes. In some institutions modularization was only skin deep: in practice the linear degree remained, as a common cohort of students worked at the same pace through similar learning experiences, supported by a small group of academics, to reach a simultaneous conclusion. In others modularity took root. Knowledge delivery, learning and courses of study were unitized, and academic life moved irrevocably away from traditional linearity and knowing the 'whole student' towards subject and functional specialism in which teams of staff delivered modules to very large numbers of students aiming for many different final awards (Trowler, 1998). In US higher education, credit accumulation rather than modular structure drives the system. Most US undergraduate students graduate with credits from more than one institution, whereas in the United Kingdom such graduates remain the exception. However, procedures for accrediting learning and facilitating transfer between institutions are increasingly well understood.

It can thus be argued that modularization and credit transfer are higher education's organic responses to the national pressures of increasing access and massification, reduced funding levels, and changing modes of national regulation and control. Also the shift from linearity through modularization to credit transfer implies a shift from 'craft' methods of teaching and learning, first to 'mass production' modularity in which the old lectures and seminars are scaled up to higher volumes, with some investment in new facilities such as larger lecture theatres. Next comes 'just-in-time manufacturing', in which complex teams of lecturers, part-time teachers, graduate assistants, instructors, technicians, programme administrators and others collaborate in complex programmes which have to be right first time, or not happen at all.

Such programmes depend on commodification of content, sophisticated timetabling systems and explicit shared rules and procedures to ensure fair and consistent treatment for students across the modular scheme. Beyond this is a continuous flow process in which the pace, content, and outcomes of the learning process can increasingly be tailored to and by the individual student.

E-learning

The apotheosis of individualized learning is perhaps that which might be accomplished by networked learning or 'e-learning'. The worldwide explosion of interest in e-learning was first driven from the bottom up, as individual academic enthusiasts experimented with commercial software or developed their own. Many of these developments are considered in the previous chapter. The UK government and the HEFCs launched the national e-University initiative in early 2000, but it rapidly ran into conceptual difficulty. Initially advertised as a means of packaging mass e-learning using the UK's most prestigious university 'brands', the e-University 'business model' suffered a long gestation period, emerging quite differently and more inclusively, embracing many institutions as stakeholders. At the time of writing it is unclear whether this concept will attract sufficient support to take off. Meanwhile most institutions continue to develop virtual or managed learning environments to transform student learning and student administration (see Chapter 13). National developments have yet to prove their relevance compared to the bottom-up activities of institutions, departments and individuals, drawing on the global availability of commercially-supported software.

STAFF

As higher education expands, most staff in most institutions would argue that 'more means worse' in terms of their working life and its rewards. (See the last section of this book.) Performance levels are intensively scrutinized, workloads rise inexorably, job satisfaction has plummeted, and stress is the major topic of conversation.

While these feelings are common, employment contracts differ markedly between institutions. After a long drawn-out dispute in the higher education corporations, academic staff accepted a new contract of employment which involved quantification of annual and weekly workload, and a definition of the kinds of work to be undertaken. In practice the contract did little to hold down workloads, as student numbers increased faster than staffing levels, and research demands also grew. In the former UFC sector the contract was different but the pressures were similar. An academic's contract was more loosely drawn, and not subject to comparison with a national template. However, it presumed both teaching and research activity, and during the 1990s the pressures for increased performance in both dimensions grew rapidly. In some universities, staff deemed to be under-performing were induced or compelled either to switch to 'teaching-only' contracts or to take severance packages and leave.

It could thus be argued that the pressures of expansion and greater accountability, rather than the forms of contract, were the key influences on the staff experience. Similar pressures also affected other groups of staff over a similar period. There were redundancies, change of employer and contract, and increasing workload among manual staff. For administrators and technical staff there were fewer radical changes in contractual forms, but perhaps even greater transformation of their work roles. There was a convergence of sorts between academic, academic-related and support roles; the previous 'academic'/'non-academic' polarity was replaced by a spectrum of different contributions to the new academic enterprise. Employment law requiring equal pay for work of equal value fuelled institutional attempts to harmonize contracts, pay and working conditions for the previously disparate groups.

The clash between academic complaints at worsening pay and conditions and constrained institutional budgets led to a national inquiry under Sir Michael Bett, a respected neutral with broad governmental and civil service experience. The Bett Report (Independent Review of Higher Education Pay and Conditions 1999) proposed a new national framework of conditions of service together with substantial increases in academic pay levels. The lack of funds to implement Bett put it on ice, but it has become a reference point for staff unions, a bargaining weapon for Universities UK (UUK) (formerly the Committee of Vice-Chancellors and Principals) in discussions over funding, and a focus for industrial action.

The continuing 'low frequency' rumbling about pay, workloads and conditions was the most important accompaniment to and constraint on most institutions' attempts to innovate in teaching and learning. It also soured discussions and initiatives which might otherwise have been more positive. Thus the dominant themes of the discourse about massification of higher education were assertions of proletarianization and deskilling (Smyth, 1995) rather than a recognition that change offered new liberty as well as new discipline (Winter, 1996). Similarly, the debate about e-learning is also coloured, at least in government thinking, by assertions about efficiency rather than educational benefit. Nevertheless academic research into the experiences of the new sector has begun to suggest a new millennium resurgence of academic autonomy (Trowler, 1998).

STUDENTS

Students are people, a fact usually ignored in most 'high frequency' policy debates about students, which disproportionately address the concerns of full-time students, or address students as full-time equivalents. (See also Chapter 3). Most higher education students pay fees and always have done. Most students are 'mature', that is, over 21, not 18 and 19-year-old school leavers. Most students are part-time not full-time. Many students register with a university without wishing to sit an examination or achieve any award. And most debate about students in higher education is conducted as if these things were not true.

However, it is true that most time and most revenue in most higher education institutions is attributable to teaching full-time undergraduates. This explains and excuses some of the disproportionate emphasis on them. But it is mistaken to assume that, even here, students constitute anything like a homogeneous group. There are higher education students in further education colleges. There are 'part-time' students for whom study is their major life concern. There are 'full-time' students for whom study is fitted in around the paid employment they need to fund their studies. Institutions have mature students whose expectations of the university are narrowly focused on its academic provision, working alongside young people whose expectations are more 'traditional': a full social and cultural life alongside their educational experience. There are postgraduate taught students seeking additional career enhancement alongside postgraduate research students training for an academic career.

Consequently it is risky to generalize about how national or even institutional developments affect student learning. However, one development with profound long-term consequences is the national school curriculum, formerly strongly influenced by university examining boards in the absence of national prescription. With a national curriculum and with university expectations relevant for 30 per cent rather than 3 per cent of the school population, a great opportunity to exploit the school–university connection has been missed. Furthermore, the introduction of fees for full-time undergraduates and the abolition of maintenance grants have encouraged consumerism and a narrow instrumentalism, jeopardizing the broader social purposes of the university and coarsening the experience of higher education for both students and staff.

INSTITUTIONS

Not all higher education institutions are the same, nor do they try to be. They vary in the services they provide, the audiences and client groups they address, and how they are organized and governed. This enormous variety is seldom apparent, even to those within higher education, whose experience is usually distinctly partial. Even where the variety is well understood it poses difficulties for action. UUK has often been criticized either for failing to give a lead, or for giving a lead that most institutions prefer not to follow. The diversity of its constituents, and the contestable claim of vice-chancellors to speak for their institutions, make it hardly surprising that UUK leads most surely only where it makes simple universal claims such as for more funding. Even then, for example a 'win' of more funds for research in the public spending round will be seen as a very uneven blessing for the sector as a whole, in which 20 per cent of the institutions get 80 per cent of the research funds. UUK is inevitably an intermediary and interpreter of higher education institutions to government, and vice versa. And institutions themselves are crucial mediators of national developments.

Diversity in institutional character and mission is a matter of institutional 'choice', constrained by institutional history and culture. But diversity of mission implies a selective attention by institutions to the complexity of their external environment. A government announcement of £1 billion for research infrastructure will be intensely scrutinized by the Russell Group but largely ignored by colleges of higher education. For a HEFC circular about funding for widening participation the reverse is more likely to be true. All universities may profess a commitment to their region and the local community, but that commitment will take a different form in a Russell Group institution with 300 local students and international blue skies research, than in a post-1992 university with 3,000 local students and a programme of applied research with local organizations.

Even apparently similar institutions may exhibit large differences in cultures, structures and processes (Becher, 1989). The debate about management and managerialism in universities has embraced both management styles and educational values. (See also Part 2.) The distinction between 'pre-1992' or 'chartered' universities and the higher education corporations of the 1988 Act, acquiring university title in 1992 or thereafter, is an unreliable guide to identifying cultural differences. 'Old' universities may be managerialist just as 'new' universities may be collegial. Other means of understanding the differences must be sought. Thorne and Cuthbert (1996) argue that autonomy, bureaucracy and competition are key themes, which permit a new kind of classification of institutions according to their insulation from or dependence on higher education market forces. The classic characterizations of the university as a loosely-coupled academic republic or collegium (Moodie and Eustace, 1974), organized anarchy (Cohen and March, 1974) or 'research-teaching-study nexus' (Trow, 1994) all depend implicitly on assumptions of resource richness which most UK institutions find increasingly distant.

Resource restriction forces more choices about priorities and brings to the surface more conflicts needing resolution. In this sense most if not all higher education institutions can be said to be moving from loose coupling towards more integrated purposefulness, albeit from very different starting points. Any middle manager in higher education needs to understand the freedoms and constraints which apply, and the basis for them, whether it be a shared educational philosophy and institutional culture, a dominant management style, a structure of centralized or devolved authority, or an external resource constraint.

CONCLUSION

This chapter has sought to provide an outline map of how national developments affect institutional, departmental and also individual practice. Theoretical perspectives on these issues are plentiful, complex and conflicting, which prompted a structure for the chapter based on entities that any reader could identify from his or her own situation. The approach has aimed to be similarly pragmatic, although aware of and informed by institutional variety and the theoretical debates, which militate against generalized conclusions. Peter Drucker famously differentiated efficiency – doing things right – from effectiveness – doing the right thing. When in doubt, the effective academic needs to do the right thing.

REFERENCES

Bargh, C, Scott, P and Smith, D (1996) *Governing Universities*, Society for Research into Higher Education (SRHE)/Open University Press, Buckingham

Baty, P (2001) LSE leads revolt against QAA, *Times Higher Education Supplement* (23 March), p 1

Becher, T (1989) *Academic Tribes and Territories*, SRHE/Open University Press, Milton Keynes

Clark, B (1987) *The Academic Profession: National, disciplinary and institutional settings*, University of California Press, Berkeley, Los Angeles

Cohen, MD and March, JG (1974) *Leadership and Ambiguity: The American college president*, McGraw-Hill, New York

Cuthbert, R (1988) Reconstructing higher education policy, in *Restructuring Higher Education*, ed H Eggins, pp 47–54, SRHE/Open University Press, Milton Keynes

Harris, M *et al* (1996) *Review of Postgraduate Education*, Report of a Review Group chaired by Professor Martin Harris, HEFCE, CVCP and SCOP, Bristol

Independent Review of Higher Education Pay and Conditions (1999) *Independent Review of Higher Education Pay and Conditions*, Report of a Committee chaired by Sir Michael Bett, The Stationery Office, London

Jackson, N (2000) Subject benchmark information: implications for curriculum design and assessing student learning, Working paper for the SACWG Conference on benchmarking November 2000, Learning and Teaching Support Network Generic Centre, York

Kogan, M (1971) *The Politics of Education* (M Kogan in conversation with Edward Boyle and Anthony Crosland), Penguin, Harmondsworth

McNay, I (1997) *The Impact of the 1992 RAE on Institutional and Individual Behaviour in English Higher Education: The evidence from a research project*, HEFCE M 5/97, Bristol

Moodie, GC and Eustace, R (1974) *Power and Authority in British Universities*, George Allen and Unwin, London

National Committee of Inquiry into Higher Education (NCIHE) (1997) *Higher Education in the Learning Society*, report of the National Committee chaired by Sir Ron Dearing, NCIHE/97/850, HMSO, London

Smyth, J (ed) (1995) *Academic Work*, Society for Research into Higher Education (SRHE)/Open University Press, Buckingham

Thorne, ML and Cuthbert, RE (1996) Autonomy, bureaucracy and competition: the ABC of control in higher education, in *Working in Higher Education*, ed RE Cuthbert, SRHE/Open University Press, Buckingham

Trow, M (1994) Managerialism and the academic profession: the case of England, *Higher Education Policy*, **7**(2), pp 11–18

Trowler, P (1998) *Academics Responding to Change*, SRHE/Open University Press, Buckingham

Winter, R (1996) New liberty, new discipline: academic work in the new higher education, in *Working in Higher Education*, ed RE Cuthbert, SRHE/Open University Press, Buckingham

USEFUL URLs

www.dfes.gov.uk
www.hefce.ac.uk
www.ilt.ac.uk
www.leeds.ac.uk/educol/ncihe/ (for the Dearing Report)
www.parliament.uk/commons/hsecom.htm
www.qaa.ac.uk
www.srhe.ac.uk
www.universitiesuk.ac.uk

3 | The Student Experience

Rob Shorrock

Students are not an homogenous group. They have a range of experiences, concerns and aspirations. The attachments they have are sometimes shared and sometimes incredibly distinct. But they all study and have a belief in education. They are also concerned about the quality and relevance of their educational experience.

NUS and students' unions are at the forefront of promoting an agenda that recognizes students can play a pivotal role in developing the curriculum, improving facilities to support learning, and implementing practices that can modify and simplify university procedures. Those institutions which embrace a partnership for change will become the university of choice for future generations of students.

(Owain James, President of the National Union of Students, 2001)

INTRODUCTION

This chapter is designed to give a perspective of the student experience in higher education, with emphasis on current imperatives such as student finances, tuition fees, the need to work while studying and the accumulation of debt. These are discussed in relation to the changing political scene in the UK. This chapter also draws attention to how students' unions are taking a greater involvement in improving and enhancing all aspects of student life in higher education, going beyond their well-known roles in welfare and representation, moving into newer territories such as the development of skills for the workplace and taking part as a consumer in enhancing the quality of student learning.

Numbers of students in higher education

It may be helpful to open this chapter by giving some information on the numbers of students in higher education. The total number of higher education enrolments in UK institutions is 1,802,500 for the year 2000/01 (HESA,

2001). This figure includes HE enrolments in further education colleges. Of this total, 66 per cent of enrolments are full-time and the remainder are part-time enrolments. Between 1996/97 and 2000/01, total enrolments in UK higher education institutions increased by 9 per cent. A final point to note is that 55 per cent of students in 2000/01 are female compared with 52 per cent in 1996/97.

STUDENT DEBT AND HARDSHIP

The accumulation of debt and hardship are important aspects of the lives of many students currently studying in higher education. There have been a number of surveys into student debt. The NUS Student Hardship Survey (1999) found that 73.3 per cent of full-time undergraduates, 71.4 per cent of part-time undergraduates and 76.6 per cent of postgraduates were in debt. The survey found that mature students have substantially more debt than other students. Such students often need more money to support dependants and may often have existing debts when they undertake a course. In this light it may be relevant to note that applications from mature students for October 2000 entry were down by 5.7 per cent compared with the previous year (UCAS, 2000).

Considering the accumulated debt of students on graduation, Barclays Student Debt Survey (1999) revealed that 1999 finalists on average expected their debt at the end of the course to be £5,286. These findings revealed that the cost to the individual of going to university has increased by 103 per cent since 1994.

DROP-OUT RATES

Student drop-out rates have increased from 14 per cent in 1983/84 to 18 per cent in 1993/94 (DfEE, 1993). The drop-out rate for full-time undergraduates across the UK for the academic year 1998/99 was 18 per cent (HEFCE, 2000: 13).

Making a direct connection between dropping out and the financial situation of students is always tempting, but the picture is actually more complex. Students drop out for many reasons. Most drop-outs occur at an early stage in a course when it might be expected that the level of debt is not so severe. However, the reasons for dropping out are more often related to consideration of appropriateness of choice of a programme of study, or problems with individual performance and motivation.

The impact of debt on behaviour is a more long-term phenomenon.

Advisors in higher education sometimes remark that a significant number of the full-time students they see have a limited conception of the level of debt that they are likely to incur. Budgeting skills can also be weak, and advisors only see students when money supplies have been cut off and money is owing to landlords and others. However, the tenacity to continue with the course is very strong, which given the alternatives is paradoxical. As one advisor explained to the author, 'It would be far cheaper for many full-time students to leave, get a job and study the same course part-time. However, prospective students aren't told about this option.'

STUDENT FINANCES

From the Robbins Report in 1963 to recent government announcements, the concept of higher education has been that all those that can benefit from higher education should have the opportunity to do so, although financial considerations call this into question. The current system of support is complex, confusing and bureaucratic, and rests on fixed assumptions that students going into higher education are young, will study full time and will be financially dependent to some extent on parents. Higher education now leads to heavy debts for many people early on in life. The addition of other life debts, such as mortgages and children, may lead to profound changes in the way future generations will want to study.

As could be expected, the issue of student financial support has been the key campaigning focus of the student movement over the last 50 years. The history of the development of financial support has been one of victory and loss. As one student commentator put it, 'It is beyond the wildest dreams of students today to imagine that students 20 years ago were entitled not only to grants, housing benefits, social security during the vacations, but also travel and book grants.' This may be a 'rose-tinted' view of the past, but there is a feeling that a previous generation of students had an experience that was both better and more secure than the present. There has been little research undertaken to substantiate this view.

Introduction of student fees

In the 1980s the Conservative government pledged to reform many of the public institutions. There was a plethora of education legislation, including key changes to the student financial support system. A particular focus was to remove students' rights to access the social security system, which resulted in the loss of entitlement to social security benefits during the Christmas and Easter vacations in 1986, and culminated in a total loss of entitlement to all social security benefits by 1990. This process of year-by-year erosion also led to the withdrawal of housing benefits, starting for students in halls of residence in 1986, and ending in a complete withdrawal in 1990.

The focus for the government in the 1980s was to try to remove the responsibility for student support from the public purse. In 1986 a review of student support led to the publication of a white paper, *Top-Up Loans for Students* (DES, 1988). This proposed a system of student loans which would be provided by banks at 0 per cent rate of interest and guaranteed by the government. However, for various reasons, in December 1989 the major clearing banks pulled out of the scheme. Consequently, in September 1990, the student loan system was introduced, which was administered by the Student Loans Company. At the same time mandatory awards were frozen and the vast majority of students had access to all benefits withdrawn. A safety net was established, called the 'access fund', providing £25 million to be administered by institutions to assist with severe cases of student hardship.

In 1993 the Government announced that mandatory awards were to be cut progressively by 10 per cent each year over three years from 1994/95 to 1996/97 and student loans would be increased to compensate. Access funds, originally a stopgap measure, would continue for the next three years, and at the time of writing they are still in existence.

In February 1996 the Committee of Vice Chancellors and Principals met to discuss whether to charge students a levy to compensate for funding cuts to universities and colleges. The decision was postponed until November 1996. At the same time the government announced an inquiry to examine student hardship and the funding of the higher education system.

It was becoming clear that the issues of student financial support and the wider funding of institutions were inextricably linked. In recognition of this, the NUS changed its policy of free education with grants for all, to a more strategic position of increased financial support for further education students, a new form of funding for higher education students which includes grants, and a form of income-contingent graduate contributions. The idea of this was to generate an unencumbered campaign against the introduction of fees.

Following the election of the Labour government in 1997 and the publication of the Dearing Report (NCIHE, 1997), recommendations were made that graduates contribute a flat rate of around 25 per cent of higher education tuition fees, on an income-contingent basis. In addition, the Dearing Committee recommended that the government introduce an income-contingent loan for 50 per cent of maintenance costs, alongside the existing grant. The Government decided to charge students tuition fees, set at a ceiling of £1,000, with the modification that fees were to be means-tested. In addition, the existing grant and loan system was to be abolished and replaced by income-contingent loans for maintenance.

The current system

In England and Wales, the position in the academic year 2000/01 is that an undergraduate student under 24 years of age and studying a standard course would be entitled to apply for a loan of up to £2,795 and a further means-tested element of up to £930. This is an area subject to Government policy and Student Advice Centres can offer the latest information on current arrangements.

STUDENTS IN EMPLOYMENT

A joint GMB/NUS survey (1996) on student employment found that 40 per cent of students are employed during term time. Of these, four out of ten are employed for 12.5 to 20 hours per week. For students who work during term time, two-thirds claim their employment affects their studies; 30 per cent missed lectures and 20 per cent failed to submit work because of their employment.

Having a job and studying is now considered to be part of the normal experience of higher education. The steady erosion of state-funded maintenance awards has been the strongest factor in bringing this about. Significant numbers of students have now worked before they enter higher education, and for them being a student involves a continuation of this lifestyle. There has been a steady increase in the number of job shops and employment centres within institutions. Some of these are run by students' unions.

Many institutions recommend limits on the number of hours that should be worked in a week, usually between 14 and 20. Jobs offered by the institution or the students' union normally have a maximum number of hours as part of the contract. Nonetheless, the need to supplement income and keep overdrafts down means that many students are working longer hours, sometimes for more than one employer.

There is an impact on student learning. There may be difficulties with time and energy left at the end of the day to devote to studying, which may mean occasional problems in being able to meet timetabling demands, or to attend teaching sessions or meetings with tutors. For students taking courses such as teaching and nursing, tensions may arise when work has to be combined with study of a highly intensive, vocational nature.

Some economies and labour sectors are highly reliant on student labour and spend much energy and resources on targeting students. Students working while studying are a common feature in many international higher education systems. The United States is a notable example. For many graduate recruiters, evidence of the student having been in employment is a strong incentive to recruitment. However, many believe that students are still poor at being able to describe skills and knowledge gained, and apply this to a new job profile.

> ### Enhancing Practice
>
> What changes have been made to courses in your department to help meet the changing needs of students as outlined in the foregoing sections?

STUDENTS IN ACCOMMODATION

It is useful to raise some of the issues relating to the student experience of living in halls of residence and other forms of institutional accommodation. In many universities and colleges this can be a point of tension and friction between managers and students.

Most institutions try to offer accommodation to first-year students. For many of the post-1992 universities with fewer places, sophisticated criteria have been developed to allocate places. Students are signed up on a licence agreement for 40 weeks per year. There are few institutions that offer full board provision, although some of the voluntary colleges are notable exceptions.

Some institutions have tendered out their accommodation provision to private companies. Special mechanisms need to be set up to deal with issues and complaints. Problems develop, possibly because of the scale of turnover and demand. During the late 1980s there were enormous problems in finding suitable accommodation, leading to emergency shelters being set up in sports halls. Students may find that they are placed with people whom they are unable to get on with, and want to move. Students often do not see the importance of carrying out a thorough inventory, and find that they are charged for damages that they assert they have not committed. These issues will often bog down local union advice services, and can be a source of conflict between students' unions and residence managers.

STUDENT LEARNING

All students should receive an induction into their course and be able to elect representatives who can voice their concerns to staff and participate in course committees. The experience that students have on courses is a key consideration for the institution and is always an important element of the Quality Assurance Agency for Higher Education Subject Reviews and audits. Students are normally asked to provide regular feedback through course committees and questionnaires on the quality of the course, issues or concerns they may have and how things can be improved. What is often missing in institutions is completion of the feedback loop by informing the student representatives what action has been taken in response to their evaluative comments. Interviews held with staff and course representatives at the University of the West of England in 1998 demonstrated some of the problems. Staff felt that students were reluctant to air concerns or problems at these meetings, or were raising issues that were beyond the powers of the meeting to deal with. Student representatives on the other hand felt that staff did not take responsibility for dealing with issues or were 'eager to refer us on to someone else in the bureaucracy', and that eventually 'there is no point in raising issues as nothing ever changes'. However, there were common areas of concern from both staff and students in terms of the pressures that were placed upon them by central authority. These included the increasing complexity of timetabling, the need for flexibility to allow students to be able to meet other commitments and also to recognize restrictions in the availability of public transport, changes in assessment regulations being properly communicated, assessments being loaded into short periods of time, delays in getting back marks and assistance from tutors in completing the work.

REPRESENTATION

Course representation is a key mechanism for hearing student views and solving problems. Staff and course representatives can achieve a great deal when there is recognition of common problems and concerns. Student representatives are trained by students' unions in identifying areas of change, negotiation skills and problem solving, and are a valuable resource if viewed positively and encouraged to be involved in the development of the course.

Course Representation – Reading Weeks in Philosophy by Jamie Darwen and Sarah Moore

The philosophy degree at the University of Warwick involves a lot of reading, but did not have a reading week. The students on the course felt that a reading week was necessary and found that all other reading degrees seemed to have one. Student representatives raised this issue through the course's Staff–Student Liaison Committee (SSLC). They agreed to conduct a questionnaire survey of all students undertaking philosophy to find out what their feelings were, when reading weeks should be, and what they would want to happen during those weeks. Academic members of the SSLC supported the survey and provided help in preparing the questionnaire, and administrative staff in the department provided support in producing and distributing the questionnaire.

The survey found that most students wanted a reading week in each of the autumn and spring terms, and that during these weeks staff should be available to students for questions and queries. In the first term for first years there should be an introductory week before lectures began, instead of a reading week in the middle of term. These results were presented to a staff meeting by one of the student representatives. Staff had reservations about cramming the work into a shorter period of time, but agreed that a reading week would be beneficial so long as it was made clear that the week was not a holiday, or a time to go home, and that work should be done on assignments during that time. It was also made clear that it was a time for students to see their tutors. The department agreed to introduce reading weeks on a trial basis for two years.

The SSLC has played a key role in reviewing progress since the reading weeks were introduced, and ensuring that the new system is successful. For example, in the first term there seemed to be problems with attendance after the reading week. Because of this, more effort was made to emphasize the purpose of the reading week in the second term, and attendance after that improved. Staff and student members of the SSLC have worked well together to make sure no other problems occur, and most agree that the introduction of reading weeks has been a success.

STUDENTS' UNIONS

Students' unions, or student associations as they are more generally known in Scotland, are membership-based organizations recognized by a college or university as the representative body of the students. Associations of students have existed in some form since the beginning of the century, but it was not until the 1960s that the organizations that we know today really came into existence. They have a set of common objectives which include:

- to advance the education of their members;
- to defend the welfare of their members;
- to represent their members to the institution and other bodies;
- to provide services for and on behalf of their members;
- to provide opportunities for recreational and social fulfilment.

Legal status

Students' unions are unincorporated associations of their members. They have no legal identity in themselves, and any legal action taken against them has to name key individuals. However, they do have charitable status, which is derived from their relationship with the institution. This is no different from the many thousands of voluntary clubs and associations in the UK. It has been an area of dispute between some unions and institutions. The dispute has centred on trying to create a clear legal identity for the union, which has resulted in some unions registering themselves as companies limited by guarantee. The University of Central England Student Union is a notable example.

Students' unions in the UK generally operate systems of automatic membership. Every student within the institution is regarded as a member. This system dates back to 1962, and agreements were made with bodies representing local authorities to agree a fee that would be paid per student as the union fee. There is now no fee paid by any funding body specifically to a student union, as students' unions receive grants as part of the institution's financial allocation cycle. However, the concept of automatic membership has remained and is guarded as a sacred principle by the student movement.

Critics and opponents of students' unions have tried to equate the concept of automatic membership with the notion of the closed shop. However, attempts by Conservative backbenchers to try to get Parliament to change the membership arrangements have been unsuccessful, mainly because of recognition from ministers that membership arrangements of students' unions are complex.

There had been no legislation relating to students' unions until the passage of the second Education Act 1994, which set out criteria by which students' unions should conduct their affairs. This was mainly recognition of practice that existed within students' unions at the time. However, this did give students the option of opting out of the students' union if they so wished, and placed a responsibility on institutions to make this known to students. Very few students take up this option.

How students' unions operate

Every students' union has a written constitution, which is agreed by the members and approved by the governing body of the institution. Each year there are elections for the executive committee of the students' union. This body manages the day-to-day affairs of the union, and its members are normally regarded as trustees of the union. Some of the positions are sabbatical, which makes them essentially full-time elected positions. The incumbent takes a year out of his or her course, and receives an allowance to work for the union full-time. University students' unions usually have an average of six sabbatical officers, covering the positions of president, finance, welfare, education, sport and recreation, and communications. The elected officers are supported by a staff team, usually led by a senior member of staff known as a general manager. This team carries out the decisions of the executive committee and is responsible for managing services such as bars, catering and retail outlets.

The executive committee is accountable to a council or general meeting of the members, and sometimes to both. For the last two decades, students' unions have been locked into an ongoing debate on participatory versus representative democracy. Proponents of participatory democracy regard the general meeting, which all students are entitled to attend and participate in fully, as key to the democratic integrity of the students' union. Those who advocate representative democracy argue that although the participatory ideal is good, the reality is that most students could not attend these meetings even if they wanted to, and a mechanism needs to be in place to hold the executive to account through the widest possible cross-section of the student population meeting together in a council. The council idea gained ascendancy through the 1990s. This has mainly been in response to the expansion of higher education institutions and the emergence of multi-site operation. For many union officers it was more practical and coherent to have a representative council than a series of general meetings on each campus. It is worth noting that most unions draw the membership of the council from course representatives.

The value of these positions in providing development opportunities for students is widely recognized. The responsibilities of officers are very wide, including budgetary responsibilities for hundreds of thousands if not millions of pounds, recruitment of staff and input into strategic and operational management.

Students' union services

Students' unions offer a range of services which can include retail, bars, childcare facilities, print shops, advice and guidance, entertainment and facilities for clubs and societies. Although paid staff often manage them, students shape their direction and development. Staff working in students' unions have either seen this as an imperative or a curse. Students' unions have started to get better at selecting staff who not only have an empathy with the union's values but also achieve a close, supportive working relationship with students. In organizations where the staff–student relationship is not clear, this can result in bitter, often public acrimony from which it can take the union years to recover.

Students' unions run mutual trading activities. During the raft of cuts in education spending in the 1980s, these became significant areas of income. Block grants had been declining in real terms and trading activities had generally been run on a break-even basis, and it was widely felt that in order to generate income these activities needed to be professionalized. Business plans were necessary to maximize potential. This was an interesting period in the history of the student movement, as there was an increase in the number of staff employed by students' unions but also the beginning of a shift in understanding of what the union was there to do. Were unions chiefly service providers, providing their members with cheap products and services, or were they campaign organizations seeking change in the education system and society at large? These questions have been fundamental to the development of modern students' unions.

Student development

The role of students' unions in providing development opportunities for students is recognized as a vital part of the education experience. The unions provide facilities and support to help students develop leadership, organization and people skills through activities such as clubs and societies and student community action, and through customized training. Many unions award students who have gone through such training or played leading roles in activities, with certificates signed by the president of the union and possibly the vice-chancellor.

Student politics

Student politics have changed significantly over the last two decades, although many of the principles that were originally embedded within the student movement still remain as key political objectives. The main change has been a shift away from declaring membership of political parties. Students' unions elections are a good barometer of this change: there has been a decline in the number of candidates standing on political platforms. Those that do are often from far-left groupings. Other candidates run as independents or on single-issue objectives.

Even if political colours are not as clear, the issues that dominate student politics remain the same. The history of change to student financial support has already been outlined. Other issues include promoting and defending student rights within the institution, campaigns against discrimination and promoting equality.

THE NATIONAL UNION OF STUDENTS

The National Union of Students UK (NUS) is the largest organized student body in Europe. It was set up in 1922, by students who had served in the First World War and had an aim of 'seeking world peace'. It was also established for more mundane reasons: to allow English universities to send delegates to an International Student Conference in Europe (Rhodes, 1990; Jacks, 1975).

The first 40 years of the life of the NUS reflected the values of students attending university during this time. During the General Strike of 1926, students were involved in running services. The NUS constitution contained a clause that did not allow it to comment upon issues that were not directly related to higher education. This was eventually changed in 1969 when the union was under the presidency of Jack Straw.

NUS UK is a confederation made up of local students' unions. Students' unions affiliate to the NUS, which entitles their student members to the NUS card. As an organization the NUS provides support to elected officers. This includes a comprehensive and effective development and training programme, detailed research on student finances, housing and education rights, and materials to support campaigns. The NUS holds an annual conference which elects a national executive and passes policy. Policies tend to focus on issues relating to student finance, higher/further education and the development of students' unions. The NUS also has additional campaign conferences for women, mature students, students with disabilities, lesbian, gay, bisexual and transsexual students, and black students. Students' unions are entitled to send delegates to all these conferences. Policy passed at a national level is not binding or mandatory on local students' unions, although it is likely that most students' unions will hold similar policies.

In recent years the NUS has focused on engendering change within institutions. Key to this has been its campaign for quality, and student involvement in quality assurance as well as promoting the concept of student rights within the institution.

Enhancing Practice

As a head of department or manager responsible for undergraduate and/or postgraduate students:

- What do you know about the services provided by your local students' union?
- Does your department have a contact with the students' union advice centre?
- Do you have student representatives on all relevant committees?
- Do you know how these student representatives are trained for their role?
- Does your local students' union provide development programmes open to all students?

BEING AN EFFECTIVE ACADEMIC

As it is concerned with the viewpoint of consumers of higher education, this chapter will close with some student views on academics. The author asked samples of students from the University of the West of England, Staffordshire University and the University of Greenwich what they thought characterized the effective academic. Their answers are in no particular order of importance or priority.

An effective academic:

- listens;
- helps to solve problems;
- understands the financial pressures placed on students;
- provides clear information about how the course will run;
- doesn't fob off students;
- follows up on issues;
- gives constructive criticism;
- works with student representatives to get things done;
- communicates with the students' union about issues on the course;
- gives students a clear understanding about what is expected to achieve the desired result;
- is flexible and recognizes that students may have to work part-time;
- is supportive of involvement in activities beyond the course;
- is available to discuss work;
- turns up to lectures;
- communicates clearly;
- is enthusiastic;
- is creative;
- is challenging and makes students think;
- returns work and marks on time.

This is a comprehensive list of expectations from the student perspective, but what is interesting is that the issues identified are entirely compatible with those in other research, for example that published by Ramsden (1992: 89), which sets out the properties of good teaching from the individual lecturer's point of view. Using this as a starting point, the significance in terms of developing systems for student support and managing quality enhancement will be obvious to heads of departments and others responsible for teaching and learning.

OVERVIEW

This chapter has provided an introduction from the perspective of the student to the students' union movement, student financial affairs, the changing expectations of the student body and the role of students in institutional life. It has drawn attention to the implications of these matters for institutions, their managers and academics.

ACKNOWLEDGEMENT

The assistance given by Graham Gaskell, NUS London Regional Officer, in planning and writing this chapter is gratefully acknowledged by the author.

REFERENCES

Barclays Student Debt Survey 1999, Barclays Bank, London

Department for Education and Employment (DfEE) (1993) *The Government's Expenditure Plans, 1993–4 to 1995–6*, HMSO, London

Department of Education and Science (DES) (1988) White paper, *Top-Up Loans for Students*, HMSO, London

Education Act (1994) HMSO, London

GMB/NUS (1996) *Students at Work*, General and Municipal Trades Union, London

Higher Education Funding Council for England (HEFCE) (2000) *Performance Indicators in Higher Education in the UK, 1997–98, 1998–99*, HEFCE paper 00/40, Higher Education Funding Council for England, Bristol

Higher Education Statistics Agency (HESA) (2001) Student enrolments on higher education courses at publicly funded higher education institutions in the UK for the academic year 2000/01, HESA SFR 48 at URL: http://www.hesa.ac.uk/Press/sfr48/sfr48.htm

Jacks, D (1975) *Student Politics and Higher Education*, Lawrence and Wishart, London

National Committee of Inquiry into Higher Education (NCIHE) (1997) *Higher Education in the Learning Society*, report of the National Committee chaired by Sir Ron Dearing, NCIHE/97/850, HMSO, London

National Union of Students (NUS) (1999) *Student Hardship Survey, 1998–1999*, NUS, London

NUS (2000) *Accommodation Costs Survey, 1999-2000*, NUS, London

Ramsden, P (1992) *Learning to Teach in Higher Education*, Routledge, London

Rhodes, FA (1990) *The National Union of Students 1922–1967* (MEd thesis, University of Manchester 1968), SUSOC

Robbins, Lord (1963) *Higher Education: Report of the Committee appointed by the Prime Minister under the chairmanship of Lord Robbins*, HMSO, London

Universities and Colleges Admission Service (UCAS) (2000) Statistical enquiry service, at URL: http://www.ucas.ac.uk/figures/archive/publist/index.html

Part 2
Running the
Business

Introduction

The Editors with Martyn Davies,
Catherine Haines
and David Allen

This part of the book considers two main aspects of academic management for heads of departments and others managing in academic environments. The section opens with a chapter on strategic and business planning by Tom Kennie. This is followed by two chapters which concentrate on people management. The first is Anne Gold's chapter 'The ethical manager: working with and through colleagues' and this leads on to 'Managing the human resource function' by Catherine Haines and Steve Ketteridge. A strong theme developed in this section is people management. It is arguably this aspect of management that many new heads and managers in higher education find the most challenging, and for which they find themselves ill prepared. Other areas of management, such as the management of finances and of information, receive very scant attention because so many of the operational details will be specific to institutions. Part 5 of this book moves the aspiring manager on to offer some ideas on continuing professional development and preparation for a future role in academic management. The emphasis throughout this section is on management; for a more detailed consideration of leadership issues in higher education, the reader is referred to Knight and Trowler (2001).

SETTING THE SCENE

The section opens with a personal perspective by a head of department in a research-led university, which raises many of the practical matters to be considered in the following chapters. Professor Martyn Davies provides a rare opportunity to discuss openly the challenges that heads can prepare for, the people who can help, and the losses and gains of the experience. His contribution will be of value to readers in reviewing their own development needs in advance of taking on a managerial role.

Professor Davies' experience is of course unique. He has taken over as head of a major and well-resourced school of pharmacy with a wide range of scientific, commercial, research and teaching responsibilities, and with all the infrastructure and history that that entails. Naturally the challenges facing other types of department will be different, but they will have some issues in common, particularly where people management and responses to national initiatives are concerned.

Personal Reflections on Being a Head of Department by Martyn Davies in Conversation With Catherine Haines

My top three recommendations for new heads of schools and departments would be to plan, to delegate and not to expect thanks! It is vital to develop a vision, an overall plan and to communicate it to the centre and the school. As head I have to delegate tasks and follow them, trying not to micro-manage everything. I try to be very interested in what people are doing. I am always watching, ready to step in, but I work hard to let the ship run.

Strategic and operational planning

The school plans annually. This process is vital. I had no experience of this before, apart from developing the strategy for my research group. This is from a much bigger perspective. There are some institutional imperatives, for example the drive for increasing undergraduate and postgraduate numbers, managing the balance between teaching and research, while making sure we increase our research income. We have cooperative links with international institutions, with overseas and postgraduate students coming to the school. It is important to make sure the school accrues some of the benefits.

In the short and medium term we set our objectives and then submit them to the dean of faculty, the pro-vice-chancellors and get financial approval for our plans. As head of school I find this planning process very useful because it gives us the opportunity formally to record our position. We have had difficult problems to solve, merging groups from two schools for the RAE submission and learning how to teach together. To some extent we know we have to persuade the centre of our operational requirements. We have a management group within the school. It is their role to 'operationalize' the strategy, delegating activities to academics with various key roles. We have to demonstrate that we have the infrastructure to carry out our plans.

The feedback I got from my management group is that I was still doing too much and so I am now trying to step back. I see my main role as making sure we reward individuals and do not overburden people. I have to encourage and reward research, teaching and administration. I like the administration to be widely and thinly spread with senior people taking on major roles. Younger staff are protected significantly. We have a senior administrator to support this.

In some ways I now accept that the school is a business. It can't stand still. This has an impact on our strategies. I set the strategic goals and then we find the mechanism to translate them into actions.

Managing finances

Financial accountability was a big eye-opener for me. The budget is now fully devolved, although the centre still has significant control. I have the budget set by the previous head. We don't have a surplus due to the new building. We have not hit our targets. I can't know it to the penny. I employ someone who has a team of people to manage this day to day.

Times have changed. I am now more in the role of a chairman or chief executive. We have a multi-million pound budget and I have to 'soft-land' these figures. We are monitored from the centre by a finance officer who reviews our monthly targets with us.

I have to be sure that these targets are achieved. I am very accountable in both directions: to the centre and to the department. I never thought that I would be thinking of academia as a business.

Managing staff

I would say that I manage with a light touch. People are organized around research groups with a lot of autonomy. People have to respond and contribute. For example, a research-driven new lecturer has things to learn about their responsibilities to the school. I see everybody for 30 minutes, one-to-one every six months to talk, mostly about themselves and their aspirations. We rely on them. I can't get the research money for them. I can't go into the lecture theatre with them. When I was a young academic I got on with it, I was an individual in a dynamic environment. I want our academics to feel the same.

The senior secretarial staff now carry out essentially administrative roles. A lot of work is now devolved down to the school, and this puts increasing demands on our office staff. We have organized staff into an IT team led by a senior academic, and employ a Web administrator.

The previous head of school made me responsible for the technical staff for a couple of years before I took up the role of head. This helped me be more aware of their needs and to encourage and value their contribution. We need to empower them and reward them for responsibilities. We encourage the academic staff to respect and recognize technical support staff skills.

The school runs science-based courses, and health and safety is critical. I am the one nominally responsible. This has changed so much recently, at all levels, with all standard operations being specified. We aim for these to be enabling not disabling but want our health and safety committee to be firm and strong, with lots of money to support it, and technical staff and all groups of staff represented.

Managing space and resource

Planning for our new building was excellent preparation for being head of school. I had to have a strategy for achieving the building, services and facilities that everyone wanted. I had to manage all the interested parties: university staff, the architects, the vice-chancellor, our own staff. I had to be a conduit of information and be firm about what was achievable. My watchword is to be prepared, to stand by and defend any decision I'm involved in taking. I had to say 'it is going to be great' to people who were deeply suspicious of change. I learnt a lot from applying for national funds from the JIF [Joint Infrastructure Fund] in a politically effective way, getting good advice on how play this game and trusting in my own judgement.

Developing staff

We are in competition with industry and that can be difficult in our subject area. We look for committed individuals, mini-entrepreneurs who are self-reliant. I manage very bright people who are lured in and out of the system. We are a high profile research department, under high pressure. They have to be able to come in and perform. We are making a key investment in them. We have extraordinarily talented people who can be extraordinarily needy for reassurance so they don't lose their perspective. We are looking to recruit people who can work well in teams. We need star researchers, and we need leaders and more rounded individuals who can become the invaluable, trusted individuals within the school.

The appraisal system helps me as head of school, in spite of the scepticism by some staff. I read all their documentation and I review action points with them at less formal meetings. It gives me a structure, a positive tool, not to act as a watchdog. It helps staff be self-critical in a positive context. Some have gone wrong. Young academics can be heavily critical and in some cases have been heavily criticized, which can be counterproductive.

We are a five star school: we want to keep as many good people as we can. I'm proud to see people progress who have been nurtured with us. I hope promotion is flexible enough to reward the right people within the school.

External pressure

We can get dispirited as so much is driven by the centre. Time and again we get given figures with very little consultation. Continuation audit is coming up soon. When will it ever end? The RAE is top of our agenda at the moment (winter 2000–01). We had teaching quality assessment last year. I have a strong sense of the UK education system driving us hard and it is my job as head of school to protect our staff and help them achieve what is achievable.

I have to fight our corner. There are no special treatment arguments from the institutional perspective. I have to make a case based on needs. We have to be accountable on budgets, yet are not able to pursue service level agreements with the centre; we'd love to be able to do that with personnel and finance.

Development for the role

I benefited enormously from being mentored by the previous head of school. He gave me advice, a new perspective on why the centre acted as it did. He was formerly a pro-vice-chancellor. He engineered roles for me outside the school to ensure I was less parochial. For example, to be the dean of a faculty is at first an extraordinary jump, a different league. I shadowed him for a year.

I did go on a specific training course, which addressed some of the issues, exposed me to good practice. I learnt a lot about myself and a lot more about how other people did things.

As far as my future career is concerned, it is too early to tell if I want to go back to being a member of school. It is certainly a strain on my research right now. Ultimately I'm good at getting research done and developing students. I have also got a company to think about. People who want to be vice-chancellors start earlier than I have.

THE INSTITUTIONAL PERSPECTIVE

Heads of department have not only to communicate with their own staff but to communicate effectively with the senior management team. A key factor in success as a head of department is rigorous interaction and representation with those at the 'centre'. On occasions there may be tensions between the needs and wants of the institution and those of the head of department which will have to be resolved.

David Allen is Registrar and Secretary of the University of Birmingham and the Chair of the Association for University Administrators. In the following commentary he presents a viewpoint from the centre on what makes for a successful head of department.

Personal Reflections on Being a Head of Department – the Registrar and Secretary's View by David Allen

Nobody goes into academic life to become a head of school or department. Heads have greatness thrust upon them. Like new Speakers of the House, they are dragged reluctantly to the role, often with no greater succession planning than 'Buggins' turn' or a process of elimination. Many come to the job knowing they will return in a few years time to the back benches and so they had better not rock the boat too much.

In a perfect world heads would be groomed for the role several years in advance, through a bespoke programme of professional development covering a wide range of management skills and issues. Too often training begins with the induction of a new head in post rather than at least a year in advance.

Given these handicaps it is perhaps surprising that so many heads do so well. Next to the quality of the vice-chancellor, the quality of heads is probably the most important ingredient of institutional success. In my experience the most successful heads:

- have the genuine respect and admiration of their colleagues for their academic achievements and personal qualities;
- demonstrate academic credibility alongside strong natural leadership skills;
- constantly communicate with their staff and students and with the 'centre';
- engage in a constructive, realistic dialogue with the centre about what is achievable;
- actively manage teaching and research so as to free the time of the most creative researchers and run efficient teaching programmes;
- seek new opportunities through multi-disciplinary collaboration, even where this may mean sharing student numbers;
- are good with people and especially handling the temperamental and the poor performers;
- are not afraid of living with uncertainty and of pushing through unpopular change;
- are adept in handling management information to improve performance;
- delegate up as well as down.

The relationship between heads and the registrar is an important one. Heads look to the registrar for impartial advice and to cut a path through thickets of bureaucracy. It is important for heads to know that there is someone who has probably seen it all before, who is there for them when the going gets tough and who has only the university's best interests at heart.

Being a head is a thankless task, but the great heads can build the reputation of their discipline in a given place at a given time for a generation. That is something worth doing.

REFERENCE

Knight, PT and Trowler, PR (2001) *Departmental Leadership in Higher Education*, Society for Research into Higher Education/Open University Press, Buckingham

4 | Strategic and Operational Planning

Tom Kennie

INTRODUCTION

Mention the 'p' word to a randomly selected group of senior academic managers and, for some, their eyes begin to glaze over. For this group, plans are of little or no value – at best a necessary evil. Despite being surrounded by visions, missions, values, performance indicators and other 'best practice' approaches they question whether this is time well spent. What if we didn't plan, they muse: would it make any difference to the outcomes? In any case it's all too difficult, the world of higher education is changing too quickly to justify spending time producing meaningless plans. Let's just do it. We're intelligent people, we'll adapt as we go. It worked in the past, it will work again.

Some of you might have sympathy with our mythical sceptic's views about the value of plans. On the other hand, you might also recognize that in an environment of limited resources, increasing competition, demands to enhance quality, widen participation and so on, processes are required to focus attention, prioritize action and check progress is being achieved. Using a simple metaphor, if you are proposing to travel to a new location, it can be very useful to have purchased or created a map, even if you then recognize that there are several different routes you can take. So although the plan (the route in this context) may be of limited value, the process of planning (using the map) can be of critical value. But how can planning be undertaken in a HE context, particularly in a way that limits scepticism and delivers benefits?

This chapter aims to deal with this dilemma in three ways: firstly, by clarifying some of the distinctions between 'strategic' and 'operational' planning (section 2); secondly, by examining a number of different perspectives on the theme of 'planning' (section 3); and finally, by offering some views on how to 'operationalize' plans and link them to what people do on a day-to-day basis (section 4).

STRATEGIC AND OPERATIONAL PLANNING

Planning is necessary at a number of levels in any organization. Often the distinction is made between planning that is strategic and planning that is more operational in nature. Mistakenly, this is often associated with the level in the hierarchy where the planning is taking place: the senior management team are assumed to deal only with the strategic, whereas (say) departments are primarily operationally focused. This simplistic distinction can lead to a lack of appreciation of the need for strategic thinking and planning to take place at all levels, and equally the need for operational implementation to be considered when senior management teams are developing an overall strategy.

One potentially useful framework for considering this issue is to explore the balance of activities illustrated in Figure 2.4.1. This framework firstly aims to illustrate some of the activities which need attention as part of the planning process, and secondly emphasizes the need to consider the balance of time

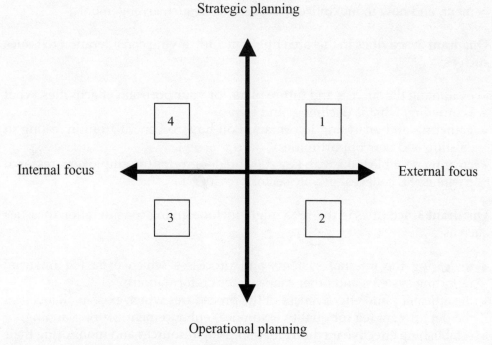

Figure 2.4.1 Balancing priorities in planning

and attention that is being given to each of the four areas. All four areas demand attention, whether the planning is at the most senior level or at other levels. However, the balance of time spent in each area will differ. In general terms, the broader the scale and scope of the area of planning (for example, on a university-wide level) the greater the weight which should be spent on the top half of the diagram, whereas the more focused the level (for example, at departmental or discipline level) the greater the emphasis on the lower half.

Each of the quadrants illustrates some of the issues requiring attention during the planning process.

Quadrant 1: activities in this area might include giving consideration to issues such as:

- conducting studies of the major changes in the external marketplace affecting higher education and the disciplines in the department;
- considering where to position the department strategically: what ultimately do you collectively want the department to be famous for?
- evaluating the nature of the competition in your areas of activity, and considering how to differentiate your department from others;
- to balance the focus on competition, also identifying on the partnerships and alliances which are, or will become, of most importance to the department, and how to maximize the return from such arrangements.

Quadrant 2: activities in this area might include giving consideration to issues such as:

- evaluating the success and future plans for your portfolio of activities: what is growing, what is declining, and so on;
- gathering and analysing information on how to benefit from investing in existing and new opportunities;
- creating tangible links with key stakeholder groups (eg employers, research partners, FE colleges, private sector providers).

Quadrant 3: activities in this area might include giving consideration to issues such as:

- reviewing the internal systems and processes which exist (eg financial reporting systems and other management information);
- the efficiency and effectiveness of the procedures which exist at all levels in the department (eg for quality assurance/enhancement, work planning;
- establishing effective methods for allocating resources and monitoring their use;

- ensuring procedures exist to gain feedback on performance, from student feedback to staff appraisal systems;
- evaluating whether you have the appropriate balance of skills and capabilities to deliver the strategic priorities for the department.

Quadrant 4: activities in this area might include giving consideration to issues such as:

- considering whether the internal governance of the department is appropriate;
- evaluating the effectiveness of the internal decision-making processes;
- determining whether the organizational structure is appropriate and relevant to the strategic direction;
- identifying opportunities to create a 'step-change' in operational terms: in other words, establish radically new ways of operating.

The issues highlighted in this analysis illustrate a number of alternative perspectives from which to consider the planning process. To help clarify these alternative perspectives, the next section considers the value to be gained from viewing planning from these multi-faceted viewpoints.

PERSPECTIVES ON PLANNING

To illustrate the different perspectives about planning, consider the following question:

Enhancing Practice

Imagine you were invited into another department which had recently won a national award for its success in teaching and research. The head of department has emphasized that their success was heavily influenced by their approach to planning. During your visit, what sort of evidence would indicate to you that the departmental planning process was of value?

Some indicators you might identify could include:

- illustrative evidence of both 'top-down' strategic direction and 'bottom-up' engagement and involvement in the process;

- clear evidence of where the department was starting from, 'the here', where the department was aiming to get to, 'the there', and evidence of the process of 'getting to there';
- different groups of staff describing their views of 'here' 'there' and 'getting there', and showing consistency in their views;
- evidence of how the department scanned the external environment and used it to inform its decision making;
- evidence that the process of developing their overall strategy was 'shared' and the various strands 'integrated' with each other;
- clear lines of accountability regarding development and implementation;
- a clear set of actions and monitoring processes to provide feedback on progress;
- clear measures of performance, together with the management information systems to gather and synthesize such data;
- a shared set of values across the department;
- evidence that the department worked as an overall system and that it was clear how the different parts interacted with and were influenced by each other.

Each of these different pieces of evidence is based on one or more mental models of what constitutes 'effective planning'. Some of the more common of these different perspectives are listed below. It is important to emphasize the need to develop a holistic perspective on the process of planning. Each perspective offers some additional insights. Ultimately, however, one of the challenges for the leaders of the planning process is to select one or more of these interpretations which offers most value. Of course this will be partly influenced by the expectations of others (eg that a formal written plan should be created), and it will also be influenced by the culture of the department and institution. In some instances, however, the approach(es) chosen may also be used to influence and modify the prevailing culture.

The formal, rational perspective

Probably the most common methodology cited in relation to planning is that based on formal, rational planning principles. For those unfamiliar with the details of the process, the recently published guidance document by the Higher Education Funding Council for England (HEFCE) (2000) offers a useful summary at the institutional level. The techniques are, however, transferable to the departmental level. A more wide-ranging review on the process of 'managing strategy' can also be found in Watson (2000).

In summary, some of the more common techniques which are used in the formulation of formal, rational 'strategic plans' might involve conducting one or more of the following analyses.

STEPE analysis

STEPE is a formal framework for reviewing the external environment, which involves considering a range of external issues that might impact upon the department or the disciplines within the department from different perspectives. This analysis can be used to help map the (S) social (T) technological (E) economic (P) political and (E) environmental influences, and enables an assessment to be made of their likely impact on the department/disciplines being considered. For example, how important is each trend and independently how certain/uncertain are you about each trend? This type of analysis offers some initial views on the significance of the changes taking place at present, and for the future.

SWOT analysis

This second analysis enables the performance of the department to be assessed in terms of both internal factors, that is its (S) strengths and (W) weaknesses, and externally in terms of the (O) opportunities available/open to it and the (T) threats confronting the department/discipline. Again this initial assessment can be of considerable value in identifying some of the strategic choices facing the department.

The competitive market positioning perspective

This second perspective on planning emphasizes the importance of 'the market'. In this example the process of planning is primarily about understanding 'the market' and matching market needs by suitable 'offerings'. One component of this approach might involve a strategic review of the department's portfolio of teaching and learning activities.

Portfolio analysis

This technique can be helpful, particularly for evaluating and reviewing teaching portfolios. A portfolio analysis might involve a review of where the different programmes are positioned in relation to subject strength and market demand.

In addition to portfolio analysis this perspective also emphasizes the importance of 'differentiation' to highlight what is distinctive about a department, a course or an area of research compared with rival departments, courses and so on. Porter (1996) suggests that to outperform rivals requires the establishment of a difference that can be preserved. He also distinguishes between differentiation based on 'operational effectiveness' and that based on 'strategic positioning'. For Porter, 'operational effectiveness' implies performing *similar* activities *better* than rivals can perform them, whereas 'strategic posi-tioning' means performing *different* activities from rivals or performing similar activities in *different* ways from rivals.

A final process which might also feature highly when viewing planning through this lens is to review the 'market sectors' in which the department has developed a reputation, and the key stakeholders/client groups who are of critical importance to the department in each sector.

This perspective works most effectively when you are working in a truly market-dominated environment. While HE has many features of a market economy, because of the provision of public sector funds in many instances decisions are made in only quasi-market conditions. In the future, however, the impact of private sector suppliers, particularly in the e-learning environ-ment, will lead to this perspective becoming even more significant.

The cultural perspective

An increasingly important interpretation relates to creating a shared culture. 'Culture' in this context relates to the shared values and ways of interacting which exist within a department or institution. The importance of these implicit assumptions about 'how things are done around here' should not be underestimated. Indeed, you may wish to challenge some of these assump-tions and use the process of planning to surface, and in time change, some of these deep-seated ways of operating. Furthermore, understanding the cultur-al characteristics of your department and the 'unwritten rules' which influence what matters is a critical aspect of ensuring plans are ultimately implemented. The works by Scott-Morgan (1996) and Price and Shaw (1998) offer some insightful guidance on how to influence the patterns of behaviour which drive the creation of powerful cultures and subcultures. For those who wish to understand more about the subcultures of different academic disci-plines, Becher (1989) is worthy of review.

The performance measurement perspective

The performance measurement perspective of planning is dominated by assumptions such as 'what gets measured gets done' and 'if you can't meas-ure it, you can't plan it'. In this territory, terms such as 'performance indicators', 'key performance indicators' and 'critical success factors' domi-nate. Two frameworks from the private sector which are gaining in popularity in the public sector (including some parts of HE) are the 'balanced scorecard' and the 'business excellence' models.

The balanced scorecard

The concept of a 'balanced scorecard' of performance measures (Kaplan and

Norton, 1996) has become fashionable in the wider commercial world. This framework has emerged to emphasize the need in the business environment to be attuned to the danger of giving too much emphasis to financial measures. To balance this focus it is also necessary to have measures which focus on people, systems and the market.

In an HE context the challenge is often to select those key performance measures which are of most significance, and for which robust data collection and analysis techniques exist to enable them to be monitored on a regular basis. In so many cases the measures selected are not linked to the overall strategy of the department and often suffer because of a lack of comparative data.

Benchmarking

One of the increasingly useful techniques which can be of considerable value in the planning process is benchmarking. In simple terms it is a process for comparing performance and more importantly for understanding and learning from the process how to enhance performance. The comparison may be quantitative or qualitative, where the emphasis might be on comparing the processes used to undertake a particular activity. Jackson (2000) provides a useful primer on the topic as it relates to an HE context.

Business excellence model

A further formal, analytical framework which is beginning to appear in the HE world is the 'business excellence' model developed by the European Foundation for Quality Management (EFQM). A current HEFCE research project (Pupius and Brusoni, 2000) is evaluating the potential of this framework as a means of enhancing institutional effectiveness. Using a standard conceptual framework (see Figure 2.4.2) the role of the planning process is to ensure that a consistent measurement methodology is utilized. This also enables comparative benchmarking to take place.

Overall the formal, rational models work best in circumstances of reasonable stability. When the level of uncertainty rises, this approach becomes less effective and needs to be supplemented by other approaches, particularly that associated with scenarios.

The sensitivity analysis perspective

The sensitivity analysis perspective comes into play as a method of illustrating, as part of the planning process, the links and interdependencies between different parts of the department or organization. For example, a model might be created to assess the impact of a range of alternative funding decisions on the viability of part, or all, of the department. Such an ability to conduct reviews of a number of 'what-if' scenarios is an increasingly important aspect

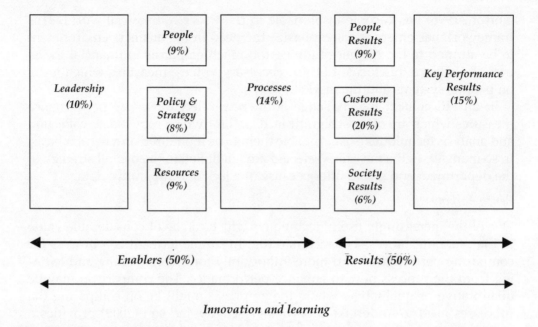

Figure 2.4.2 The business excellence planning model

of the planning process. Small changes in student numbers, or of the level of recovery of overheads on research contracts, or of the level of profit on a commercial contract, need to be understood fully as part of the planning process. In addition, the cumulative impact of a number of alternative scenarios might also benefit from such analyses.

Sensitivity Analysis Modelling Using PROFSIMTM by Tom Kennie and Chris Ward

A recent innovation which uses sensitivity analysis to model the impact of a range of alternative financial and organization decisions in a higher education context has involved the use of the PROFSIMTM simulation software. As part of the recently established Top Management Programme for Higher Education (TMP@HE), a management development programme for senior managers in academic institutions, PROFSIMTM was used to create a model to simulate the characteristics of a commercial e-university. The model, entitled DONS.COM!, provided a tool for senior managers to consider the impact of a wide range of operational decisions on the overall profitability of a commercial e-learning enterprise. Over 150 spreadsheets linked together in Microsoft Excel enabled the participants to test out a range of possible scenarios and evaluate many different planning decisions, but without the normal risks.

As parts of the higher education world become more attuned to the need for risk analysis of both a financial and non-financial nature, the need for this type of sensitivity testing software may well become of more significance.

Building such financial and organizational models does require effort; however, the benefit is that they offer those making planning decisions a means of assessing the cumulative impact of a range of possible decisions.

The 'emergent' perspective

In response to the rapidity of change and in recognition of the limitations of a centralized planning model, the 'emergent perspective' school of thought developed. The prevailing assumption on which this approach is based is that what matters is creating the conditions where the plan can 'emerge'. What matters is 'good process', not just 'good practice'. Create the right environment and an appropriate plan will evolve.

In this context what is crucial is creating the conditions in which an appropriate plan can be developed. At one level these conditions might be as simple as having a clear timetable for developing and implementing the plan: a planning cycle. However, more often there is a real need to create conditions in which individuals can be creative. This implies giving serious time and thought to the conditions within which planning takes place. At one extreme (although it is more common than it should be), a plan is drafted in isolation by one individual, is distributed very close to the completion deadline, and minor amendments from others are eventually included. Alternatively, in order to really engage people's interest and attention it is necessary to allow time and space, preferably away from the physical context of daily operational activities. However, simply arranging a departmental 'away-day' by itself is rarely sufficient. What is more beneficial is to create the conditions in which the constant shaping and reshaping of the plan is a shared activity, conducted in a manner in which consultation is genuine and creative ideas are encouraged and recognized.

The scenario perspective

The scenario perspective on planning has emerged into the HE context in recent years, primarily as a response to the increasing uncertainty associated with the process of planning. In a world where forecasting the future is highly problematic, where the impact of changes elsewhere in the 'complex system' can lead to unexpected consequences, many of the traditional planning processes become quite inadequate.

To deal with such increasing uncertainty the process of scenario planning emerged into the commercial environment in the last 20–30 years (Schwartz, 1996). A number of different approaches to the process exist. However, typically the process involves a number of phases including:

1. A means of gathering data on the key trends in a particular sector (eg using a STEPE analysis).
2. Some assessment of the degree of uncertainty associated with each trend, and a further assessment of the impact of each trend.
3. A clustering of these trends in order to identify a number of dimensions of change.
4. The development of a narrative to describe the alternative 'scenarios' which might arise.
5. The identification of some lead indicators which might give a degree of pre-warning that a particular scenario was becoming more likely to occur.
6. An evaluation of existing formal plans against each of the scenarios in

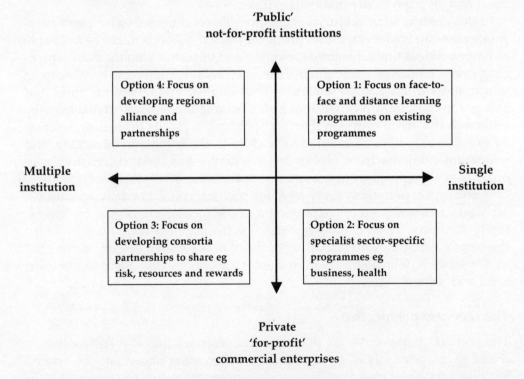

Figure 2.4.3 Identification of dimensions of change and potential scenarios

order to consider whether any changes to the existing plans are necessary to ensure they are sufficiently responsive to possible future scenarios.

To illustrate a possible outcome of step 3, the sets of axes shown in Figure 2.4.3 emerged from a recent scenario building exercise.

Using Scenario Planning at the Discipline Level
by John Ratcliffe

Ratcliffe (2000) illustrates how the concept can be applied to a discipline, in this instance surveying. He identifies four possible scenarios for real estate education which he characterizes as follows:

'*All the talents*': there is a high level of funding for research and a high demand for real estate education. All options are open, all things possible, and 'all the talents' can be harnessed to promote and progress research for the real estate industry. The question is choice by all concerned.

'*Take your pick*': there is a high level of funding for research, but real estate education is not attractive. Those wishing to pursue real estate programmes or commission property-related research can 'take their pick' from among a range of competing institutions. Quality, reliability and service are paramount.

'*For sale to the highest bidder*': there is low funding for research, but real estate education is popular. It is a marketplace, where academic institutions offer real estate programmes and research services to those who can best afford them.

'*Antisthenes reborn*': there is low funding for research, and little demand for real estate education. A downward cycle of decline traps the property profession, and a diminishing number of institutions chase shrinking budgets and falling roles. A dismal picture.

To illustrate the development of a more detailed narrative for each scenario he offers the following in relation to the final scenario ('Antisthenes reborn').

Narrow short-term thinking has led to an absolute paucity of funds for research. What monies there are, are directed towards the high technology industries and the commercial end of genetic engineering and pharmaceuticals. The real estate market is disaggregated, disenchanted and disappearing in a structured form. Disintermediation has struck at the heart of the earnings base. Technology-driven knowledge-based expert systems have rendered much previously 'professional' work to a merely 'technical' level. Real estate education is generally unattractive.

There is a sharp polarization of academic institutions. The 'best' universities are forced to raise fees, and just manage to recruit an ever diminishing pool of property oriented students. 'Lower division' universities are forced to dismantle courses and amalgamate or modularize real estate programmes almost out of recognition. Many abandon real estate education altogether – and departments of business, economics and finance gobble up the remains. There are deferred maintenance, non-renewal of equipment and cuts in staff and staff development almost everywhere. Early retirement deals for older faculty, vacant positions and the use of part-time and temporary staff proliferate. The professional body, the RICS, reintroduces examinations and withdraws recognition from all but five centres of excellence in the UK and seven others across Europe. On top of all this, the RICS Research Foundation withholds support from university based research and, in conjunction with a 'consortium' of top firms, establishes its own Research Institute.

Similar thinking could no doubt apply to a number of related disciplines. What scenario planning cannot do is predict the future: what it can offer is a process for considering a range of possible futures and using this to encourage academics to plan for some or all of these possible futures.

OPERATIONAL PLANNING

The process of taking the really creative ideas which emerge during the planning process and turning these into effective operational plans requires careful thought, particularly to minimize a lack of integration.

Integrating the elements

Avoiding a lack of integration within the planning process requires, to adapt a current government mantra, a high level of 'joined up-ness'. Broadly speaking, the parts which need linking together include:

- the statements which clarify and make explicit the overall direction, that is, '*the strategy*' for the institution and for the department;
- the processes and statements used to manage financial resources, that is, '*the budget*' for the department;
- the processes and statements which describe specific actions to be undertaken across the department, that is, the '*operating statement or plan*' for the department;
- the processes and documents which are used on a one-to-one basis to summarize the priorities and objectives for staff across the department, that is, the '*performance appraisal*' system.

Figure 2.4.4 illustrates the links between the first three of these elements.

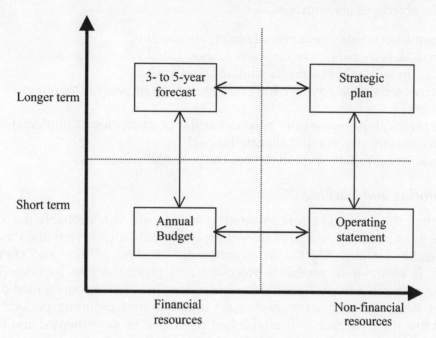

Figure 2.4.4   Aligning financial plans with operational and strategic plans

Setting objectives

The second component in the creation of an effective operational plan is a method of translating general statements of intent into specific objectives and actions. Whether these are at the level of objectives for the department or for individuals, it is important to ensure clear measures of success exist, with clear lines of accountability. It can be useful jointly to review objectives against the following SMART framework. Are the objectives:

S   Specific: is the objective specific enough, or should we break it down into more manageable parts? Have we clearly specified who is accountable?

M   Measurable: have we considered what direct and indirect measures could be used to assess whether progress is being made?

A   Action oriented: have we identified clear actions which need to be progressed?

R   Resources: have we fully considered the resource implications of the objective?

T   Time: have we clarified the time limits for achievement of the objective?

The STAIR test (Grundy, 1995) can also be a useful means of cross-checking that the objectives are appropriate:

S   Simplistic: is this objective sufficiently demanding?
T   Tactical: is this objective tactically relevant, and have we considered how it fits in with other tactically similar objectives?
A   Active resistance: have we fully considered the impact of this objective on others?
I   Impractical: have we fully considered the practicalities of implementing this objective (within the allocated time)?
R   Risk: have we fully explored all of the potential risk factors?

Monitoring and learning

Providing the time and effort required to monitor plans is probably the area where most planning processes have the greatest difficulty. All too often those responsible for planning fail to recognize the amount of time and energy which is required to establish processes and procedures to monitor and review plans on a regular basis. How often does the plan become a filed document which is rarely examined again until the next planning period? To avoid this it is vital that well-established processes are documented and that time is set aside to review, learn from and update the plans.

The lessons from a recent study by Beer and Eisenstat (2000) highlight 'six silent killers of strategy', including:

- top-down or *laissez-faire* senior management style;
- unclear strategy and conflicting priorities;
- ineffective senior management team;
- poor vertical communication;
- poor coordination across units;
- inadequate down-the-line leadership skills.

Harvey, in his expert commentary, offers some further insights into the planning process, suggesting that mere application of planning tools is not sufficient to bring about real institutional improvement. The subsequent points he offers provide a useful contextualization for this whole chapter.

Expert Commentary: Strategic Planning in HE – The Worm's Eye View

---

Scepticism abounds in higher education. Nowhere is it more evident in daily institutional life than in the area of planning. Strategic, operational, tactical, academic and non-academic planning: all trigger bucketloads of scepticism. Departments, heads and hard-pressed administrators are sceptical whether all the reams of data requests churned out by 'the centre' actually provide information of relevance to planning, and question whether planning *per se* is actually conducive to a better university. Eyes roll and anguished pleas accompany the annual business planning round and the roll-forward of the institutional plan: the timetable is too compressed; we've given all this data to you already; it's totally inappropriate to set individuals or groups performance targets; what use are you going to make of all this anyway? I bet they don't do all this at Oxford and Cambridge.

Vice-chancellors, registrars and academic secretaries blench at the sight of the steady-state world of institutional planning as seen by the funding council. The clinically clean managerial environment that is the backdrop to the rolling corporate plan and the annual operating statement are far removed from the cut and thrust of daily decision taking, where the difference between landing or not landing Professor Smith from Harvard in the Department of Bio-informatics is the real difference between taking the department to the cutting edge or dooming it to five years of poor leadership and stagnation. In this business where almost everything depends on the quality of people, their creativity and the conditions for enabling them to succeed, the absence of pristine documents, annually updated, integrated and quantitatively consistent, is unlikely to be the cause behind the senior management insomnia. Box-ticking on forms and careful and costly prose are worlds away from the real institutional success stories. In these places academics and researchers are liberated from the administrative grind that seeks to turn their creativity and innovation into cash targets, performance measures and benchmarks.

Or are they? Is strategic planning really only an administrative ruse for justifying the existence of the bean-counters in Senate House or just an expensive means of giving the administration or the civil servants the information needed to grind another axe? Is planning something other than the management and information office at the end of the corridor where much goes in but little comes out?

Tom Kennie's instructive tour d'horizon of the tools of the planning trade would suggest that there is. This chapter does much more than iterate seven key perspectives on organizational planning and the techniques each encompasses, valuable as these are in themselves. Some key messages in the text go to the heart of actual planning practice in HE today:

- We do require planning to focus attention, prioritize action and check progress.

- We do have to think carefully about the best means of turning strategy into operation.
- Strategic planning is too often seen as the purview of senior management and not something that engages people at all levels of the organization.
- Institutional leaders do need to understand why various perspectives on planning exist and how they interact in the planning process.
- Using techniques to draw up narratives or paint scenarios to enable the consideration of a range of possible futures is a more fruitful planning activity in fast-changing environments or in large complex organizations where there are multiple missions and destination points.
- Paying attention to the conditions under which planning takes place moves the planning process away from a linear set of stages to be followed and instead focuses on the context that best enables individuals to be creative: a planning process that is likely to engage people and produce greater ownership of what it produces.
- The 'silent killers' of strategy should be written in large letters on all our doors.

Kennie's key messages are the essential glue to effective organizational planning. Without understanding them and their interaction, managers – whether they be academics or administrators – will turn the handle on the planning cycle and produce documents and spreadsheets that do little for real institutional improvement.

As Michael Shattock has so clearly demonstrated (Harvey, 2001), successful universities like Warwick University in the 1980s and 1990s operate in an untidy world where competitiveness, opportunism, fleetness of foot, good judgement and good communication, characterize high performance. Control and clear structure in an artificially formal/rational world are insufficient ingredients for success and getting things done.

Dr Philip Harvey
Academic Secretary
University of Exeter

CONCLUSIONS

In common with all management processes, planning should not become an end in itself. It is vital to maintain a sense of perspective and ensure that it is constantly used positively to enhance the performance of the department, rather than seen as an inappropriate heavy-handed tool of 'management'. The role of those responsible for coordinating the process is to create the context where people can engage in informed debate and discussion in a creative and positive manner. Viewed from this perspective, the techniques outlined in this chapter are simply helpful mechanisms for data analysis, framing of options or the translating of intent into action.

REFERENCES

Becher, A (1989) *Academic Tribes and Territories: Intellectual enquiry and the cultures of disciplines,* Open University Press, Milton Keynes

Beer, M and Eisenstat, RA (2000) The silent killers of strategy, *Sloan Management Review,* Summer

Grundy, T (1995) *Breakthrough Strategies for Growth,* FT Pitman Publishing, London

Harvey, PK (2001) 'Exeter University: Going back to the future?' in *The State of UK Higher Education: Managing change and diversity,* ed D Warner and D Palfreyman, SRHE/Open University Press, Milton Keynes

Higher Education Funding Council for England (HEFCE) (2000) *Strategic Planning in Higher Education,* Higher Education Funding Council for England, Bristol

Jackson, N (ed) (2000) *Benchmarking in Higher Education,* Open University Press, Milton Keynes

Kaplan, R and Norton, D (1996) *The Balanced Scorecard,* Harvard Business School Press, Cambridge, Mass.

Porter, M (1996) What is strategy?, *Harvard Business Review,* November/December, pp 61–80

Price, I and Shaw, R (1998) Shifting the patterns, *Management 2000*

Pupius, M and Brusoni, M (2000) 'Comparing and contrasting the EFQM excellence model and the EQUIS accreditation process for management in higher education, paper presented to the International Conference, Quality in HE in the New Millennium, University of Derby

Ratcliffe, J (2000*) The Future of Work: Changes, Trends Property and Education,* RICS Education Conference 2000

Schwartz, P (1996) *The Art of the Long View,* Wiley, Chichester

Scott-Morgan, P (1996) *The Unwritten Rules of the Game,* Blackwell, Oxford

Watson, D (2000) *Managing Strategy – A guide to good practice,* Open University Press, Milton Keynes

The Ethical Manager: Working With and Through Colleagues

Anne Gold

INTRODUCTION

This chapter is not prescriptive, beyond suggesting that effective management is usually ethical management that works with and through other people. It lays out some of the context in which people manage in higher education in the United Kingdom (see also the next chapter and Chapters 1 and 2), and suggests some issues to be taken into account while managing the internal and the external tensions.

This chapter urges managers (of courses, research projects, a group or a department) to articulate their management priorities, in order to thread their way creatively through what often seem to be conflicting demands. It begins by defining management, and suggests ways in which managers may ensure their management decisions are underpinned by their own principles as well as those of their organization. It encourages reflection on self-management, on managing with others and on managing within the organization.

DEFINING MANAGEMENT

The experience of the author in running management courses for people working in higher education is that running separate courses for those with more and less managerial experience is helpful. Although they may fruitfully consider similar issues, there are distinctive differences in the attitude of the two types of participant towards management and managing. Beginning, or first time, managers need to spend time in the programme deciding whether they *should* be managers and whether they *really* are managers. Sometimes they are ideologically unable to describe themselves as managers because, for them, the term brings with it concepts of authority and control which they find disturbing. Management and leadership bring powerful and often emotional overtones which can encourage resistance in those who are managed, and guilt in those who are to manage.

Terms such as 'management', 'leadership' and 'administration' are used differently in different countries and in different management situations. Sometimes they are seen as interchangeable, and sometimes they are seen as hierarchically related. For this chapter, the following definitions are adopted, from Oldroyd, Elsner and Poster (1996):

- Leadership: the process of guiding followers in a certain direction in pursuit of a vision, mission or goals; making and implementing and evaluating policy.
- Leader: a person who exercises power, authority and influence over a group derived both from his or her acceptance by the group, and his or her position in the formal organization.
- Management: a) the structure for and process of planning, coordinating and directing the activities of people, departments and organizations; getting things done with and through other people; b) the individual or group of individuals who manage an organization.
- Manager: an individual responsible for the planning, coordination and direction of people, a department, or an organization.
- Managerialism: the assumption that management is the solution to many organizational problems; often a pejorative term directed at those who see management as an end rather than a means, particularly in the publicly funded services.
- Administration: the processes required to support the implementation of policies in organizations.

In other words, in higher education a manager is taken to be someone who works with other academics, researchers and administrators to ensure that knowledge is produced, reproduced and disseminated effectively. Management is a neutral term: it is how it is done that makes it either disturbing or empowering.

CONCEPTS OF MANAGEMENT AND THEIR HIGHER EDUCATION CONTEXT

Many people have a concept of management that is particularly difficult in a higher education context, because although external frameworks and demands have changed enormously over the last twenty years (see Chapters 1, 2 and 6), internally, there is often strong resistance to being managed in response to these external requirements. Diana Leonard (2001) shows how people working in universities in the UK have moved from having such central concerns as social responsibility and scholarship to recognizing national competitiveness and a view of themselves as working in enterprises which are concerned with quality and effectiveness. She suggests that concerns such as professional accountability, supported by ethics and integrity, have been replaced by central state control which ties outcomes to budgets by means of external evaluation of research and teaching against 'objective' criteria.

Enhancing Practice

- What external audits and frameworks will your university be working with in the next three years?
- How many of them will affect your own work?

PRINCIPLES INFORMING MANAGEMENT DECISIONS

Against the backdrop of the internal/external organizational tensions, managers in higher education find themselves mediating between the needs of the individual, the task and the organization. Often there are difficult choices and stresses: for example, when the institution or department is about to become the subject of an external audit such as a subject review or a research assessment. It is tempting to subsume the needs of individual employees into the immediate organizational needs: time for reading or writing is used up to ensure that administrative tasks are complete and well presented. In another scenario of imbalance, it could be that a key and formerly creative and internationally recognized member of staff is no longer functioning adequately. He or she may be preventing the effective production, reproduction and dissemination of knowledge (for example, undergraduate and doctoral students are receiving poor teaching and supervision, and little research is taking place). At what point does a manager intercede to support the students and the needs of the organization, while apparently challenging the professional practices of a renowned and respected member of staff?

At such points of stress, managers make the most balanced decisions if they have had the opportunity to articulate their values and principles about working with and through colleagues, and about empowering them to work most productively. They are then able to link those values to concrete plans and strategies which take account of the context for the organization. These values and principles are not developed in an intellectual or sociological vacuum: they are usually the products of managers' 'journeys' to their present professional position. They shape the managers' understanding of power and patriarchy, and they influence the way they work with other people when they themselves are given power in their organizations.

Effective and ethical managers have an understanding of power relations, and of their effect on those colleagues with whom they work and for whom they have management responsibility. Thus, although western European society privileges white, middle-class, able-bodied heterosexual men, it is clear that some men who fit all these categories do not manage in a patriarchal way. And when women, or people who come from other sites of apparent or potential disadvantage, reach positions of power, they do not always work in an empowering and collaborative way. So what makes the difference? How have these people interrupted the inevitability of managing in preordained ways?

In the first place, an understanding of power and the effects of power on other people is of the greatest importance. Most people who have felt less than powerful at some stage in their lives find it relatively easy to understand the effects of disempowering management styles. They know at first hand what disempowerment feels like. But knowledge and understanding are not enough. Rather like Kolb's (1984) learning cycle, it is necessary to have a reflective intervention, and also to have the opportunity to plan to do things differently. In other words, it is important to:

- understand the effects of disempowerment;
- articulate a set of principles to alleviate those effects;
- develop strategies to put those principles into practice.

People who work through all of these stages – feeling (or observing empathetically) the effects of the misuse of power; reflecting upon those effects; drawing up principles that counteract those effects; putting strategies in place based on the principles; then observing to see whether the strategies work to empower rather than disempower – are most likely to work with 'power for', rather than 'power over'.

> ### Enhancing Practice
>
> - What values underpin your work in higher education?
> - What values underpin your management practice in higher education?
> - Is there similarity in your answers to questions one and two above?

Empowering managers tend to work educatively with those they manage: they are clear why they have chosen to manage with colleagues the way they are managing, and their central concerns in management are connected with the development of those with whom they work. In this way, they endeavour to prioritize their management activities so that the colleagues with whom they work have considerate and ethical attention.

This prioritizing affects the way managers deal with paperwork and how they order their own work. It may be that they set aside regular 'surgery' hours for colleagues to come without an appointment, have an open-door policy at regular times, or always make a point of visiting common rooms and being accessible to colleagues. Whatever way they decide to signal their accessibility, it shows that they see managing people as part of their task, and not as interruptions to their main task.

Many managers carry an internal diagram in which they position themselves in relationship to those they manage. It may be that they see themselves as leaders, facilitators, or models of professional academic behaviour. It may also be that those they manage are happier with authoritative managers who tell them what to do, or with consultative managers who ask them for their opinions, but make the final decisions themselves. However this internal diagram presents itself, it has an effect on the interactions and the relationship between the manager and those who are managed.

Three important management principles emerge from the above:

- The manager takes responsibility for developing staff.
- The manager sees accessibility as part of the main management task.
- Clearly communicated expectations about management style make for fewer misunderstandings.

> ### Enhancing Practice
>
> Do you agree with the three principles mentioned above? Are there other principles that also underpin your management style?

MANAGING SELF

Given that managers have articulated a set of principles about higher education and about management, it is important to make sure that those principles inform the way they manage themselves as well as their colleagues. The 'greedy university' described by Currie, Harris and Thiele (2000) is very demanding of all workers in higher education, and managers must learn to set boundaries for themselves around their work and the rest of their lives. Higher education does not encourage individual or group discussions about resisting the intensification of work; rather it allows for competition for the moral high ground about who has worked the longest hours.

Managers who manage themselves well, who manage the interface between personal and professional lives effectively, and who are clear about their boundaries, present excellent role models for younger colleagues.

One way in which the interface between the personal and the professional has become blurred in the last few years is a very visible (and intrusive) link between personal and professional lives: electronic communication. Managing e-mail and the fax machine (both of which are joining the phone in entering everyone's homes) is a skilled balancing act which signals to colleagues how accessible the manager is even during previously private personal time and territory.

Another visible way in which the self-management of managers affects the well-being of colleagues is how resilient (or tired) they are. The drive in most professions at the moment is to overwork and to allow work life to take over all other lives. Colleagues recognize stress and poor attention, and sometimes they lose confidence in their managers if stress is very visible. They fear that if the manager is not functioning, they themselves will soon be 'infected by' the same inability to cope. The manager needs to model a balanced life in order to encourage colleagues to welcome that balance.

MANAGING WITH OTHERS

It seems to be taken for granted that teamwork is a 'good thing', and that managers should strive towards building teams among those they manage. Certainly the word 'team' appears in the language of many higher education institutions: course teams, team meetings, management teams and so on. However, in higher education many staff work individualistically, and they are resistant to attempts to get them to work in teams. Managers need to be persuaded that it is worth coaxing people to join in teamwork.

Gold and Evans (1998) suggest that an educative leader works constructively with teams of people rather than just individuals. Reasons for working with teams include:

- They are a democratic and consultative way of working.
- They share the load.
- They go further than one person alone could.
- They are a good arena for professional development.
- They allow two-way communication so that managers are able to hear what those who are managed have to say.
- When they are well managed, team meetings are exciting, creative and stimulating.

When recruiting new people to a working team, or when trying to accommodate major differences of opinion, it is tempting to ignore diversity and to go for the comfort of working with people most like existing team members: people who mirror their social and academic background. In practice, this often means that new recruits to working teams, or new appointments to fill vacant posts, are chosen because they 'fit', or are most like the existing team members. There is little space in this framework for new ways of operating or for the introduction of team members who function differently. If acknowledging and celebrating diversity is a principle of both the organization and the manager, there are clear issues to be addressed by managers when selecting and working with teams of colleagues. There are also issues of stagnation rather than innovation and change if the status quo is perpetuated *ad infinitum.*

Managers also need to appreciate that there are several different dynamics going on in teams, which require understanding and management by team leaders. For example, Belbin (1993) shows that for a team to function effectively, team members need encouragement to operate in ways that may initially annoy their fellow team members. Belbin writes about the ideal ways of operating that team members may have (each having at least two ways of operating). But in order to function well, a team must have someone who is prepared to pay attention to the process rather than the content of a team meeting – a chair. Teams need people with several other ways of operating, such as shapers – people who are challenging and dynamic and who thrive on pressure – and completers who are painstaking, conscientious and anxious. Belbin shows that an effective team needs people with both these ways of functioning and several others. It is up to the team leader to help members to value each other or at least to understand that their creative production will ultimately be better when they work together.

It is also necessary to recognize that teams go through life cycles, and that they need to be managed differently at various stages of their life cycle. There has been much writing and research about group development since the 1930s. Teams may go through:

- *Forming*: a short 'honeymoon' period very early in their lives as a team. Team members behave formally and politely, are anxious and ask many questions of the team leader and about the task, and seem to be trying to work out the rules to achieve the task.
- *Storming*: this can be a very uncomfortable time for team leaders *and* team members. Conflict and sub-groups emerge, and the authority of the leader is challenged. Opinions polarize and individual team members resist the efforts of the team leader or the group, to gain control. This is an emotional stage where basic values and the achievability of the task are questioned.
- *Norming*: the group begins to work together more agreeably, developing mutual support, reconciling some differences and celebrating others. Cooperation begins in order to work on the task, ground rules are agreed, and communication of views and feelings develop.
- *Performing*: this should be a very satisfying stage. The group organizes itself into a team in order to form an appropriate structure for the task to be completed. There is a general air of progress as team members move flexibly between group roles. There is a positive, energetic ethos to the team at this stage.
- *Adjourning*: many groups in higher education have to end, for example when the task is done or the academic year is over.
- *Mourning*: some teams need to go through this stage before they begin to *form* or *reform*. Team members constantly refer back to their previous teams, and show signs of sadness and an inability to accept the need for a new team.

Understanding these stages can make it easier for team leaders to stay hopeful about the team even when it is at the uncomfortable stages of its life. It is often helpful to remember that even one new member can change the dynamics of a team so that it feels as though it is a new team embarking on the whole life cycle again. If the team leader has imported a new team member in order to make the team more effective, re-forming the team and going through some of the more uncomfortable stages can have positive outcomes. The aftermath of the storming stage is a very productive stage; usually a team must go through the storming stage before it becomes effective.

It is important to lead the team through the storming stage so that it does not stay in that stage unproductively and painfully for too long. If a team seems to be caught in the storming stage, it could benefit it to talk about the stages of team life.

The adjourning stage is easier to cope with if it is acknowledged. Educational organizations are not very good at endings. An effective team leader can plan ahead for ending celebrations that suitably acknowledge the achievements of the team.

> ### Enhancing Practice
>
> Think about the teams in which you work. You may have management responsibility for some; you may be a long-term member of others; and you may be very new to some.
>
> - What team role do you play in the teams in which you work and for which you have responsibility.
> - Are the teams functioning well, or is there a key team role missing?
> - What stage has the team reached in its development?

Many managers are dismayed by the prospect of managing conflict. However, it may be helpful to remember that conflict is probably necessary in order to encourage creativity and originality. An important skill is to develop strategies to manage conflict. One fear about managing conflict is what happens when physiological reactions precede rational ones, as we are biologically programmed. In other words we blush, become tearful, shake, shout or grow pale long before we have had the opportunity to think about and make sense of what is causing these reactions. Most advice about managing conflict, therefore, involves taking time to allow rational thought to come through the physiological reactions. Try:

- talking things over with someone who is not involved;
- making an appointment later in the day or the next day to go over the issues;
- making careful plans and rehearsing the conversation;
- separating the person from the issue – focusing on the present difficulty rather than previous history.

It is important for managers to ensure that conflict is managed before it becomes painful and destructive.

This chapter has suggested that ethical managers have an understanding of power relations and that they tend to work educatively with those they manage. Part of their educative culture is the creation of a no-blame ethos in which mistakes can be admitted and used as a basis for learning. Such an ethos, in an educative organization, will be underpinned by a commitment to continuous professional development for all staff. Kolb's (1984) cycle of learning from experience is a useful framework for the manager to consider, where the person who is managed can be thought of as a learner whom the manager is assisting to develop. The cycle need not be followed slavishly, but its basic shape is:

- *Concrete experience*: planning for learning must include the opportunity for concrete experience.
- *Reflective observation*: reflection on that experience.
- *Abstract conceptualization*: an introduction to relevant reading and research findings.
- *Active experimentation*: the possibility to plan changes to the concrete, or real, experience, next time.
- *Time* to think and talk about that concrete experience.

(Adapted from Gold, 2000)

In other words, managers who are committed to encouraging reflective practice in their colleagues will be aware of the need for talk, of the connection of talk, reading and practice, and for time for talk.

Enhancing Practice

- How often do people in your department or group meet to talk about their work?
- Are there opportunities for meeting informally?
- Is talking in corridors encouraged or discouraged?

Corridor conversations can be repetitive and unproductive. They may be the place where problems and issues are rehearsed and repeated without resolution. Or they can be inspirational conversations, where colleagues ask questions and make contributions that take each other much further in their thinking than they may have gone alone; they may be 'learning conversations' (Brookfield, 1987). Brookfield has characterized these as follows:

- Good conversations are reciprocal and involving. In a good conversation, the participants are continually involved in the process; they are either talking or listening. Developing critical thinking is a process in which listening and contributing are of equal importance.
- The course of good conversations cannot be anticipated. When we begin to ask people to identify assumptions underlying their habitual ways of thinking and learning, we do not know exactly how they are going to respond.
- Good conversations entail diversity and agreement. A measure of diversity, disagreement and challenge is central to helping people to think critically. Unless we accept that people have views very different from ours, and that a multiplicity of interpretations of practically every idea or action is

possible, we will be unable to contemplate alternatives in our own thoughts and actions.

(Adapted from Brookfield, 1987: 238–41)

Managers who understand how reflective practice is best encouraged will be most likely to ensure that learning conversations are taking place between and among themselves and those they manage.

MANAGING IN AN ORGANIZATION

Successful managers will understand their own organization and the international and national imperatives that impinge on it. (See Chapters 1 and 2.) They will understand how the organization works, how formal and informal decisions are made, and where the official and unofficial power bases may be found. The manager's principles and values will help determine whether to use the informal and the unofficial, but there is no doubt that the manager should be able to 'read' the organization. It is necessary to be able to manage outwards from the section that is a direct management responsibility and into the rest of the organization. The liaison between the immediate area of responsibility and the larger institution is key because it is the conduit for information and change. It is vulnerable to micropolitical struggles, and it helps to define the potential for action that can be taken by the area of immediate responsibility. 'Micropolitics focuses on the ways in which power is relayed in every-day practice' (Morley, 1999: 5).

It is difficult to read the unofficial decision-making routes in an organization one is new to: micropolitical influence is secret and well hidden, and it has usually taken many years to develop. It then takes years for new staff members to read and understand the alliances that make up unofficial decision-making groups. Micropolitical influence depends on unofficial power relations: for example, the sharpest wit, the person who has been there the longest, those who drink together regularly, or those who travel together appear to have influence. These unofficial groups often grow from a set of accidental circumstances, but they can become powerful unofficial decision-making bodies, where the business of the official group is decided and planned out. They are hardly ever truly open-access, and they are anti-democratic while often wielding enormous power and influence. The main decision for ethical managers is whether to use the formal decision-making processes, or to use the covert, micropolitical ones. The former may ensure continued presence on the moral high ground, but the latter may be used to make sure that decisions are actually taken and followed through.

It is necessary for a manager to know the statutes and policies that make up the legal framework of the university. Some apparently commonplace decisions are made for quite apparently tangential reasons. Woodward reminds one of this when writing about institutional equal opportunities policies, but she could be writing about any institutional policy:

> Change... may be precipitated by a range of factors. First, the institution's mission may have undergone review, leading to pressures for change from the highest level of management... Alternatively, there may be a strategic shift in direction, again set at this senior level, in response to changing external conditions such as an opportunity (for example, a funding council initiative offering additional income or extra funded student places) or a problem (for example, a downturn in student applications and recruitment from the customary social groups for that institution).

> *(Woodward, 2000: 146)*

University committees are often the place to challenge irregularities such as lack of equity or misuse of power. But knowledge of the workings of committees is required, which includes understanding the relationship between different committees, and having a well-developed ability to be heard in meetings. Committees can be forbidding and hierarchical places where speaking requires courage and aplomb. There are often unwritten micropolitical rules about having a voice, to such an extent that people who are new to a specific committee rarely speak the first time they attend (unless they have officer responsibility). If new managers find themselves representing their constituency on a committee, it may be easier for them to speak if they acknowledge that they are there as representatives. Other helpful factors are to remember that committees are probably still the main arenas for challenging the status quo in higher education, and that most people are awed by ceremony.

OVERVIEW

Giving prescriptive steps towards good management has been resisted. Rather, readers are urged to search for the principles that might underpin their own vision of management in higher education.

Those who agree to be a manager should understand that certain issues, informed by the manager's values, signify ethical management. These include managing teams and understanding how they function, having commitment to developing team members, understanding the organization and its power bases, and developing a voice in committees. These are all ways of managing with other people in order to develop them and the organization.

REFERENCES

Belbin, M (1993) *Team Roles at Work*, Heinemann-Butterworth, Oxford

Brookfield, S (1987) *Developing Critical Thinkers*, Open University Press, Milton Keynes

Currie, J, Harris, P and Thiele, B (2000) Sacrifices in greedy universities: are they gendered?, *Gender and Education*, **12**(3), p 269

Gold, A (2000) Quality and school-based continuous professional development, in *Quality and Educational Management*, ed E Balazs, F van Weiringen and L Watson, Wolters Kluwer, Budapest

Gold, A and Evans, J (1998) *Reflecting on School Management*, Falmer, London

Kolb, D (1984) *Experiential Learning*, Prentice Hall, New Jersey

Leonard, D (2001) *A Women's Guide to Doctoral Studies*, Open University Press, Milton Keynes

Morley, L (1999) *Organising Feminisms: The micropolitics of the academy*, Macmillan, London

Oldroyd, D, Elsner, D and Poster, C (1996) *Educational Management Today: A concise dictionary and guide*, Paul Chapman, London

Woodward, D (2000) The role of middle management, in *Managing Equal Opportunities in Higher Education*, ed D Woodward and K Ross, Society for Research into Higher Education/Open University Press, Buckingham

6 Managing the Human Resource Function

Catherine Haines and Steve Ketteridge

The aim of this chapter is to provide new heads of departments and managers with an overview of essential information on managing human resources (HR). Many novice managers find this function the most daunting to master. The chapter is selective and will draw upon carefully chosen topics that will be of immediate relevance and use. It consists essentially of specially commissioned expert commentary written by leading HR professionals working across the higher education sector. This chapter will address strategic and operational aspects of HR management.

At a strategic level, information will be provided on:

- HR strategies;
- managing performance;
- Investors in People.

At the operational level, there is information that will be needed to take advantage of opportunities and cycles in HR management for:

- recruitment and selection;
- appraisal;
- job evaluation.

Similarly, HR experts have been commissioned to advise on some of the inherited situations which may limit the productivity and creativity of staff:

- dealing with poor performance;
- handling disciplinary matters;
- harassment.

INTRODUCTION

Human resources, like other resources, have to be managed, and it is interesting to note that out of total expenditure in UK HE institutions, staff costs for the year 1998/99 accounted for 57.8 per cent (HESA, 2000). In some institutions staff costs may be devolved to some extent to departments, in the same way as other financial resources, but in others they may all be held centrally so that the senior management team can maintain tight control on this major element of expenditure.

The new head of department may also find that apart from academic staff there are a number of other categories of staff in the department. Academic staff (non-clinical) account for just 32.9 per cent of staff employed by universities (Bett *et al*, 1999), and there is a variety of other staff groups covering, for example, clinical academic staff; administrative, professional, technical and clerical staff; and manual staff. At the time of writing, each of these groups works under differing terms and conditions of appointment, which may include different salary scales, working hours, maternity benefits, entitlements to annual leave, and possibly even London Allowance paid at different rates. To help guide the new head through this bewildering array of detail, it is important at an early stage to build a close relationship with the HR/personnel manager and to seek specialist advice on these matters.

Increasingly the term 'human resource management' (HRM) is being used in the sector in place of 'personnel management'. Some authors may argue that the terms are freely interchangeable, and others would consider that there is an essential difference between the two. This is discussed by Crosthwaite and Warner (1995: 3), who offer the following definition:

> HR management is that part of management which is concerned with the effective utilization of the human resources of an organization. All managers conduct it: principals/senior managers at the strategic level, personnel specialists in advisory and auditing roles and line managers at an operation level.

> *(Crosthwaite and Warner, 1995: 3)*

HRM is becoming a familiar term for the wide range of tasks which go beyond 'hiring and firing' and deal with maximizing the potential of the staffing resources to deliver strategic objectives for the organization. Thus, many universities have now redesignated staff in this area as HR professionals in recognition of this complexity.

HR specialists can offer professional advice and support in three main areas of activity (Hall, 1996):

- *Resourcing*: ensuring that appropriate numbers of qualified staff are available to enable the organization to achieve its corporate objectives. This clearly includes provision of institutional policies and procedures for use in recruitment and selection, redundancy and dismissal, and in some institutions where these matters are not devolved, assistance with the processes. This may also cover support with other related matters such as organizational development, job design and evaluation.

- *Relations*: ensuring that the organization's staff are appropriately rewarded, are optimally productive and adequately protected. This will include development of institutional policies and procedures on remuneration, promotion and review, reward, industrial relations, discipline and grievance.
- *Development*: ensuring that the workforce has the necessary skills to meet the needs of the organization. This includes training and development of staff, and appraisal. In some higher education institutions, some or all of the staff and management development functions may be located within a separate unit. Many different models exist across the sector, with different reporting lines, different levels of integration and cohesion of the various roles in the HR development function.

TAKING A STRATEGIC APPROACH TO HR MANAGEMENT

Higher education is moving away from operating through various freestanding HR policies and procedures towards a more strategic approach to HR management. A major driver is the initiative *Rewarding and Developing Staff in Higher Education*, funded by the Higher Education Funding Council for England (HEFCE) (2001). This is consistent with other trends in higher education in which separate strategies have been developed to cover teaching and learning, estates and communications and information technology. Among the purposes of an HR strategy are:

- to ensure that human resources are developed in a way that contributes to the corporate objectives;
- to provide an integrated framework for current and future initiatives;
- to assist in identification of problems that will need to be addressed in the short and/or longer term;
- to provide a vision for the future based on assessment of current and future context.

(UCEA, 2001)

The head of department will need to interpret the institutional HR strategy for detailed planning at departmental level. Expert commentary 1 by Larry Bunt advises on the need for heads and managers to inform the development of the HR strategy, and draws attention to the fact that the various elements in HR management must all work together if the strategic objectives are to translate efficiently into measurable outcomes.

> ## Expert Commentary 1: Human Resource Strategies Within Higher Education

Once unheard of, Human Resource (HR) strategies are now recognized as central to the delivery of excellence in higher education services. The paper *Rewarding and Developing Staff in Higher Education* (HEFCE, 2001) requires from each university a closely costed strategy specifically to address the following:

- recruitment and retention difficulties;
- staff development and training including management development;
- development of equal opportunities targets, including equal pay/equal value;
- review of staffing needs/balance between categories of staff;
- annual performance reviews linked to rewards;
- action to tackle poor performance.

This list covers a spectrum of common goals. But the core of any HR strategy, in any organization, is to ensure that we have the *right* staff with the *right* skills and *right* motivation, in the *right* jobs, and at the *right* time. Of course what is 'right' for one organization at any time will be different from the needs of another. Nowadays greater emphasis is placed upon collective issues such as corporate culture and values. So today's academic managers should influence their institution's strategy at the developmental stage to ensure that it is sensible, and will deliver when called upon to translate plans into tangible action.

The traditional levers used by strategies are pay and rewards, organizational restructuring, and processes designed to improve efficiency and effectiveness. Depending on the prevailing ideology, the latter might focus on *systems* (ISO 9000, TQM, business process re-engineering) or on *people* (for example, performance management, appraisal or empowerment). In either case, the golden rule is that 'what gets measured gets done'. The most elegant system will fail if there is no means of monitoring its effectiveness, or if the outcomes are not perceived as important enough by staff.

HR strategies should be transformational, but vested interests and fears about change must be identified and overcome if they are to succeed. This requires an understanding of the *real* rewards system, not just pay. For professional staff, money is not the primary source of job satisfaction, and its motivational value is short term only. However, it has a major symbolic influence as a measure of how one is valued relative to one's peers, so that inadequate remuneration, or worse still, the perception of unfair pay and hence *recognition*, creates recruitment and motivational difficulties. Most professional staff take a long-term career view of their earning capacity, so job security, training and development are also key. In practice the real rewards systems, and thus barriers to change, are often symbolic and much more subtle. Examples are titles, research time/autonomy, access to privileged facilities or trappings, or proximity to the hierarchy.

Implementation requires the tacit support of the majority, so mechanistic or 'big bang' changes are often less effective than those piloted with local champions to generate some early rewards. Finally, most HR strategies require changes in behaviour, attitudes, skills or competence, and these require major investment in training and development. Staff in higher education are often resistant to such corporate initiatives and therefore they must be of high quality and led from the top. This means that senior staff should lead by example, demonstrating personal commitment to staff development.

Larry Bunt
Personnel Director
University of Westminster

Another issue raised in the HEFCE (2001) initiative is the question of managing and rewarding performance. In the light of this, many universities may review their schemes for assessing the contribution made by the individual to the team, the department and the institution, and may also be considering linking some element of pay to performance. In higher education, institutions have had mixed success in the introduction of such schemes, which lead to performance-related pay (PRP). This is a complex issue when dealing with academics, since the rewards that motivate such staff may go beyond pay alone, and because it may be difficult to separate the contribution made by individuals from those of teams. The post-1992 universities in particular have more experience of working with PRP schemes, notably as part of the remuneration packages for senior managers. In expert commentary 2, Andrew Snowden reviews various factors that need to be considered when implementing performance management schemes if they are to be effective in higher education.

Expert Commentary 2: Managing Performance – The HR Director's View

It has become commonplace to describe academics as difficult to manage, although managers in the creative industries, in research institutions, in software houses or in social services, would point to their own challenge of managing creative professionals. Nevertheless, the training and motivation of academic staff lead them to be individualized, critical, competitive, independent and, in many ways, resistant to management.

Managing for enhanced performance is a much more difficult concept than managing underperformance. The academic reluctance to accept management extends to academic managers and leaders themselves, who can be embarrassed about their management role. They gladly talk about their administrative tasks and will reluctantly accept that addressing poor performance might be something they cannot avoid. But managing academic teams in order to maximize team performance seems well beyond the job description. The evidence of the impact of effective leadership (not to be confused with management) on enhanced teaching performance in the compulsory education sector is convincing. In universities there is increasing awareness of the importance of enhancing learning and research through team activities, and therefore this implies an increased emphasis on appointing and developing academic leaders with direct responsibility for the performance of their teams. This is a huge development challenge for universities. The process of setting and agreeing performance objectives, agreeing any prerequisite development activities, and then reviewing and resetting objectives may look good on a corporate management development programme, but it does not begin to address the culture change required.

Increasingly, academic managers will be asked to make judgements about academic performance. Performance-related pay (PRP) and performance bonuses may continue to be resisted because there is clear evidence that they are far from motivating and do little to enhance performance. Evidence from the universities in the United States, where performance pay as an element of pay increases is widespread, suggests strongly that while such schemes satisfy boards of regents and governors, they have little positive effect. The trick in designing the best schemes is merely to make them minimally demotivating. However, the recent HEFCE initiative *Rewarding and Developing Staff in Higher Education* (2001) requires universities to show how rewards will be linked to performance in higher education.

Partly such schemes pander to political pressure. And they forget the real link between performance and reward. The majority of staff believe that they are above average and would expect the rewards on offer. If they are disappointed, the negative impact far outweighs the positive impact. On the other hand, if you refuse performance pay where appropriate, or deny incremental progression, to ensure that underperformers are in effect penalized, the high performers will often be satisfied. This may be a pessimistic view of human nature, but certainly the design of any reward scheme should take these factors into account.

There is something in the claim that since PRP assumes a system of setting and agreeing objectives and formally reviewing the outcomes, then the system itself, irrespective of any performance payments, will lead to enhanced performance.

Universities have to develop both leadership and management skills. There is growing research that effective transformational leadership can enhance the performance of teams within universities. This implies inspiring a shared vision, empowering individuals to work to achieve that vision with significant autonomy, modelling the way forward in one's own behaviours and styles, and dealing firmly and fairly with staff. This is a style of 'performance management' that may be acceptable to academics.

Andrew Snowden
Director of Personnel
University of Wolverhampton

A useful framework which brings together a number of different aspects of HR management in relation to the delivery of strategic objectives is the Investors in People Standard (IiP). John Doidge, in expert commentary 3, evaluates the applicability of IiP to higher education institutions. This is not a new scheme and has been more readily adopted in some institutions than others. Two principal strategies have been used. Some universities have chosen to adopt the standard across the whole organization. Others have found a more useful approach to be the 'brick-by-brick' approach, in which they work for the standard in selected academic and administrative departments. For example, many of the large catering and residential services units employing large numbers of support staff have found it useful to work towards the IiP standard, and it has been adopted by at least one large academic department in a major research-led university. Higher education institutions as principal employers in regions around the UK are under pressure to adopt the IiP standard. Those interested in achieving IiP standard may also find Taylor and Thackwray (2001) a useful source of general information.

Expert Commentary 3: Investors in People

Investors is the most widely recognized tool for organizations to plan for the development of their staff to meet business aims; systematic staff development against the IiP standard will improve business performance.

(The Learning Age, DfEE, 1998)

As a respected benchmark for good practice in the training and development of people to achieve organizational goals, Investors in People (IiP) has had a somewhat patchy history of acceptance and progress in higher education, but national reports and government targets consistently champion IiP as an effective tool for staff development. IiP was launched in 1990 and has survived, unlike some other measures, across all employment sectors. Government targets for 2002 are for 45 per cent of all medium or large employers to have achieved the standard (National Skills Task Force, 3rd Report, DfEE, February 2000).

The experience of IiP in higher education led to the view that to be wholly accepted within the sector, given all the other quality initiatives and requirements around in the mid-1990s, some amendment of the standard was necessary. Together with advice and pressure from other sectors, this enabled changes and simplification of the standard, particularly in the assessment process. The revised standard (April 2000) still requires organizations to demonstrate that they:

- are committed, from the topmost level, to the standard;
- have communicated this throughout the organization, and shared management's vision and objectives;
- have planned effectively but flexibly to meet these objectives, identified training needs and how they will be met;
- have taken action to implement the plan, involving managers at every level;
- have evaluated its effectiveness and impact on the business (organization).

These are fundamental processes which might characterize any good employer, and which apply easily to the HE context. Stripped of the unfortunate business jargon of the early days, few HE employers could raise fundamental objections to them, but there is a cost, not least in undergoing the formal assessment. Processes no longer need special documentation but, as with all quality assurance, they do need evidencing.

At the beginning of 2001, 23 whole higher education institutions had achieved the standard, with many more having individual departments recognized. The IiP process allows both and the incremental, departmental process, though expensive in individual assessment fees, has proved itself to be more amenable generally to the HE context, especially in devolved institutions where standardization of procedures is not the norm.

At a time of continuing pressure, from the QAA subject (academic) review, RAE 2001, continuation (institutional) audit and professional accreditation, it is difficult to press the benefits of IiP onto an organization, particularly for academic departments. Many higher education organizations have found it more productive to use the standard in the first instance for administrative departments. IiP can be a springboard to review fundamental management processes – appraisal, communication, managerial effectiveness, training and development – but the award itself can be useful as a marketing/business tool, especially for commercial operations within institutions.

The pressure is still on for QAA and the funding councils to recognize the role of IiP in ensuring standards, as part of the 'lighter touch' framework. While it is not clear how this will work, it is certain that those organizations with robust processes in line with IiP requirements will already have the evidence required to meet the most vigorous scrutiny.

For more information, and to view case studies of various higher education organizations that have achieved the award, visit the HESDA Web site at: http://www.hesda.org.uk/nation/iip.html.

John Doidge
Director of Staff Development
University of Leicester

OPPORTUNITIES AND CYCLES

The head of department will inherit a 'team' or 'group' of staff at the time of appointment. Many of these may be close colleagues, and suddenly the relationship has changed because s/he has now acquired managerial responsibility for them. A distinctive feature of academic management is that this relationship may only last for three or four years, after which the manager may well revert back to the status of a senior colleague. Another tension may be that the previous head (or heads) still plays a significant role within the department.

One of the opportunities of being the head is the chance to renew or refresh the department through new appointments. In some disciplines this may be a rare event, as opportunities for staff appointments occur infrequently, or because financial imperatives have limited the option of selecting new colleagues. In contrast, in other disciplines in which there is a strong market demand for well-qualified individuals, the situation may be reversed and the head is faced with 'recruitment' (and inducement) rather than 'selection'. In these cases a significant proportion of the head's time may be spent in the vitally important recruitment and selection process, which may limit attention that can be given to other HR management roles.

In expert commentary 4, Steve Pashley highlights key points in the recruitment and selection process which need careful consideration and which in the world of higher education may sometimes get overlooked. Recruitment and selection is one area of HR management in which the novice head of department will need to take advice on legal aspects of the process from an HR specialist in the institution.

Expert Commentary 4: Recruitment and Selection

The recruitment of a person into any organization is an opportunity to renew and refresh a department or team. It is also an opportunity to 'get it wrong' and end up making a costly mistake, which can take a long time to put right and possibly even lead to litigation.

All organizations will have well-developed policies concerned with recruitment and selection, which should be transparent, designed to ensure equality of opportunity, and support effective operation of the process. These will ideally be supported by some staff development to give recruiters the right attitudes, skills and understanding. It is vital both that these policies are followed, and that they should also be reviewed from time to time.

There is always a tension between the desire to fill a vacancy as quickly as possible and the perceived administrative burden of advertising, selecting, making the offer of a job and so on. The trick is to get the balance right so that rather than being a bureaucratic hindrance, the process can be streamlined and supported by the essential documentation, which is designed to assist rather than frustrate. Key staff in the education sector are in a competitive market, so the ability to move swiftly with an offer at the end of an efficient recruitment campaign can pay dividends.

It is often a good idea not to rush straight in to recruitment and selection. The manager or head of department needs to think about the post and the type of person required. For example, do you need to recruit at all or are there ways in which existing roles can (or should) be restructured? Seek out the views of others.

It is also worth spending time thinking about how to assess the candidates against the specification that has been drawn up. Interviews are the mainstay of the recruitment process, but they are often brief and shallow affairs, particularly when each member of a panel of (say) eight is allocated five minutes each for questions. Take time in the interview to drill down a little deeper. Sometimes interesting facts are only obtained after the discussion has been going for half an hour. Is it worth considering other forms of assessment such as psychometric tests, presentations/lectures, or group discussions with other candidates? These options will not be appropriate for all vacancies, but at least consider them, preferably with your HR department, as alternatives that can be used for assessing applicants' knowledge, skills and personal attributes.

Once the best candidate has been identified, prompt follow-up action will be needed. All managers or heads of departments want to retain good staff; therefore careful consideration must be given to the important issues of pay, reward, development and other areas of HR management outside the scope of this particular study. But at the very least it will be necessary to plan the induction of new staff into the team/department, and to ensure that they take part in any corporate induction programme, so that their early experiences of you and their new employer are generally positive.

Steve Pashley
Director of Human Resources
Leeds Metropolitan University

At an early stage the head of department will discover that at regular points in the academic year there are a number of important HR management tasks to be undertaken. These will include:

- the annual review of all staff for regrading, promotion and possibly consideration of merit awards and bonuses;
- consideration of staff with respect to probation;
- the regular appraisal of staff or consideration of staff as part of a performance management scheme;
- assessment of staff training and development needs;
- induction of new staff.

These activities in the cycle will differ widely from institution to institution, and the amount of leeway given to heads will be dependent on institutional policies and practices, and on the extent to which staffing costs are devolved to the head. The financial health of the institution may also limit the amount of resource that can be invested in these activities.

In higher education the term 'appraisal' is used to describe the regular and systematic review of staff at which performance is reviewed against objectives, previously agreed by negotiation with the appraiser. It is primarily a developmental process. In expert commentary 5, Liz Allen from the National Association of Teachers in Further and Higher Education (NATFHE) evaluates the use of the appraisal process in the management of staff. Although the emphasis in this commentary is on academic and teaching staff, in most institutions appraisal has been implemented across all or many grades of staff. New heads should note that appraisal can be a powerful tool for enhancing two-way communication with support, technical and manual and other grades of staff who may not otherwise have a forum in which to express their views and concerns.

Expert Commentary 5: Appraisal

In the early 1990s, academic opinion was largely suspicious of the idea of staff appraisal. A process of negotiation and discussion has resulted in the emergence of developmental schemes, potentially supportive of staff, and in many cases has succeeded in promoting a sense of ownership of appraisal and in raising expectations of its impact.

Despite this, over the last decade appraisal has been subject to widespread 'benign neglect' (as described by Hughes, 1998). Factors such as competing demands on time, lack of strategic management and a lack of clarity as to what it is 'for' have led to appraisal cycles not being met and reports going nowhere.

In practice, successful appraisal requires not just a good, mutually owned scheme, but committed resources for training (appraisers and appraisees), quality time to undertake appraisals, and ensuring identified outcomes are met. With this level of commitment, appraisal can be an invaluable tool in helping staff identify areas for development, and in giving them feedback and a sense of being valued in their work. It can also help academic managers in enhancing the skills base, managing staff through change and organizational development.

In a strategic sense, appraisal in higher education could be more ambitious. This is not to suggest that the sector embraces the performance pay agenda, which would link appraisal processes to pay and performance monitoring, thereby destroying the consensus that has built up around peer ownership of professional development. Only by retaining developmental schemes, which are clearly separate from other institutional procedures, will staff be willing to expose uncertainties and areas of relative weakness, and to learn from peer support.

Currently appraisal very often applies only to full-time and permanent staff. There are strong arguments for extending it to hourly-paid and fixed-term staff, and to part-time tutorial assistants. It is a way of getting feedback from groups of staff, who may be committed to teaching or research, but who have no other input into planning or review procedures, even though they may have a particularly valuable perspective on their areas of work. For postgraduate tutors, appraisal can form an important element of career planning and development. Part-time lecturers now have some statutory entitlement to training and development, and at the very least should be offered the option of participation in appraisal, ideally with payment for attendance. In terms of the overall quality of the student experience, it makes no sense to exclude such a significant group of staff from a key quality enhancement process. Of course, increasing the number of appraisees does mean that more appraisers are needed, and strengthens the case for peer appraisal.

Appraisal can also be a very important tool for mapping and delivering aspects of equal opportunities. At the very least the process needs to be imbued with a degree of equal opportunity awareness, and this should form an element of appraisal training. Appraisers should be aware of potential gender and ethnic differences in coming to self-assessment and the assignment of value to various activities and even personal styles. But appraisal is not just about 'appraising equally'; it is also an opportunity to track development opportunities: for instance to monitor the relative take-up of management and research development activities and, potentially, to support certain groups of staff in taking up opportunities where they may be under-represented.

The challenge to academic managers is no longer to defend the concept of appraisal, but to meet high expectations of it, for the individual staff member and for the team or department.

Liz Allen
NATFHE Universities Department

The process of job evaluation is becoming increasingly important in higher education and has been given new impetus through the HEFCE initiative *Rewarding and Developing Staff in Higher Education* (2001). The purpose of job

evaluation is to ensure equal pay for work of equal value (a legal requirement), using an institution-wide system to assess the size and complexity of a
given role. The Universities and Colleges Employers Association, UCEA
(2001) has provided a useful overview of the importance and scope of job evaluation. Many institutions are considering implementing analytical job
evaluation schemes, which may operate at local, regional or national level.
Managers may find increasingly that they will need to make use of job evaluation schemes to assist them in objectively determining appropriate levels of
pay and grade. Such job evaluation schemes are also vital in supporting equality of opportunity through ensuring equal pay for work of equal value.
Pamela Hampshire has been involved in the development and piloting of the
HERA (higher education role analysis) scheme of job evaluation, and in expert
commentary 6 she summarizes some of the aims and experiences of using
such schemes in the sector.

Expert Commentary 6: Job Evaluation

Job evaluation is an approach used to help determine the relative size of
jobs within an organization, in a consistent and systematic way. The aims
of job evaluation schemes are to:

- establish comparative worth between roles so that equal pay can be
  provided for work of equal value;
- facilitate consistency in pay and grading decision making;
- provide a rational basis for the design and maintenance of an equitable
  and defensible pay structure.

While there are a number of different approaches to job evaluation, the
most common, and that used by employment tribunals, is analytical job
evaluation. This involves comparing information about a particular job or
role against a set of standards for each of a number of factors. Traditional
job evaluation schemes use factors such as knowledge requirements,
responsibilities (for staff, for decision making, etc) and physical demands.
Others use qualitative measures, such as impact or outputs. A recent
trend, particularly in the public sector, has been for organizations to
develop their own schemes which reflect their own values, priorities and
culture. The trend is now towards the use of skills and competences,
rather than traditional factors, to ensure that what individuals are able to
do and the standards expected of them are built into the scheme.

Data about role content and requirements are collected systematically
in a structured process, often via a questionnaire. The data are assessed

against different factors for the scheme, and a score or rating is arrived at for each individual factor and for the role as a whole. While not automatically determining the pay of a job or role, this score provides a basis for establishing equitable pay differentials between roles.

HERA (higher education role analysis)

A number of different job evaluation schemes has been used within higher education over the years. The most notable of these has been the 'Blue Book' used for technical staff in the pre-1992 universities since the early 1970s.

In the early 1990s, it became apparent that existing pay structures within HE were inadequate to meet the needs of the sector, in terms of flexibility and diversity of employment. In 1994, over 100 UK higher education institutions formed themselves into a company, which has produced HERA. This is a competency based, computerized role analysis scheme, which can be applied to all roles in higher education, to assess their relative value in a consistent and equitable manner. It is valuable because it provides a fair, equitable and transparent means for an individual employer to assess the relative value of all its employees' roles; it can address anomalies, particularly those relating to gender, which may exist in current pay structures, and can help employers to meet their requirements for equal pay for work of equal value. It can be adapted to reflect priorities and business needs.

HERA has been developed with Towers Perrin Management Consultants, over a total period of five years, to reflect the values of the sector, following extensive research, involving over 2,000 staff. The development has also involved academic experts in equal value, job evaluation and competences, and the main trade unions have been informed and consulted. HERA has been piloted in six universities and colleges representative of the sector as a whole.

Pamela Hampshire
Educational Competences Consortium Ltd (the owner of HERA)

INHERITED SITUATIONS AND HR PROBLEMS

Most of the staff working in departments are conscientious and professional in their duties. However, new heads may often find they have inherited one or two situations which have affected the productivity or creativity of the department or team, and which have been allowed to continue for some time. Such problems may concern the performance of duties, competence, professional conduct and even attitudes of staff. These problems can involve any of the categories of staff in the department, including researchers. At an early stage new heads may have to prioritize which of these situations can be improved within their term of office.

All institutions will have established procedures for dealing with cases of poor performance, and the head will need to note that the procedures for academic staff may well be different to those for other grades. In expert commentary 7, Claire Barnes presents some guidance on dealing with poor performance, and counsels on the need to work closely with one of the HR professionals in the institution.

Expert Commentary 7: Dealing with Poor Performance

Most managers can instantly recognize poor performance. In the most general terms, poor performance is achievement below an acceptable level. But achievement of what, and what is meant by an acceptable level? In higher education, both these aspects tend to be understood implicitly, although some staff will understand the expectations differently from others. Academic staff and senior researchers have more freedom to determine their own work content than probably any other group of staff, but junior researchers, technical and other support staff are largely comparable to other employees in the world at large. Therefore managing the poor performance of academics and senior researchers can present certain difficulties not faced by managers of other types of staff.

It is important to read the section on 'managing performance' before dealing with poor performance. Only when performance is managed is it possible to deal confidently with poor performance. To identify poor performance it is essential to consider some fundamental points:

- To which staff group does the person belong (eg academic, administrative)?
- Does the employer have a procedure for dealing with poor performance for this staff group (often called a 'capability procedure')?
- Is the poor performance a recent issue or has it always been so; is the poor performance deteriorating or has it reached a plateau?
- Define the components of poor performance (eg for academics: poor student feedback on teaching, poor interpersonal relationships with

colleagues and/or students, minimal research output; for administrators: not prioritizing work, poor attendance, not doing as requested, missing deadlines). With academics in particular, avoid petty reasons. The issues should be substantive.

- Define the possible reasons for the poor performance. These could include not knowing what is expected; being accustomed to minimal output being acceptable; lack of necessary skills; lack of ability; mental health problems; personal problems. Occasionally poor performance is a disciplinary matter because it is wilful, but this is rare.
- What is the nature of your relationship to the staff member? Have interpersonal relationships deteriorated, perhaps because of this problem? It is much more difficult to deal with this type of problem if you have a poor working relationship.

Having made this informal analysis, you should discuss the way forward with your human resources manager (HRM). Any action taken involving staff could result ultimately in an employment tribunal, and professional advice is necessary throughout. The most important cautionary word is that initiating a procedure such as that below will feel extremely threatening to the employee and may result in a complaint of harassment. It could also result in a resignation, which may be very welcome, but not if it is followed by a claim for constructive dismissal! Always act supportively and without blame. Read the institutional harassment procedure (if there is one).

The following advice may be offered by your HRM. Meet with the staff member concerned to discuss your concerns, explaining your perception of the performance issues and seeking their response. Explore the possible reasons; seek to identify his or her views. Discuss ways in which you can help, and support the individual's proposals to reach acceptable standards (which must be made explicit). Follow up the meeting with a letter which confirms in writing the performance issues identified; outline any support you have agreed to give (eg skills training, mentoring arrangements) and detail an action plan for reaching an acceptable standard (which you will have discussed and, ideally, agreed) with a timetable. Give a date for your next meeting to review the situation. Often these meetings can go on monthly for many months and the outcome of each should be recorded.

If there is no improvement forthcoming, it may be necessary to explore the ways forward with your HRM. The staff member may be in a job inappropriate to his or her abilities, and it may be sensible to seek to redeploy him or her; the employee may be suffering from a mental illness (such as depression) and occupational health professionals may need to be involved. Be aware of unusual reasons for apparently poor performance. The author has discovered two such occasions where academics have simultaneously held down two full-time jobs! Sometimes it may be necessary to action dismissal proceedings. This can be fraught with difficulty in pre-1992 universities, particularly with academic and often research staff because of their 'model statutes'. Often staff will offer to resign in return for a severance package. This may be acceptable to your employer, but always use a 'compromise agreement' to ensure there will be no subsequent successful legal action. Again your HRM will advise you.

Claire Barnes
Director of Personnel
Queen Mary, University of London

In cases where unacceptable levels of performance exist, the head of department may be forced to consider initiating the 'capability procedure', if one exists in the organization. It is important to realize that the capability procedure is meant to be used as an aid to achieving improvement and is not intended to be punitive. In other instances, the head of department may need to go down the path of initiating disciplinary procedures, in which case the head will need to seek advice from an HR professional and must be sure to follow the institutional procedure to the letter. In her expert commentary below, Susanne Byrne briefly discusses the scope of disciplinary rules and offers some sound advice on the operation of disciplinary procedures.

Expert Commentary 8: Handling Disciplinary Matters

Disciplinary rules set the standards of conduct at work. All staff should know in outline, if not in detail, what may be regarded by their employer as a disciplinary offence and that the management has disciplinary powers which are liable to be exercised if the need arises. Most disciplinary issues that arise are relatively minor and can generally be resolved on an informal basis between the head of department or manager and the employee. Where a more serious issue arises, however, and a more formal response is called for, a formal procedure should be followed.

Formal disciplinary procedures provide a method of dealing with any serious disciplinary issues arising from performance or conduct. Most organizations model their formal procedures on those contained in the ACAS (Advisory, Conciliation and Arbitration Service) *Code of Practice on Disciplinary and Grievance Procedures*. Your personnel or HR department should be able to provide you with a copy of your own institution's formal procedure, if you do not already have a copy.

According to the code, the guiding principles of any formal disciplinary procedure are that:

- No action should be taken against an employee until the case has been fully investigated.
- The employee must be advised of the nature of the complaint and must be given the opportunity to state his/her case before any decision is made.
- The employee has a right to be represented by a trade union representative or work colleague during the disciplinary interview. (This is now enshrined in the Employment Relations Act 1999.)
- There is right of appeal against any disciplinary penalty imposed.

Most procedures indicate the types of offence which would be regarded as gross misconduct and could lead to the suspension and ultimately the dismissal of an employee: theft, fraud, sexual/racial harassment and falsification of records are typical examples. They also stipulate what level of management has the authority to take the various forms of disciplinary action, including dismissal.

In accordance with the ACAS code, most procedures also set out the various stages in the disciplinary process; these generally involve progression from an oral warning to a written warning to a final warning. The level of warning to be given will depend on the seriousness of the offence, and except for instances of gross misconduct no employee is dismissed for a first offence.

In the case of academic and academic-related staff in the pre-1992 universities, the Education Reform Act 1988 specifies that the arrangements for their discipline should be spelt out in the statutes of the university. This was a result of the insistence of the government of the day that all pre-1992 universities should have a consistent model of discipline. This model cannot therefore be varied without the consent of the Privy Council. There is no corresponding provision for non-academic grades of staff.

For heads of departments initiating disciplinary measures there are two essentials. The most critical is to know your institution's disciplinary procedure and follow it to the letter. (Employment tribunals can find dismissals to be unfair because of failure to follow an agreed procedure.) The second is to take advice from one of your HR professionals where necessary.

Susanne Byrne
Personnel Manager
Queen Mary, University of London

The final commentary in this chapter concerns harassment and bullying. Institutions will have policy statements on harassment and bullying, and it is the responsibility of the head to ensure compliance. It is worth noting that harassment and bullying can transcend hierarchical structures, and instances have been known where heads of departments have been bullied by their own staff. In expert commentary 9, Marie Morehen stresses the importance to managers of maintaining an environment in which academic activities can flourish free from harassment and bullying.

Expert Commentary 9: Harassment

It is the responsibility of every employer and service provider to have in place equal opportunities and harassment policy statements to ensure a working environment where the dignity of men and women at work is respected. These policies need to place a positive duty on all staff, managers, supervisors and students not to tolerate or condone harassment or bullying. Where it does occur there should be a procedure in place to make a complaint and for the institution to provide support. Communications and awareness training is an important part of both introducing and operating a harassment policy. Complaints of bullying and harassment can sometimes be associated with poor supervision or management of staff or students, and therefore these issues can usefully be included in awareness training.

Creating and maintaining such a culture could be said to be a critical success factor in higher education institutions where working relationships and staff/student relationships are essentially collegiate and not overly regulated. Where trust and confidence break down as a result of harassing or bullying behaviours between staff, or between staff and students, it is an inevitable consequence that individual creativity and productivity are adversely affected. Protection of individuals from harassment on grounds of gender, sexual orientation, race or disability underpins the principle of diversity, and provides a model to young people of valuing diversity, as part of their learning experience.

Complaints should always be taken seriously and acted on promptly and confidentially, and it is important not to prejudge the decision whether or not the alleged conduct amounts to harassment or bullying. Both experienced and inexperienced managers and supervisors might benefit from specialist assistance from personnel professionals in handling concerns or complaints of harassment. There is evidence that the skilled handling of an independent investigation of a complaint has a significant impact on the satisfaction with the outcome from the perspective of both the complainant and the subject of the complaint. Universities may wish to consider establishing a mediation service where issues between individuals can be resolved before reaching the magnitude of a formal complaint.

In addition to the practical and everyday problems resulting from harassment, the legal responsibilities and liabilities for universities as employers and education providers regarding discrimination are increasingly complex, and again specialist advice is necessary. Unlawful discrimination in the form of harassment which subjects an individual to detriment may be complained to an employment tribunal under the Sex Discrimination Act 1975, Race Relations Act 1976 and the Disability Discrimination Act 1995. The Race Relations (Amendment) Act 2000 places general and specific duties on public authorities to promote racial equality. Arguments relying on European Court of Human Rights case law are now likely to affect court and tribunal decisions regarding sexual orientation, and UK legislation prohibiting discrimination on grounds of religion and sexual orientation must be in place by 2003, followed by UK legislation prohibiting age discrimination in employment by 2006. Claims can also arise ranging from breach of contract, criminal liability and personal injury in respect of complaints concerning harassment or bullying.

It is imperative that higher education institutions strive to provide environments free from harassment or bullying to achieve maximum creative and learning experiences for both staff and students.

Marie Morehen
Director of Personnel
University of Nottingham

Enhancing Practice

Having read this chapter, what do you consider are the three most powerful messages that you will take away and use to enhance your own practice in managing human resources?

OVERVIEW

This chapter has covered a number of aspects of HR management for heads of departments and managers, which indicate what a complex and demanding task this can be. To be effective, the manager must operate institutional procedures which will increasingly be brought together within the framework of an HR strategy. Heads will also need to work closely with the HR professionals within the institution, to ensure that their own practices are fair and non-discriminatory, and that their actions will not lead to legal problems. It is important for the manager not to underestimate the time that can be spent on this aspect of the role. There can be tremendous rewards in terms of success and motivation through getting it right. Conversely, failures can take a very long time to resolve.

ACKNOWLEDGEMENT

The authors are indebted to Claire Barnes, Director of Personnel at Queen Mary, University of London for her expert advice in writing this chapter.

REFERENCES

Crosthwaite, E and Warner, D (1995) Setting the scene, in *Human Resource Managment in Higher and Further Education* ed D Warner and E Crosthwaite, Society for Research into Higher Education (SRHE)/Open University Press, Buckingham

Department for Education and Employment (DfEE) (1998) *The Learning Age*, The Stationery Office, London

DfEE (2000) *National Skills Task Force, 3rd Report*, February, DfEE-Prolog, Sudbury, Suffolk

Hall, A (1996) Personnel management, in *Higher Education Management*, ed D Warner and D Palfreyman, SHRE /Open University Press, Buckingham

HESA (2000) *Higher Education Statistics for the UK 1998/99*, Higher Education Statistics Agency, Cheltenham

Higher Education Funding Council for England (HEFCE) (2001) *Rewarding and Developing Staff in Higher Education*, 01/16, Higher Education Funding Council for England, Bristol (also available through URL: www.hefce.ac.uk)

Hughes, P (1998) *Appraisal in UK Higher Education*, Universities' and Colleges' Staff Development Agency, Sheffield

Independent Review of Higher Education Pay and Conditions (1999) *Independent Review of Higher Education Pay and Conditions: Report of a committee chaired by Sir Michael Bett* (the Bett Report) The Stationery Office, London

Taylor, P and Thackwray, B (2001) *Investors in People Explained, 4th edn*, Kogan Page, London

Universities and Colleges Employers Association (UCEA) (2001) *Rewarding and Developing Staff in Higher Education: A guide to complying with HEFCE 01/16*, UCEA, London (URL: http://www.ucea.ac.uk/guideto0116.pdf)

Part 3
Creating Intellectual
Wealth

Introduction

The Editors with Leela Damodaran

Part 3 examines the ways in which universities strategically view the creation of intellectual wealth, to include the promotion of research teams and 'growing one's own' researchers via the higher degree route. For much of the 20th century, the notion of the lone researcher was accepted as common practice in the arts, humanities and social sciences, with graduate students following this route, taking as long as required to complete their PhDs. Although this model was not so prevalent in science and engineering, the impetus in recent years has been to minimize the social isolation of research students and staff with the evolution of strategic research teams. The advent of the research assessment exercise (RAE) and subsequently the research councils and the Quality Assurance Agency (QAA)'s code of practice on research supervision have furthered this impetus, as large, powerful research teams capable of generating international recognition (and the accompanying high-ranking RAE rating, with the funding attached) are much sought after. As we move into the 21st century, adopting a strategic approach to managing the whole research agenda – in terms of kudos, knowledge generation and financial reward – has become increasingly important.

Chapter 7, written by Stan Taylor, examines the management of postgraduate research supervision, paying particular attention to the QAA code of practice, and offering some templates against which managers of research students may wish to compare their own practices. Chapter 8, 'Managing high-impact research groups', by Ewan Ferlie, Janet Harvey and Andrew Pettigrew, considers factors which make for effective research teams. Finally in this section, Chapter 9 by Ken Young explores the notion of developing a strategic culture for research, stressing that this is not a 'mere managerial challenge', but instead an intellectual one.

The personal perspective of Professor Damodaran (Head of Human Sciences and Advanced Technology Research Institute, Loughborough University), derived from her cumulative experiences as a career researcher, chartered psychologist and consultant, together with extensive teaching practice in education and commercial sectors, enables her to offer a grounded insight into the world of contract researchers: a significant group involved in creating the nation's intellectual wealth.

A Personal Perspective by Leela Damodaran

The views presented in what follows are derived from a career spanning 12 years as a contract researcher, and a further 20 years in various roles with responsibility for research management. Globally, research institutes are deemed to be the powerhouses in terms of knowledge generation. But paradoxically, in the UK these creators of intellectual wealth appear to be marginalized by disenfranchising human resource policies. As this section of this book is focused on the creation of intellectual wealth, it is worth highlighting some particular factors with respect to the unsatisfactory nature of the short-term employment of research staff (for them and others) which leads to difficulty in building and retaining research teams. Additionally, within higher education today there are a number of issues surrounding the creation of intellectual wealth, most notably those associated with its funding and the subsequent deployment of resources. The scenario below offers a fairly typical set of common practices further to receipt of funding for research (and will hopefully stimulate concern amongst readers to address the fundamental issues raised):

- Each time a new research grant is won by an academic, a *recruitment process* has to be carried out to find a contract researcher to work on the project. This is usually prolonged and expensive and delays the start of the project.
- The costs of *advertising*, *interviewing* and *selecting* are paid out of central Higher Education Funding Council for England (HEFCE) funding, not usually by the research council (or other funder).
- The *skills match* of the new recruit to the needs of the research project is usually inadequate.
- To compensate for this *skills deficit* the grant holder must spend more time on the project than planned (subsidized by HEFCE); the researcher must spend time (paid by the research council) acquiring the requisite knowledge and skills before the planned programme of work can begin effectively.
- Part-way through the project, and particularly as the end date comes into sight, anxiety about future employment sets in resulting in the *researcher starting to explore future job opportunities*.
- Towards the end of a grant, *the intellectual engagement of the grant-*

holders and research staff with their research material should be at its peak: interpreting the findings, understanding the implications, crystallizing new knowledge, building theory and publishing in order to maximize research output and research quality. *Instead*, too often significant efforts are diverted into updating curricula vitae, scanning *employment opportunities*, completing job application forms and attending interviews.

- The *researcher leaves*, often to pursue work in a different area, not of his/her choosing.
- Frequently the imperative to stay in employment means that the researcher leaves before the end of a project. This means that the *grant holder must put in more time to complete the project*. HEFCE pays the salary of the grant holder in most cases.
- Data that the researcher collected and understood is lost or under-analysed and thus the research *quality is compromised* (but this will not of course be reported in the final report).
- The research council and (indirectly) HEFCE investment in developing the specialized skills and deep knowledge of the research staff is lost.

This scenario is repeated endlessly in many universities and begs many questions. Firstly, why, in a sector where numerous mission statements refer to the creation of knowledge and achievement of research excellence, is there such a dearth of accountability for the loss of established expertise? Sometimes centres of specialized knowledge with a long track record of success in winning grants hit a trough in research income, although their domain is still relevant and important and their staff highly skilled. Without temporary support and short-term investment of resources by their host institutions, decades of investment can be lost as staff leave. The loss of human capital is not considered and no one is held to account for it.

A second critical question is why the myth of the stereotypical research associate is so prevalent. It seems often to be assumed that all research staff are young, transient, possessing few skills and therefore a disposable and easily replaceable asset. This is far from the reality, but there is little empirical data available to be authoritative about the categories of research staff and relative numbers in each. What is not in question is that there are many very able researchers who bring credit to and promote the reputations of their institutions. For example, these individuals contribute significantly to winning research grants, conduct much of the research and management tasks on projects, complete project deliverables, represent their centres on standards bodies and advisory committees, are members of expert panels, reviewers for research councils and expert evaluators for the European Union. Some have been returned in the 2001 Research Assessment Exercise. That they are asked to do all these things, and to do them successfully, suggests they have deep knowledge of their specialist domain, are well respected externally and a major asset to their host institution.

It is to be hoped that this publication will, through the good practice it promotes, pave the way for research staff to receive the recognition and institutional support appropriate to the contribution they make to knowledge and to the knowledge economy.

Managing Postgraduate Research Degrees

Stan Taylor

The aim of this chapter is to provide an overview of current ideas and good practice in the effective supervision of research degrees. It will be of interest to those with responsibility for the management of research degree programmes, as well as new and experienced supervisors of research students. The account focuses on the key areas of:

- recruitment and selection;
- induction, training and support of research students;
- induction, training, and support of research supervisors;
- monitoring of student progress;
- evaluation of the quality of the research student's learning experience;
- reviewing research programmes.

INTRODUCTION

Historically, the management of postgraduate research degrees has been delegated to individual academic staff, who have recruited and selected students, inducted, trained, supported them, and supervised their research. While in many cases this system worked well, from the mid-1980s onwards concerns began to be expressed about low completion rates in some disciplines, the links between the quality of supervision and completion and failure rates, and the quality of the student learning experience.

These concerns were fed into the review of higher education conducted by Lord Dearing, which recommended (NCIHE, 1997) that they should be addressed through a national code of practice to which all institutions would be expected to adhere. The task of devising a code was given to the Quality Assurance Agency for Higher Education (QAA), which in 1999 published a section dealing with research programmes. Subsequently, the QAA has been monitoring the extent to which the code has been implemented as part of Continuation Audit/institutional review.

In order to meet both the concerns about postgraduate research education and the precepts of the QAA code, it has become necessary effectively to manage research programmes at a higher level than just by the supervisor, for example at departmental or graduate school level. This has led to the development of a new academic role, the manager of research programmes.

RECRUITMENT AND SELECTION

Under this heading, managers of research programmes may have to ensure that prospective students have the relevant information to make an informed judgement about applying for a research degree, and to manage selection processes to ensure that they are fair and are effective in identifying applicants who have the potential to successfully complete the programme.

Recruitment

Here the key question is what information a prospective applicant – who may be on the doorstep or the other side of the world – needs to know in order to decide whether to make an application. The former Higher Education Quality Council (HEQC, 1996: 7) has compiled a useful checklist for supervisors and managers of:

- the broad academic areas within which the department/school has the relevant expertise and resources to supervise research projects;
- requirements for entry (including language requirements);
- fees payable for the programme of study by the student or on his/her behalf;
- where appropriate, the possible sources of internal and external funding and any restrictions or conditions attached to such awards;
- the regulatory framework for the award;
- departmental and institutional points of contact for further information.

Useful additions might include:

- the research training programme;
- requirements for assessment, including any taught elements;
- exit points from the programme, eg MRes, MPhil and PhD along with any credit requirements;

- selection procedures;
- for non-native English speakers, provision for enhancing linguistic competence.

Further, as the QAA (2000a, 2000b) implements the national frameworks for higher education qualifications in 2001–05, it will be useful to have:

- a statement that the programme conforms to the relevant level of qualifications framework.

Selection

Once applications have been received by the institution, they then have to be put through the selection process. In many cases, this is prescribed at institutional level, but it is not unusual in the case of postgraduate research programmes for the selection process to be managed in whole or part at lower levels by staff responsible for research programmes. They will have the responsibility for ensuring that selection processes adhere to the QAA code for research programmes (QAA, 1999), which seeks to ensure that they are fair, effective and conform to standard good practice.

Fairness, of course, means that selection processes should be non-discriminatory. For this reason, it is recommended in the code that selection processes should involve the judgement of more than one member of staff and that selectors should be aware of equal opportunities principles and legislation and of the need, where appropriate, to take account of special needs.

Effectiveness means recruiting students who are appropriately qualified and/or prepared and whose research can be potentially supervised and supported to a successful conclusion. Effectiveness entails ensuring that applications are considered by selectors who have the expertise to evaluate them, normally including the postgraduate admissions tutor and the prospective supervisor(s). It also entails having policies and procedures for selectors to follow. These should include a policy on taking up and receiving references prior to considering applications; a policy on interviewing and procedures in cases where applicants cannot be interviewed, for example with many international applicants; guidance on interviewing; criteria for making a final decision, and a requirement to record the reasons for decisions before communicating them to the institution and the candidate.

INDUCTION, TRAINING AND SUPPORT OF RESEARCH STUDENTS

Once research students have arrived at the institution, there is a need to induct them, train them in research and offer them appropriate support as they begin their studies.

Induction

A key precept of the QAA Code of Practice is that:

> Research students should be provided with opportunities by the institution to enable them to commence their studies with an understanding of the academic and social environment within which they will be working.

(QAA, 1999: 8)

At institutional level, such opportunities should include induction to the institution and its postgraduate portfolio; to its regulations governing research degrees, including registration, enrolment, progression requirements, and assessment, complaints and appeals procedures; to its arrangements for research supervision; to its guidelines for academic conduct; to its policies on equal opportunities, health and safety, data protection and intellectual property rights; to its generic learning support infrastructure including computing and library facilities; to its welfare systems for research students, and to its provision for career development.

At departmental/school level, induction should cover the main research activities; resources and facilities for research; opportunities for meeting staff and other research students; representation for research students; social facilities, and local health and safety requirements.

At programme level, it cannot simply be assumed that students necessarily know what is involved in undertaking a research programme: many have little idea of what they are letting themselves in for. An hour spent outlining the processes involved and a recommendation that students read one of the excellent guides available (eg Cryer, 1997) can help students to appreciate what is in store and prepare them better for the experience.

Students also need induction into specific aspects of the research programme. These may include the aims and intended learning outcomes; the research training; any programme-specific regulations, such as those governing transfer from an MPhil to a PhD, and the arrangements for monitoring, reviewing, and evaluating the programme.

Additionally, induction has to meet the needs of international students, particularly those studying for the first time in the UK. Socially, the 'culture shock' and other bewildering experiences of landing for the first time in another country are well documented (see eg Furnham, 1997: 13–29; Kiley, 2000: 91–92), and it is important to provide an orientation. Useful guidelines for what should be included may be found in the CVCP (1995) *Code of Practice for the Recruitment and Support of International Students in UK Higher Education*. Also, such students may, as Macrae (1997: 140) has argued, be unfamiliar with the UK higher education system and its expectations of students, and this may be appropriately dealt with in a well-prepared induction programme.

Enhancing Practice

- What induction is provided for your research students at the institutional, departmental/school and programme levels?
- Does it cover all of the topics above drawn from the QAA code of practice?
- What provision is made for international students?
- Does it cover both the social and the academic needs of such students?

Training

While research students may have previously undertaken small-scale projects, few have the range of expertise necessary to undertake larger-scale ones, and it is widely recognized that they need an initial training in the early stages of their research programme. Such training may be strongly encouraged by major research sponsors and in some cases required as a condition of recognition for studentships (see eg ESRC, 2001).

In principle, an initial research-training programme is effectively a taught component of the degree and, as such, subject to the same requirements as any other taught programme. So research-training programmes should have clear aims and intended learning outcomes. Outcomes should, in accordance with the QAA code (1999: 10) normally include:

- a knowledge and understanding of the context of research in the discipline(s), the design of research projects, conceptual frameworks, relevant empirical methods, intellectual property rights, research ethics;
- general research skills, including where appropriate writing a research proposal and a research plan, managing a research project, academic writing, presenting the results of research;
- specific research skills relating to the discipline(s);
- key (transferable) skills which are learnt and practised in the research programme but which have general applications in employment, eg teamwork, communication, time management.

These learning outcomes should be reflected strategically in curricula for the programme, in methods of teaching and learning and, where appropriate, assessment.

Additionally, devising an initial training programme involves careful consideration of the needs of international students. They may need assistance to improve their English (see eg Kiley, 2000: 92–93), and possibly support in understanding and applying what may be novel approaches, methods and concepts as well as, at a more practical level, in operating unfamiliar equipment in new environments.

It is unusual (but not unknown) for research students to be invited to undertake teaching and demonstrating duties in their first year, but they may well be in their second and/or third. This can be difficult for research students; as Hill (1996: 47) has put it:

> Being asked to teach students, while basically still a student yourself, puts you in a rather strange position... It's incredibly useful, rewarding and so forth. But for me (and I imagine this to be quite common) the weeks before my first seminars saw me in a state of growing terror that I did not possibly have the maturity, knowledge, experience, or authority to do this...

If suppressed terror is not good for research students, it scarcely makes for a high quality learning experience for undergraduates either. It can therefore be a responsibility of the manager of research programmes to ensure that research students who have been asked to undertake teaching or demonstrating duties receive a proper training. Of course, if postgraduates are to undertake assessment – formative and/or summative – appropriate training is an essential prerequisite.

It may be noted that, as well as supplying initial research training and training for teaching, many institutions are offering further training in the second and third years of study. So, for example, at the start of their third year students may be offered a session on 'Completing your PhD' dealing with the writing-up process, or towards the end of their third year, on 'Preparing for your viva'. Useful resources for these purposes include *Thesis Writing* (Murray, 1997), *The Viva* (Murray, 1998), and *The Postgraduate Viva: A closer look* (Green, 1998).

Support

The primary academic source of support to research students is, of course, their supervisor(s). But there may be occasions when supervisors are unavailable for extended periods or when students are studying away from the institution. One of the key tasks of the research programme manager may be to ensure that, in such circumstances, appropriate supervisory support is available to the student.

In the case of supervisor absence, this is clearly much easier to cover if there is joint supervision or supervision by a committee. Otherwise, it is necessary to have mechanisms for notification of supervisor absence and to trigger the appointment of a temporary supervisor. The latter obviously needs to be experienced and trained, and should be fully briefed by the departing supervisor about the research project, what the student has done, and what objectives have been agreed for the period of supervisor absence.

In the case of student absence, it is necessary to ensure that there are effective mechanisms to maintain supervisory support. These may, for example, include agreed contact procedures with the supervisor(s), for example by e-mail, or the appointment of an additional supervisor at the place where the student is undertaking their research. It is worth noting that, while supervision can be delegated in this way, the responsibility for it remains with the institution at which the student is registered. The latter needs to ensure that additional supervisors have the relevant expertise, are trained and able to offer appropriate support.

As well as arrangements for ensuring the continuity of supervision, it is also necessary to have arrangements to cater for the eventuality that the supervisor–supervisee relationship breaks down, that is, one or both feels that they can no longer work together. In practice, most institutions have policies in place, often involving initial mediation by the head of department and then usually with further recourse to a more senior member of staff. It is important to recognize that, in such cases, both students and supervisors may need support until either reconciliation is achieved or a new supervisor appointed.

In addition to academic support, research students may also need pastoral support. In many institutions, this function is also undertaken by the supervisor, in which case s/he is supposed to act as the student's personal tutor. But this can create difficulties insofar as there may be conflicts between the requirements of the two roles, and some institutions have established other arrangements for the pastoral care of research students, for example through an independent postgraduate tutor.

While the supervisor or other tutor can supply support from 'above', research students also need support from other sources. One of the most consistent findings of the research literature on research students (see the summary in Delamont *et al*, 1997: 96) is that they suffer, to a greater or lesser degree, from intellectual and social isolation. But as the authors point out, while a degree of intellectual isolation is inherent in undertaking an original research project, 'there is no reason for this... to be accompanied by social or emotional loneliness' and indeed this can be detrimental to the success of the research. So it is important to ensure that there are opportunities for students to mix with others. These might include a regular postgraduate seminar, a graduate student society, common development and training programmes, or participation in conferences or professional associations.

Again, in this context, it is worth stressing that particular consideration needs to be given to supporting international research students. They are more likely to feel socially and culturally isolated than home students, and they may find it more difficult to ask for support from supervisors or to make friends with fellow students. It is, as Ryan (2000: 81) has argued, important to ensure that staff take an interest in the well-being of international students and assist them to join social networks. Where international students are accompanied by their families, consideration also needs to be given to involving spouses and children in social activities. They can feel marooned in an alien environment, and it is important to include them in departmental social activities and point them in the direction of relevant institutional societies and clubs.

In considering the support of research students the particular needs of part-time students and students with disabilities should also be included.

INDUCTION, TRAINING AND SUPPORT OF RESEARCH SUPERVISORS

Historically the assumption has been that, provided academics have a research degree or equivalent experience of research, they should be capable of supervising research students. But it is increasingly recognized, not least in the QAA code, that while qualifications and/or experience of research are a necessary condition for good supervision, they are not sufficient, and supervisors need appropriate induction, training and support.

Induction

Particularly if they are new to the institution, research supervisors need induction into the research degree, the regulations governing it and formal requirements relating to their role.

Historically, one of the defining characteristics of universities has been the power to award research degrees, including those of MA or MSc by research, MPhil, and PhD/DPhil/MD. But while the nomenclature may be the same, there are variations between institutions in the ways in which criteria for awards are defined. Supervisors need to be informed about these criteria in their institution to understand exactly what they are supervising their students to achieve. Supervisors also need to be inducted into the regulations governing degrees. Such regulations normally cover registration, enrolment, matriculation, requirements for progression, complaints procedures, procedures to be followed in the event of a breakdown of the relationship, assessment and examination, and appeals. A knowledge of these is necessary both to advise students and to ensure that supervision is undertaken within the regulations.

Additionally, supervisors have to be inducted into the formal requirements relating to their roles. These will normally include:

- meeting formally with the student on a minimum number of occasions in the academic year;

- ensuring that a record is kept of such meetings;
- advising the student on his/her progress;
- reporting formally on the student's progress to the university at specified (usually annual) intervals;
- reading drafts of the student's work;
- advising the student on submission or, in some universities, permitting them to submit;
- recommending examiners;
- arranging the examination;
- being available for consultation at the time of the viva (or, in some cases, sitting in on the viva);
- communicating the results of the viva; and, in cases where the degree has been awarded subject to minor changes, certifying to the university that they have been made.

Supervisors must be aware of all of these requirements, but particularly those relating to the frequency of formal meetings, policy on recording meetings, and progression requirements. In the – unlikely – event of legal proceedings, failure to observe these can cost the student, the supervisor and the institution dear.

Enhancing Practice

- How do you induct supervisors into the requirements for research degrees in your institution?
- How do you induct them into the regulations governing the degrees?
- How do you make them aware of their formal responsibilities as supervisors?

Training

The purpose of initial training is to make supervisors aware of good practice in performing their functions. The importance of this has been recognized in many universities which have established training programmes, in some cases leading to certification. The provision of training is recommended in the QAA code (1999: 11) and, in recent years the research councils have begun to take a much closer interest in the quality of training and, as will be seen in one case, to develop a framework for accreditation within their own institutions.

The list of functions to be covered in training programmes might include:

- establishing and maintaining a professional relationship with students;
- helping to induct students into research in their discipline;
- where appropriate, assisting with the choice of a topic;
- where appropriate, helping them devise a research proposal and plan;
- supporting their initial progress;
- encouraging them to write regularly;
- assisting with academic problems with their research;
- assisting with personal problems with a bearing on the research;
- reviewing the progress of the research;
- advising on drafts of the thesis;
- advising on submission;
- assisting in preparation for examination.

Until recently, managers of research programmes or supervisors looking for information and advice about these areas could be pointed to the general literature (see eg Delamont *et al*, 1997; Graham and Grant, 1997; Wisker and Sutcliffe, 1999) and then had to trawl through a range of sources to find other materials particularly in relation to supervision in specific subject areas. However, the task of researching good practice has been revolutionized through the 'gateway to research supervision' Web site developed by Professor Pat Cryer (2001). The site provides a 'one-stop' portal for information and advice about research supervision both generally and in specific subject areas, and as such is an invaluable resource for research training programmes.

Training should, of course, not be confined to the start of careers in research supervision. Supervisors should be encouraged regularly to update their knowledge and skills, and hence there needs to be refresher training and development.

It is important in devising training programmes to incorporate the dimension of international students. Supervisors need to be aware that there is now a considerable volume of research (see eg MacNamara and Harris, 1997; Ryan and Zuber-Skerritt, 1999) showing that such students may have very different expectations of the supervisory role and of their own role as research students; different styles of learning; different styles of writing; difficulties in writing in English, and other academic and social difficulties stemming from unfamiliarity with the culture. Accounts of good practice in supervising international students are to be found in the volumes cited above, as well as Ryan (2000: 69–75).

Biotechnology and Biological Sciences Research Council (BBSRC) Training and Accreditation Programme for Postgraduate Supervisors (TAPPS)

Increasingly, academic staff are undertaking professional development in teaching and learning which leads to accreditation by, for example, the Institute for Learning and Teaching. The genesis of the BBSRC TAPPS initiative is that the same process should be extended to research supervision. The scheme for accreditation was initially developed by Dr Peter Mertens at the Institute for Animal Health, and then made more widely available.

TAPPS provides support for both new and experienced supervisors in the forms of dedicated workshops, discussion groups and other forms of training. Supervisors who have successfully completed the training may then submit a 'claim for accreditation' based upon achievement of seven key 'outcomes' and six 'personal values'. The claim has to be substantiated by a portfolio of evidence. The claim and portfolio are assessed by two examiners appointed by the BBSRC Institutes Management Committee, and there is an external examiner.

The TAPPS framework is easily adaptable for use in other institutions and, while most interest has been from science-based disciplines, there is no reason why it cannot be applied to supervisors working in other disciplines.

For further information, see http://www.iah.bbsrc.ac.uk/TAPPS/

Support

Initial training can indicate potential good practice in research supervision, but it needs to be reinforced by exposure to actual good practice. For this reason, it is beneficial if new supervisors 'shadow' experienced ones for a year before taking on their 'own' first research student.

Once supervisors have successfully supervised a few students, they may have little need for continuing support in the role itself, but they may need support of another kind in terms of being allocated time to offer high-quality supervision. It is still not unknown for departments to assume that, simply because a supervisor is researching in a particular area and has students working in it, supervision is a relatively costless activity. But this is not the case; effective research supervision involves a significant commitment of time, and over-burdening can lead to stressed supervisors and/or disappointed students. One task of managers of research programmes is to make sure that supervisors are not overloaded, and this is in fact a precept of the QAA code (1999: 11).

There is a further precept covering what has also been a historically neglected area, namely support for the supervisor(s) in cases 'where serious concerns of student ability or application to the study programme have been identified' (QAA, 1999: 11). This may be picked up by formal monitoring procedures, but these may only be undertaken at long intervals, and it is obviously better for supervisors to be able to tackle problems as and when they arise rather than wait. So if a student's work does not seem to have the potential to meet the standard or if a student is clearly neglecting his or her studies, supervisors need a clear route to report this upwards for action at a higher level.

MONITORING STUDENT PROGRESS

All institutions have formal procedures for monitoring student progress, usually at or approaching the end of each year of study. Such monitoring should normally take place against explicit criteria, reflecting the stage at which the student is, or should be, in their research project. So, for example, criteria for a first-year PhD student might include evidence that the student had successfully completed the relevant research training, identified a clear 'trigger' for the research, had evaluated the literature relating to the topic, considered the appropriate methodology/methods to be used in the study and was aware of the strengths and limitations, and had satisfactory plans to develop the project. For a second-year student the criteria would relate to the continuing progress of the research topic in terms of data collection and analysis, while for a third-year student the criteria might include the production of an outline of the thesis and an indication of how it was likely to meet the university's requirements for the degree.

Procedures for the application of such criteria vary both between and within institutions. They may include: a report by the supervisor(s) on the student's progress; separate reports by the supervisor(s) and the student; joint reports; the presentation of evidence, written and possibly oral, to a panel including the supervisor(s); or a presentation to a panel excluding the supervisor(s). While, in the past, written reports by supervisors alone or jointly with students have been the norm, many institutions and departments have now instituted panels to introduce a broader perspective on student progress to try to help keep projects on track. A number have also included interviews and/or oral presentations in monitoring procedures to improve the quality of evidence on student progress and also to give students practice relevant to their later oral examinations.

The outcome of monitoring procedures is a recommendation whether students should or should not be allowed to continue with their research programmes. In most cases, progress is satisfactory, and this decision needs to be communicated to the supervisor and to the student (and possibly the sponsor) with suitable feedback.

Where progress is not deemed to be satisfactory, most institutions have procedures for informing the student of requirements for improvement and setting deadlines for further review. At the deadline, additional evidence is presented and decisions are taken whether to permit the student to continue with the programme, whether to allow him or her to re-register for a lesser research degree, or whether to terminate his/her registration. Particularly given the increasing tendency to litigation in higher education, research managers need to be aware of these procedures and to make sure that they are followed to the letter.

EVALUATION OF THE QUALITY OF THE STUDENT LEARNING EXPERIENCE

As well as monitoring the progress of students, managers of research programmes may also be responsible for evaluating the quality of the learning experiences of research students. In the case of the taught components of their programmes, this can normally be done using the conventional methods of questionnaires and/or focus groups to generate evaluation data. Such methods can also be used to evaluate other aspects of the student's experience, such as the usefulness of pre-entry information and both the general and the specific facilities to support research projects. Data thus collected can then be fed into appropriate mechanisms for quality assurance and enhancement.

These conventional methods are, however, much more difficult to apply in evaluating the quality of research supervision. Supervisors may still see their relationships with their research students as private ones between consenting adults and resent public intrusion; students are aware that, particularly if their supervisor only has a small number of research students, responses to questionnaires/comments in focus groups can be traced back to them, and may be unwilling to be frank. So, on grounds of principle and/or the difficulties of obtaining reliable data, many departments do not seek to evaluate the quality of research supervision during the student's period of study.

While this reluctance is understandable, it is worth noting that it may entail costs to all concerned. Research students are effectively disenfranchised in terms of being able to offer an opinion on the quality of their experience and, in serious cases, they may be left with the alternatives of giving up or pursuing a formal complaint. Supervisors are deprived of feedback – positive or negative – on their performance and of the chance to improve it. The department is deprived of early warnings that things might be going wrong with a particular supervisor and student and of the opportunity to put matters right at an early stage. Also, without an evaluation system, it is difficult to present the kind of evidence increasingly demanded by research sponsors that the organization is assuring and enhancing the quality of supervision. So it is at least arguable that supervision should be evaluated, preferably by mechanisms that command the confidence of supervisors and students. Mechanisms are more likely to do this if they:

- are universal and fair, that is, they apply equally to all supervisors and all students so that none feel singled out by the process;
- are transparent, that is, they are based upon clear, explicit, and agreed criteria which are relevant to the stage of study being assured and enhanced;
- involve a third party trusted by both supervisor and student, such as the research programme manager, in evaluating the quality of supervision;
- guarantee confidentiality in the treatment of specific information relating to the supervisor and the supervisee in reports, for example to the head of department.

In addition to evaluating the experiences of research students during their studies, increasingly and very much in line with developments in taught programmes, there is a trend to try to evaluate their overall experience by administering exit questionnaires to successful graduates of the programme. Such students can be encouraged to reflect upon their experience over the two, three or more years of their studies and deliver a considered verdict on the programme as a whole. In the UK, at least one major research council – the BBSRC (undated) – is already using such an exit questionnaire to elicit evaluations from students it has sponsored.

Finally under the heading of evaluation, and bearing in mind the increasing saliency of the employment agenda in research programmes, it is worth considering contacting students a year or two after graduation, and asking them how well their postgraduate experiences prepared them for employment. Such surveys often indicate a gap in terms of team-working skills, particularly among graduates in the arts and social sciences where research students tend to work in isolation. Evidence of this kind can be used to improve the acquisition of skills, for example in the research training programme.

Enhancing Practice

- What mechanisms are in place in your institution to evaluate the quality of the taught components of research degrees?
- Are there mechanisms for evaluating the quality of research supervision during the student's period of study? If not, would it be possible to introduce such mechanisms of either a direct or indirect kind?
- Are there mechanisms for evaluating the overall experience of research students? If not, would it be possible to introduce one?
- Are there mechanisms for tracking graduates who have been in employment for a year or two? If not, could such mechanisms be established with a view to improving the programme?

REVIEWING RESEARCH PROGRAMMES

While taught programmes tend automatically to be reviewed by course teams, this is not always the case with research programmes. But, in order to maintain their viability and to assure and enhance their quality, research programmes require review, and this is embodied in the QAA code for research programmes (QAA, 1999: 14).

Reviews of research programmes can usefully cover:

- pre-entry information;
- trends in applications;
- trends in conversion rates (applications turning into registration for the programme);
- the effectiveness of the induction programme (for UK, EU, and other international students);
- language support (for non-native English speakers);
- the research training programme;
- the quality of research supervision;
- progression rates;
- submission rates;
- pass and failure rates;
- feedback from external examiners;
- feedback from sponsors;
- the higher education qualifications framework.

Reviews along these lines should be undertaken annually, and the results reported upwards to enable institutions to show compliance with the QAA code.

OVERVIEW

The role of managing research programmes is, in many institutions, a fairly new one. Its origins lie in demands, particularly from research funders and sponsors, for public evidence of the quality and standards of research programmes. The role can entail undertaking a very wide range of responsibilities including managing recruitment, selection, the induction, training and support of research students and research supervisors, student progression, evaluation and the review of research programmes. In exercising these responsibilities, it is necessary for the managers of research programmes to show a high degree of sensitivity and tact in mediating between the demands of the outside world and an inside one in which a professional relationship – that between the supervisor and the student – plays a key part in success. But if that balancing act can be achieved and the demands of public accountability squared with preservation as far as possible of the traditional relationship between supervisors and students, then it is not only a necessary role but one well worth undertaking.

REFERENCES

Biotechnology and Biological Sciences Research Council (BBSRC) (undated) Exit Questionnaire regarding my PhD supervision, Biotechnology and Biological Sciences Research Council, Swindon. URL: http://www.iah.bbsrc.ac.uk/TAPPS/ Student%20 Exit%20Questionnaire.htm

Cryer, P (1997) *The Research Student's Guide to Success*, Open University Press, Buckingham

Cryer, P (2001) Gateway to Research Supervision, URL: http://www.iah.bbsrc.ac.uk/ supervisor_training

CVCP (1995) *Code of Practice for the Recruitment and Support of International Students in UK Higher Education*, Committee of Vice-Chancellors and Principals, London

Delamont, S, Atkinson, P, and Parry, O (1997) *Supervising the PhD: A guide to success*, Society for Research Into Higher Education (SRHE)/Open University Press, Buckingham

Economic and Social Research Council (ESRC) (2001) *Postgraduate Training Guidelines*, ESRC, Swindon

Furnham, A (1997) The experience of being an overseas student, in *Overseas Students in Higher Education*, ed D MacNamara and R Harris, Routledge, London

Graham, A and Grant, B (1997) *Managing More Postgraduate Students*, Oxford Centre for Staff Development, Oxford

Green, H (1998) *The Postgraduate Viva: A closer look* (video pack), Leeds Metropolitan University, Leeds

Higher Education Quality Council (HEQC) (1996) *Guidelines on the Quality Assurance of Research Degrees*, HEQC, London

Higher Education Funding Council for England (HEFCE), Committee of Vice Chancellors and Principals (CVCP) and Scottish Committee of Principals (SCOP) (1996) *Review of Postgraduate Education (the Harris Report)*, HEFCE, CVCP and SCOP, London

Hill, K (1996) My first seminars, in *In at the Deep End*, ed D Allan, Unit for Innovation in Higher Education, Lancaster

Kiley, M (2000) Providing timely and appropriate support for international students, in *Good Practice in Working with International Students*, ed G Wisker, SEDA Paper 110, Staff and Educational Development Association, Birmingham

MacNamara, D and Harris, R (1997) *Overseas Students in Higher Education*, Routledge, London

Macrae, M (1997) Induction of international students, in *Overseas Students in Higher Education*, ed D MacNamara and R Harris, Routledge, London

Murray, R (1997) *Thesis Writing* (video pack), Centre for Academic Practice, University of Strathclyde

Murray, R (1998) *The Viva* (video pack), Centre for Academic Practice, University of Strathclyde

National Committee of Inquiry into Higher Education (NCIHE) (1997) *Higher Education in the Learning Society* (*Dearing Report*), HMSO, London

Quality Assurance Agency (QAA) (1999) *Code of Practice for the Assurance of Academic Quality and Standards in Higher Education: Postgraduate Research Programmes*, QAA, Gloucester

QAA (2000a) *The Framework for Higher Education Qualifications in Scotland*, QAA, Gloucester

QAA (2000b) *Framework for Higher Education Qualifications in England, Wales and Northern Ireland*, QAA, Gloucester

Ryan, J (2000) *A Guide to Teaching International Students*, Oxford Centre for Staff and Learning Development, Oxford

Ryan, Y and Zuber-Skerritt, O (1999) *Supervising Postgraduates from Non-English Speaking Backgrounds*, SRHE/Open University Press, Buckingham

Wisker, G and Sutcliffe, N (1999) *Good Practice in Research Supervision*, SEDA Paper 106, Staff and Educational Development Association, Birmingham

8 Managing High-Impact Research Groups

Ewan Ferlie, Janet Harvey and
Andrew Pettigrew

INTRODUCTION

This chapter examines some of the organizational and managerial issues
which arise at the level of the research group within higher education institutions (HEIs). In management terms, the research team can be seen as an
operational or middle management level of organization, which can be contrasted with the strategic management of the larger academic department. The
unit of analysis within this chapter is the whole research group, including
both the research director and other research staff (especially senior research
staff who may become important theme champions in their own right). We are
attracted by the notion of 'shaping' rather than 'managing' such groups, in
recognition of the collective and historically dependent nature of the process
of organizing. They quickly develop niches and move along tracks from
which it is difficult to shift. While some develop strong reputations and flourish within the research and development (R and D) 'market', others languish
in obscurity or may even fail to raise the funds they need to survive. Further
to the contextualization provided in the introduction, this chapter (based on
research carried out in the healthcare sector) moves on to consider: firstly, the
factors which appear to typify high achieving research groups; secondly, factors which are inhibitors to developing a strong research group and culture;
and, finally, discussion of higher-level themes which should be considered
when looking to promote success.

What do we know about the formation and maintenance of 'high-impact'
research groups' (we acknowledge that 'impact' is a complex and multi-
dimensional construct which will be unpacked later in the chapter)? While

universities are endeavouring to organize and manage research more deliberately (Robson and Shove, 1999), effective strategic management at the departmental level will fundamentally rest on the presence of such research clusters at this lower level, so it is an important question.

Some writers have recently drawn attention to macro-level shifts in the organization and management of knowledge (Gibbons *et al*, 1994; Ziman, 2000) from conventional academic knowledge (mode 1) to forms of knowledge which are more applied, more open to end users, collectivized and multidisciplinary (mode 2) in nature. This applies also to our own field of organizational and management research (Pettigrew, 1997; Tranfield and Starkey, 1998). Looking across the higher education system as a whole, there are trends towards a new 'soft money' system in which larger numbers of contract research workers compete for grants at the periphery of the traditional university system: research groups are transformed into small business enterprises. The metaphorical forum of scientific opinion is turned into an actual market in research services (Ziman, 2000: 76). Within the public policy literature, there are calls for universities to undertake more 'relevant' and applied research and to link more effectively to firms within the context of the knowledge based economy (Leadbetter, 2000). Universities are here seen as key motors of the post-industrial economy rather than producing knowledge for its own sake. Some of these dynamics have been explored at the level of the whole university (Clark, 1998). Clark identifies as a characteristic of 'entrepreneurial' universities the growth of what he sees as a novel periphery of non-traditional applied research units which cross conventional boundaries and link with external organizations.

So it is interesting to explore the more local processes of knowledge production which take place within research units. This chapter will draw on some recently completed empirical work the authors have undertaken on the determinants of 'high-impact' research groups within medical schools (Harvey *et al*, 1999, 2001) so, in a sense, offering a substantive case study in terms of the data generated by this research. However, the findings may be relevant to other disciplines (notably in the natural and social sciences) which demonstrate a pattern of collective organization, contract research and a greater stress on applied research capacity. (The humanities may present a different pattern, as some have argued that they are characterized by a lesser degree of collective or corporate organization: see Becher, 1989: 109.) The following themes which emerge from our study may be worthy of general consideration in other natural and social science research settings:

- the role of research 'leadership';
- innovation and entrepreneurialism;

- the management of scarce human resources;
- networking.

'HIGH-IMPACT' RESEARCH TEAMS

The empirical data for this study was drawn from the field of healthcare. The NHS Executive West Midlands commissioned the undertaking of an audit of the output of medical research groups within the region (Harvey *et al*, 1999) which might be useful in performance assessment. As the empirical material, collected through a combination of postal surveys and four comparative case studies, was analysed, so we became intrigued by possible changing patterns in the way in which research knowledge was being produced (Harvey *et al*, 1999). We were particularly interested in why some groups appeared to be more 'effective' in producing research reputations.

It is acknowledged that the definition of 'effectiveness' is complex. It is argued that 'effectiveness'(Harvey *et al*, 2001) is related to indicators of research group performance and implies competitive advantage over comparable groups. Effectiveness is also related to the ability to acquire resources in accordance with the goals pursued by the group. Effectiveness will therefore reflect objective sector-level measures (such as research assessment exercise (RAE) performance) and also subjective strategy fulfilment (that is, meeting internally derived strategic aims and goals which are accepted by the group). (See Donaldson's 1999 discussion of performance measurement and top teams.)

The initial postal survey identified research groups that were high profile in their field and had high output in orthodox academic terms (such as refereed journal articles and with recognized and highly visible 'star' performers). This was achieved using survey data: our case studies sought to explore the organization and management of these groups both historically and currently in a more qualitative fashion. Selection of the cases was further informed by reference to the 1996 RAE ratings and also sought to include groups who had received substantial amounts of peer reviewed funding (as a further quality control).

A comparative case study analysis was undertaken of four medical research groups: an endocrinology department and a genetics department located in large teaching hospitals; a primary care department situated in a university and the main research institutes located in a specialized orthopaedic hospital, also with university linkages. All four cases involved research groups with strong university affiliations, usually with group members holding part-time academic posts, and one of the research groups was directly located within a university. A total of 27 interviews were conducted across the sites, using a semi-structured pro forma. We were interested to see whether common themes emerged inductively across the four cases.

HIGH-IMPACT RESEARCH GROUPS: FIVE KEY FACTORS

The following five factors emerged repeatedly as associated with high achievement across the four cases.

Strong leadership

Strong leadership was linked to the need for high-level strategic direction. Research groups are more strategically driven both internally and externally than was previously the case; that is, there is more emphasis on the acquisition and use of resources, and research is much more managed within macro-level evaluative frameworks which make visible and seek to assess performance.

Strong leadership was associated with good research practice in that it provided focus, direction, vision, coherence and ideas (a much wider and energizing conception of leadership than control, although it did include elements of control). At best, the leader provided a pioneering and innovative orientation, for example, the leader positioned the endocrinology group at the forefront of molecular endocrinology, generating the intellectual, financial and political support to mobilize this vision. The leader needs to be able to spot emerging research directions and recognize their implications for research activity: intellectual innovation remains at the core of the research leader's task. This includes spotting new ideas or mobilizing themes around which a collectivity can work productively. Innovation is in part also an aspect of entrepreneurialism, a willingness to take risks when the research outcome remains unpredictable (Clark, 1998). Leaders of research groups were able to generate a supportive, flexible and entrepreneurial academic environment (in the endocrinology and primary care cases in particular).

Leaders also connected the research group with the host university, and nationally and indeed internationally with the wider research community. Enterprising leaders engaged in 'boundary spanning', reaching across old university boundaries to link up with outside organizations and groups. Our cases suggested that the skills needed to be an effective leader of a research group are changing, as research leaders now have to interface with and manage a more complex and business-orientated environment. Different eras may indeed require different leadership styles: for example, in the primary care case the qualities of the former leader (who had built up the group as a teaching department during a more stable financial period) were different from the current leader, who needed to be highly entrepreneurial and politically astute.

'Leadership' could also take a more collective form, with the development of second-tier research theme champions who could energize particular areas, under the overall direction of the research director.

Finding, motivating and retaining talent

Given increased external performance pressures, research leaders needed to configure their resources to add maximum value. As human capital is the core asset of research groups, so hand-picked expertise lay at the heart of high-achieving research groups. Some of our cases exhibited carefully constructed packages of expertise, including a portfolio of people as well as of projects. For example, the endocrinology group 'pump-primed' people as well as projects from internal resources. Instances were given of individuals whose salary had been 'bridged', so that they could achieve the research experience and expertise they needed to be credible candidates for research fellowships. The importance of sustaining research groups over time was stressed, both to consolidate the initial training investment and to maintain a critical mass in particular areas.

There was a need to develop second-level 'product champions' (principal investigators – PIs – below the centre director level) to lead and mobilize particular thematic ideas and to build subgroups around them. Many of these second-level PIs are themselves on temporary contracts and have to raise funds not only for junior staff but also for themselves. In both the endocrinology and primary care cases, thematic subgroups have developed, championed by individual 'key players'. The emphasis, therefore, was on finding, motivating and rewarding talent. Externally funded medical fellowships (both local and national) were seen as an important resource within this process, while external research project grants were more associated with allowing the possibility of diversifying research interests and intellectual innovation. The problem of recruiting suitably qualified prospective 'product champions' emerged in a number of cases. The primary care group had managed to 'bridge' researchers by extending researchers' competences by moving them into new but related areas, facilitating the reconfiguration of research resources in response to changing demand patterns.

In addition to the possession of complementary skills, the cases also suggest that positive interpersonal relations are important to the internal workings of research groups. There were instances of considerable disruption where those recruited had not fitted in to the group.

Strategic related diversification

In addition to the conscious diversification of the range of skills possessed by individuals and available within the group, it was important for groups to be able to diversify into new areas. This is best achieved through related diversification, which can ensure continued coherence in the research portfolio, maintains critical mass in addressing cognate research problems, and also maintains a clear internal core competence and a strong external group identity.

The use of internally-funded pilot studies to construct a bridge into new areas was a tactic which was often employed. Diversification might also entail alliance construction with an established outsider who could add to the group's track record. Strategic diversification might entail the growth of a more diverse workforce internally (for example, the appointment of a specialist statistician to complement clinical research work).

A significant 'driver' to related diversification within endocrinology appears to have been the lack of a dedicated funding body, so that the group had to apply in the 'open pool' of funding and a more competitive marketplace. This appears to have acted as a spur to diversification. What might initially have appeared to have been a disadvantage in fact provided impetus for moving forward. This driver, combined with the 'tone' set by the head of department, encouraged the research group not to see endocrinology as a 'ridged box' but as having 'fluid boundaries', and reinforced the trend to cross-boundary working.

Strongly linked theory (scientific base) and practice (clinical practice)

The cases also pointed to the presence of a strong interplay and cross-fertilization between the clinical service and the scientific base in facilitating high impact research. This represents the interplay of theory and practice within the medical domain. This relationship has two aspects: the material (involving the supply of human material such as bone, bone marrow, body fluids, tissue) from clinical practice for use in science, and the intellectual (this allows scientific discoveries and results to be interpreted within the wider domain of clinical practice). The latter is seen as affecting the direction of laboratory work as it supplies an initial orientating frame of reference.

In some cases, the collaboration of a clinician and a scientist with the same general substantive interest allowed both parties to access a slightly different area, providing the opportunity for innovative and complementary work: this occurred, for example, around work concerning metabolism within the endocrinology department. In all of the case study groups, we were told that there was a good intellectual (as well as material) exchange between scientists and clinicians.

Network connectedness

One of the crucial functions of research group leaders is to provide network connectedness both within the institution and nationally/internationally within the research community and beyond. The drive to build purposeful networks arises from various factors which include:

- emphasis (in some cases insistence) of the research councils;
- concentration of resources and expertise: this is associated with specialization, coupled with collaboration to allow access to specialized resources;
- intellectual 'drivers' rooted in the growing complexity of knowledge and hence the need for collaboration with specialists in particular areas;
- availability of new communications technologies (such as e-mail) which reduce the importance of geographical distance.

Within our four cases, networking appeared to be especially significant in the following areas:

- The research leader needs to be well connected both in the host university and externally.
- The recruitment of clinical staff and the selection of able research leaders.
- There might be some trading between groups in relation to shared facilities such as use of tests.
- The norms of reciprocity and construction of 'win win situations' were apparent in relation to such shared use of specialized facilities.
- Such trading facilitated collaboration between the key research 'players' within a particular field.

Departments are under pressure to become more 'outwards facing', with senior staff being expected to develop strong interpersonal links. The quality of the networks which individuals and the group as a whole have is a critical success factor: as one clinician put it, 'If you don't network, you're dead!'

Inhibitors to developing a strong research group and culture

Four counter-factors emerged as inhibitors of the development of a high impact research group:

Excessive reliance on short-term contracts

Excessive reliance on short-term contracts could undermine the staffing continuity needed to build up long-term research themes and prevent critical mass from emerging.

Excessive financial insecurity

There has been a shift from long-term and protected modes of funding to a 'soft money' system in which groups are expected to compete on a project by project basis. Even 'soft money' was difficult to obtain and required a lot of scientist time being spent on bid preparation and returns (as well as on ful-filling the requirements of more elaborate audit systems for the NHS R and D function such as the 'Culyer returns').

Conflicting demands

Academic research groups operating at the interface of the NHS and the uni-versity system have to balance an increasing number of different (even contradictory) institutional demands: the need to raise funds versus the need to secure academic output; the demands of the NHS versus the demands of the RAE. Both the university and NHS systems also generate a number of 'strategic initiatives' which constrain the behaviour of individual research groups (the introduction of the so-called Culyer R and D system designed to measure research performance and enhance accountability for the use of NHS R and D funds); changes in the NHS education and training system such as the introduction of specialist registrars; the greater stress on entrepreneurial-ism and protection of intellectual property within the university system).

Inter-occupational tensions

In a few cases, there was evidence of tensions between scientific and clinical staff which could retard effective cooperation between the two functions. Such tensions as existed appeared to be status and power based, with some detect-ing clinical dominance over research projects. Such tension is illustrated in the case study below.

High-Impact Research Within an Orthopaedic Hospital

This case study related to a number of research institutes within a spe-cialist orthopaedic hospital. The long tradition of research excellence was a feature of this case, being transmitted across successive generations of researchers. The specialist nature of the hospital gave it a concentration of clinical expertise, and this was associated with a strong scientific base. The large number of research departments on site and the central support facility which has grown up to aid them are considerable strengths. The organization's integration of specialist areas allows one speciality to feed into another. It gained a 5* in the 1996 RAE, in conjunction with another research group/university located about 90 miles away.

The hospital is located in a very rural setting, but because of its spe-cialized nature, draws its patients from a wide catchment area. While it is physically remote, it is intellectually well connected. There has been clinical research on the site from its foundation (about 1900), with scien-tific research emerging later. The former chief professor was a charismatic leader who developed a research infrastructure on the grounds that, 'If you are going to be in the forefront, you've got to have some research.'

There is a strong tradition of networking, drawing in clinicians from outside (and getting them up from London) to debate clinical practice and later research. The early research was 'very hands on' (that is, highly clinically based) and it continues to be clinically driven. Basic research contributes to the clinical treatment of patients (for instance, HRT treatment). The site now has a very wide funding base, including charitable funding, research councils, industrial funding and NHS funding. Regional NHS funding has more recently been an important source of 'pump priming' money, facilitating preliminary work and an early 'track record' in areas the organization has been trying to grow. (Often a pilot study has been funded in-house prior to applying for regional money.)

The site also has a long history of raising substantial sums from charity, and a dedicated fund raiser has been in post for a number of years. In the past, there were large block grants from the Department of Health but these have more recently become 'rolling contracts' (an interim arrangement), facilitating a transition to applying for individual project grants through competitive bidding: 'Since then, as with other research groups, we have had to fend for ourselves in a big way!' This has resulted in some losses of unfunded staff or those unwilling to accept such financial insecurity. However, the hospital believes that it is still able to attract well qualified staff, because of both its national reputation and the attractive rural location.

Paradoxically, the geographical isolation of the orthopaedic hospital appeared to strengthen the emphasis on national and international network building. Staff recognized that they had to make a conscious effort to establish and maintain a network of linkages, using contacts with former staff, conference attendance, personal links and their high reputation.

CONCLUDING DISCUSSION

The collective pattern of organization and management of research groups, at least within the field of medicine, may influence their level of 'effectiveness' as it has been defined here. In this section, we comment on three higher level themes which also emerged across the four cases:

Entrepreneurialism

Entrepreneurialism emerged as a central aspect of high-achieving/high-impact research groups. It comprised two major aspects:

- commercial entrepreneurialism, related to the market;
- intellectual entrepreneurialism, related to innovation around ideas and their process of development.

Commercial entrepreneurialism

One definition of an entrepreneur is someone who enters into a business with a chance of making a profit or a loss. Research groups are now operating in a far more market-driven framework which entails greater competition (as well as some collaboration) between groups and increased contextual uncertainty and complexity. The 'marketization' of research (through the soft money mode of finance and the emergence of performance measurement systems); the 'bidding' system employed in competing for research funding and the growth of 'nearer to market' research (where funders have a greater input in specifying more focused research questions) have all become pervasive. In addition, there are ever more elaborate post hoc audit systems (Power, 1997) also designed to measure performance and assure quality.

So research groups too have to decide where to place limited resources to best effect. This entails strategic 'juggling' in order to satisfy various audiences and keep researchers in work, with research groups almost acting as small R and D businesses. This was also apparent in the words used to describe research activities: for example one product champion talked of a 'loss leader' (small-scale research pump-primed 'in-house') in the hope that it would then attract significant research funding. Some groups were also taking action to protect themselves against excessive market pressure, trying to stabilize the labour market.

Intellectual entrepreneurship

Intellectual entrepreneurship derived from ideas developed over time, as part of the process of strategic related diversification. Sometimes this involved 'putting a new slant on the already established', in order to open up novel lines of enquiry and funding: novelty was felt to be attractive to funders. One needed to cross boundaries, to be flexible yet at the same time keep a strong core competence within the group.

Complexity

Research groups operate in a more complex environment and themselves have become complex small organizations. Such groups increasingly incorporate *multi*-faceted projects, involving *multi*-faceted collaboration between *multiple* disciplines. They employ multiple funding bases, *multiple* methods, and *multi*-disciplinary, *multi*-project working (researchers working across more than one project). The trend to multi-faceted working was driven both by the market but also by the increasing complexity of knowledge – in turn related to both specialization and collaboration. Diversity was seen as a strength, but had to be balanced against the need to retain a core competence and mobilizing a research theme for 'branding' purposes.

Collaboration

Increased complexity, specialization and the emergence of very high cost facilities in turn creates a requirement for collectivization and collaboration (Ziman, 2000). This was reinforced by the funding councils, such as the Medical Research Council (MRC), with their emphasis on the cooperative group rather than the lone researcher. Multi-faceted projects therefore need the cooperation of sub-specialist or adjacent field experts, and a greater concentration of related expertise. The 'downsides' of collaboration were felt to be high transaction costs and that it may be artificially 'forced' by funders. At its best, collaborative working is associated with a multiplier effect, through creating cross-boundary insights which add value.

The issue of cross-disciplinary working is related directly to thematic rather than disciplinary working. Our cases suggested a movement to thematic working, although not as strongly as has been depicted in some of the literature (Gibbons *et al*, 1994; Tranfield and Starkey, 1998; but for a more cautious view see Huff, 2000). Our empirical material suggests that thematic working does occur, but that participants are still working from a strong, disciplinary, expert base. The credibility of the researcher within multi-disciplinary collaborations (and attractiveness to partners) derives ultimately from his or her specialized disciplinary background.

A thematic approach therefore appears to bear the same relationship to discipline as flexibility does to coherence: that is, the ability to engage in the first must be rooted in the credibility of the second. Thematic working also requires a problem-solving orientation and is again facilitated by the degree of network connectedness a research group possesses, which emerges as perhaps the core dimension of high impact.

CONCLUSIONS

This study of high-impact research groups found a number of interrelated factors to be critical to their success, namely:

- strong leadership;
- finding, motivating and rewarding talent;
- strategic related diversification;
- strongly linked theory and practice;
- and in particular network connectedness.

High-performing research groups exhibit strong leadership and have 'product champions' as second-level leaders heading up research streams. There is a problem of succession planning, as groups can become dependent on one or two well known investigators who are difficult to replace, should they move on. Strong leadership is also associated with well defined strategic direction, strong linkages between theory and practice, and related diversification (but around a coherent strategic core). High performance is also related to finding, motivating and retaining complementary talent and skill mix, although it is difficult to develop second-level product champions. This provides the human resource flexibility to manage an increasingly complex external environment.

High-performance research groups display many of the characteristics associated with 'mode 2' knowledge production (Gibbons *et al*, 1994). They are increasingly employing collaborative strategies, and there is some shift to multi-disciplinarity, although we would suggest to a lesser extent than some of the literature suggests, as participants are still working from a strongly disciplinary base. Our position is then closer to that of Huff (2000). Indeed, partners become attractive to multi-disciplinary collaborations precisely because they can bring with them strong disciplinary reputations.

Both intellectual and commercial forms of entrepreneurship are evident, driven by the more competitive and complex environment. This can also be seen in terms of the 'marketization' of the research group, along the small business model. At the very hub of this complex web of interrelated factors is network connectedness, which we suggest is central in mobilizing the other factors involved.

Research and policy agenda

These conclusions are based on exploratory work and so further work is needed to confirm them. It would be interesting to see whether these factors are also apparent in other settings besides the bio-medical sector. Further research is also needed to elaborate the relationships between the different elements of our model. For example, exactly how does network connectedness enhance and facilitate strategic related diversification?

Our model has been built on assessment of one definition of 'effectiveness' (as already outlined), namely academic output and RAE rating, ability to secure peer-reviewed funding and reputation. Others might contest this choice and argue that links with practice (or other 'mode 2' indicators) might form an alternative and legitimate dimension of output, particularly given the growth of 'mode 2 research.'

Is there a downside to more entrepreneurial modes of research? Are there elements of 'market failure' in R and D funding? What happens to advances in basic theory or methodology? Does critical or speculative work get crowded out? This project focused on 'high-impact' units; but there may also be a number of 'low-impact' units where little or no work of significance is produced. The dynamics of failure may be as interesting as the dynamics of success, although it would be more difficult to secure access. It would be interesting to review the evolution of research fields in the 1990s (for example, we have a particular interest in health services research but there are many other examples), and assess the extent to which key influential works were produced by 'near to market' units or by alternative knowledge producers.

Clark's (1998) argument that 'an expanded developmental periphery' is emerging which is much more outwards facing that the traditional academic core is not altogether supported by this study. For example, the endocrinology group was situated firmly within the department of medicine within a teaching hospital, yet developed many characteristics of an entrepreneurial research group. The academic and disciplinary-based core may then be able to transform itself to a greater extent that some have imagined, even without the creation of novel intermediary mechanisms (such as technology transfer offices).

It may be that in other fields (for example, business studies) free standing and outwards facing units may be more prominent than in the medical field where a strong disciplinary base seems to remain important. We also remain unclear how these research units interact with the host academic institutions, particularly in respect of long-term career and labour market management.

The fashionable drift to marketization and entrepreneurial skills may need to be balanced against a different requirement for longer-term horizons and labour market stability. Where do universities draw this balance? Are they seeking to protect research units against excessive market forces or do they take the view that research entrepreneurs should take risks, and can be allowed to fail? Or will academic output and RAE rating continue to be the criteria by which we judge research groups? It will be interesting to follow the debate post-2001 RAE result publication.

ACKNOWLEDGEMENTS

The authors wish to acknowledge the financial support of the NHS Executive (West Midlands) in conducting this research.

REFERENCES

Becher, T (1989) *Academic Tribes and Territories*, Open University Press, Buckingham

Clark, B (1998) *Creating Entrepreneurial Universities: Organisational pathways of transformation*, Pergamon Press, Oxford

Donaldson, L (1999) *Performance Driven Organisational Change: The organisational portfolio*, Sage, London

Gibbons, M, Limoge, SC, Nowotny, H, Schwartzman, S, Scott, P and Trow, M (1994) *The New Production of Knowledge: The dynamics of science and research in contemporary societies*, Sage, London

Harvey, J, Pettigrew, A and Ferlie, E (2001) *The Determinants of Research Group Performance: Towards mode 2?*, Centre for Creativity, Strategy and Change, University of Warwick

Harvey, J, Pettigrew, A, Ferlie, E and Stewart, J (1999) *Auditing Output and Understanding The Processes and Synergies of the Research Cycle*, Centre for Creativity, Strategy and Change, University of Warwick

Huff, AS (2000) Changes in organisational knowledge production, *Academy of Knowledge Review*, **25**(2), pp 288–93

Leadbetter, C (2000) *Living on Thin Air*, Penguin, London

Pettigrew, A (1997) The double hurdles for management research, in *Advancement in Organisational Behaviour: Essays in honour of Derek Pugh*, ed T Clark, Ashgate, Basingstoke

Power, M (1997) *The Audit Society*, Oxford University Press, Oxford

Robson, B and Shove, E (1999) *Interactions and Influence – Individuals and Institutions: A summary report of six pilot studies*, ESRC, Swindon

Tranfield, D and Starkey, K (1998) The nature, social organisation and promotion of management research: towards policy, *British Journal of Management*, 9, pp 341–53

Ziman, J (2000) *Real Science*, Cambridge University Press, Cambridge

9 Developing a Strategic Culture for Research

Ken Young

This chapter reviews a number of aspects of the development of a strategic approach to research. The emphasis is on approach, not on output, and especially not on the kind of research strategy document that, with the next research assessment exercise (RAE) a couple of years away, is typically presented for the consideration of a university's academic community. Strategy is a process, not a product.

The first section of the chapter acknowledges the problems of generalizing about the diverse world of research, while the second calls attention to the common pressures that nevertheless operate upon it. The third section focuses on the department as the primary unit within which academic management and leadership has to be exercised, and sets out an approach to that task. The fourth section considers the implications of developing a strategic approach to research at the institutional level. Throughout, a cautious approach is taken to concepts of 'research culture' that, I argue, have to be considered alongside, and in interaction with, issues of power and process.

THE SEVERAL WORLDS OF RESEARCH

To a perhaps greater extent than any other aspect of academic life, the subject of research offers a dangerous enticement to over-generalization, or to the extrapolation of experience into areas where it may be an unreliable guide. Let me begin, then, by declaring the auspices under which I write, and forestall, so far as possible, the accusation of presumptuousness. As a social scientist, historian and engineer manqué, I have no direct experience of scientific research. I have seen enough of it at second hand to know that the values, routines, working practices of research in the natural sciences – that is, those matters that are thought to constitute its culture – differ markedly from those in the humanities. The large grant, the research team, the post-docs, the equipment budget, are a foreign land to the historian, and I recall now with a certain wry sympathy the vice chancellor who, on appointing me to a chair, enquired as to what laboratory space I would require, and whether I would be bringing technical staff with me.

At first sight, then, the two cultures are alive and well. But the realities are not quite so stark. Those engaged in social research lie perhaps somewhere between the two extremes, even if only a minority of those who make up social science faculties have experience of working in research groups. For example, Ferlie, Harvey and Pettigrew's account of 'high-impact research groups' in Chapter 8 illustrates a style of operation that is shared with engineering, if not the basic sciences. But these are the exceptions, and the divisions are greater than the commonalities. Maybe not 'two cultures' after all, then, but certainly a continuum, and we are none of us able to bestraddle more than a fragment of it.

If the world of research is segmented by discipline, it is even more segmented by institutional setting. A great deal of research takes place outside the universities, in research institutes of one kind or another, free standing or publicly funded, and in social and economic matters it is increasingly undertaken by consultancy firms. The university researcher has the dubious benefit of an external reference group just within his or her peripheral vision. The researcher may have, as I have, spent some years in that sector, and have thereby first hand experience of a world in which there are no distractions from research. It is a single-minded world. Yet there are obvious drawbacks to that monocultural existence. I used to keep a notice on my wall reading 'The project is dead. Long live the project!' as a comment on its relentlessness. Those working outside the university sector are also insulated from any obligation – or deprived of any opportunity – to transmit, as well as create knowledge.

The contrast serves as a reminder that academic life is a matter of balancing competing demands. How those demands are experienced will differ from institution to institution, and often between departments in the same institution. But although the generality of demands in a research-led university in the Russell group will differ from those in a former polytechnic, the expectations levelled against an individual in either may be equally intense.

RESPONDING TO NEW PRESSURES

Research in the university has never been more important to both individual and institutional fortunes. Paradoxically, it has probably never before been under so intense a threat from competing pressures. What has been aptly termed 'the audit explosion' has subjected universities, departments and individual staff to regular monitoring of everything from the specification of their course learning objectives to their allocation of time, month by month. Just as once the professionalization of university teaching turned commitments of conscience into obligations, so has the imposition of audit turned those obligations into requirements. Meeting requirements becomes everyone's preoccupation, and in this way the priorities of those who make policy for the system as a whole are translated into the (perhaps reluctant) priorities of those who deliver teaching and undertake research.

Inevitably, the priority attached to the research requirement will be weaker than that attached to the processes of teaching and learning, where internal and external audit alike may bring the spotlight to bear on individual shortcomings. This effect varies by discipline, with research assessment having a far more profound effect in the humanities then in the natural sciences, where it has been just one among several pressures for rationalization and qualitative discrimination.

The corollary of these competing pressures is that academic managers need to manage them by intervening in the ways in which activities are prioritized. Here is a source of tension. The science dean who protested that academics 'want to do research, they want to teach, they want to run their own scientific agenda and not to be told what to do by a middle manager' (Henkel, 2000: 238) was voicing the curiosity and independent-mindedness that brought most of us into academic life in the first place. Yet the self-moved scholar, though still to be found throughout the system, is no longer the universal norm. For the rest of us, the call to face up to the challenges of academic management cannot be ignored.

I do not suggest that research management is in itself a threat to the core values of scholarship. The relationship is more complex, and outcomes in flux. As Henkel (2000) summarizes it:

> The RAE had sustained important aspects of professional self-regulation in UK higher education. It had also reinforced the basic structure of the university system and the values of academic authority and excellence supporting it. At the same time, it was evidence of the advance of managerialism: towards the concentration of resources in pursuit of efficiency and effectiveness, towards evaluation against output, towards transparent measures of performance and towards clearer demarcation of the functions of research and teaching... Professional obligations had been more clearly defined and the allocation of rewards made more public. The RAE was a trigger for the creation of new institutional structures and changed institutional cultures. The balance of influence between the individual, the discipline, the department and the institution had become disturbed.

> *(Henkel, 2000: 143)*

So the balance is altered, not entirely as intended, by the RAE, which has proved to be a 'change driver' of unexpected power.

In essence, relationships are reconfigured in favour of the collective: the department and the larger institution of which it is a part; and the external discipline (or rather spokesmen for it) as the arbiters of quality. Put another way, the fates of individual academics are yoked together as never before by this process of assessment and reward. Members of a department indeed find themselves sinking or swimming together. For the first time, an individual's career prospects (or even the possibility of continuing employment) may be shaped not just by his or her own efforts, but by those of colleagues also. A collective fate calls for collective norms, for a sharing of aspirations and values, if the worst is to be avoided or the best realized. It calls for a common research culture. But can a culture of research actually be brought into being? Or is it necessarily a form of spontaneous order with a dynamic of its own?

'When I hear the word culture', Hermann Goering is widely misreported as saying, 'I reach for my Browning' (actually 'Brauning' – a clever pun on the name of a German playwright). Few concepts in the social sciences have been subjected to systematic abuse to quite the same extent as this one, and people who use it casually have taken a raincheck on critical thought. How did this situation come about? It is a common – but misplaced – belief that the way to enhance performance is to transform the organization's culture. This emphasis on cultural change and the management of corporate cultures derived originally from studies of organizational change and resistance. It was a short step from here to the notion that the prevailing realities of a situation in the workplace could be regarded as a 'culture' to be 'managed', and a new orthodoxy was born (Handy, 1978; Peters and Waterman, 1982). Problems arise, however, when leaders are enjoined to 'manage the culture' (Young, 1997). For much of what is said about organizational culture actually refers not to culture at all but to something quite different: organizational climate or, in ordinary language, the way it feels at the workplace (Taguiri, 1968; Barker, 1994).

One sadly familiar result of misjudged attempts to manage the culture are fall-offs in morale, disaffection, evasion; that is, a general deterioration in the climate of the organization. The run-up to the 2001 RAE, perhaps a make or break assessment for many, produced no shortage of examples of strain, truculence and disaffection in many departments throughout the country. Individuals felt themselves to be pressed to publish for assessment, when their instinct was to publish only to share their ideas and findings with others. 'Creating a strategic culture of research', then, is a business fraught with risk. To understand the nature of the challenge, it is first necessary to delineate more clearly the nature of academic management (or leadership, as I prefer) at the primary unit of organization: the department.

MANAGING DIVERSITY AT THE DEPARTMENTAL LEVEL

While it is likely to have been the research impulse that brought young postgraduates into academic life, the everyday reality of their lives in a department becomes inescapably teaching-led. Research may have to be *undertaken* (although the strength of that expectation will vary), but teaching has to be *delivered*. The departmental meeting that discusses research across the board is probably a rarity; the departmental meeting that does not discuss to exhaustion its teaching programme and timetable probably does not exist. It did not need the scrutiny of the QAA, and the corresponding rise of quality assurance units within the universities to achieve this pre-eminent status for teaching. They simply increased the intensity – and frequency – of these discussions. The expectation that individual teachers would pull their weight in terms of load, attend diligently to their pastoral responsibilities, and keep their own courses and reading list under continuous review, is longstanding.

Even where courses are not team-taught – something more common in the new universities than the old – teaching is seen as a collective endeavour. It subsists within the implicit contract between the student as customer and the department, as the responsible part of the providing institution. Its rewards are rarely individualized, despite the application of some ingenuity in attempting to make them so. The result is a tendency for staff to coalesce into some semblance of a team.

Research, by way of contrast, is seen as an essentially competitive individual endeavour. Rewards are highly individualized, and research acclaim provides the most certain route to promotion, especially in the 'scholarship track' of reader/professor. There is – inescapably – an invidious quality to research success, and the applause bestowed upon the successful colleague is rarely entirely free from ambivalence. Similarly, the allocation of research leave, that precious resource that reflects actual rather than promised achievement, becomes sensitive – even bitter – the more discretion is vested in heads of department to grant it. Success is rewarded, and so positions the beneficiary for further success. The result is a differentiation of staff. An older generation of middle-ranking academics, often with enviable records of achievement in teaching and a respectable sufficiency of publications to their name, often feel threatened by these unwelcome developments. These colleagues are as indispensable a part of the university as the hard-nosed grant-getting instrumental research academic intent on publishing his or her way to the top. Each has their place, and a research strategy has to be inclusive if it is to get the best out of both.

These are the two very different dynamics that operate upon the competing pressures to teach and undertake research. They are tendencies, no more, but the tension between them poses a challenge to academic management at the departmental level. The art of management is acting through the agency of others, and for managers to become effective leaders they have to shape the actions of others to meet organizational goals by setting direction, by defining values, by raising motivation to realize those values, and by inspiring belief in their ability to deliver. So much is commonplace. Given the tensions between the competing pressures of teaching and research and the way in which they manifest themselves differently among the individuals who make up a department, a declarative style of leadership will not suffice. Instead, it is useful to conceive of the challenge as one of balancing the needs of *task*, *group* and *individual* (Adair, 1996).

A head of department is obliged to maximize these three divergent values simultaneously. The task is in this case to build an effective research organization. The group value resides in the unity and *esprit de corps* of the department itself. The individual value requires respect and support to be given to the very different qualities of each member of staff, so that each in turn can give his or her best and achieve a degree of fulfilment. Every head of department will know that these three drive in opposing directions. Clumsily pursued, the goal of grade enhancement at the RAE (to define task narrowly) can shatter the group spirit of the department and drive individuals into misery; the climate changes for the worse. An obsessive concern with the integrity of the group on the other hand may sacrifice actual performance, as well as being experienced by the individual as a crushing, stifling pressure to conform. Too loving a concern for the individual may similarly sacrifice performance and create an atomized department of self-seeking individuals who enjoy a benevolent climate, but who do not belong to a common culture and who are unlikely to achieve the task. As Figure 3.9.1 shows, each value pulls against the other two, yet no one of the three can be allowed to dominate the others.

Those are the inescapable realities, and the effective head of department learns to read, as well as lead, the department, sensing where the imbalances arise, and throwing his or her weight in favour of task, group or individual as the moment requires. It is a process of dynamic balancing. Not only does the situation refuse to remain static, it is inherently unstable, and an intervention in favour of one value will sooner or later need to be balanced by an intervention in favour of another. Seen in this way, academic leadership is an abstruse art and its practice a rare skill. Training and development for heads of department tends to neglect this kind of dynamic analysis in favour of procedural competences that, at the end of the day, do little to support heads in developing the ability to read, as well as lead, departments.

So far I have portrayed departmental leadership as something akin to keeping an unstable vessel upright and afloat when the crew's concerns lie elsewhere. But the task amounts to something more than keeping an even keel. It must be about setting, maintaining and pursuing direction, and that is where the management of a department (or, indeed, a research institute) requires a competence in strategy.

This is the right moment to return to the question of 'managing the culture',

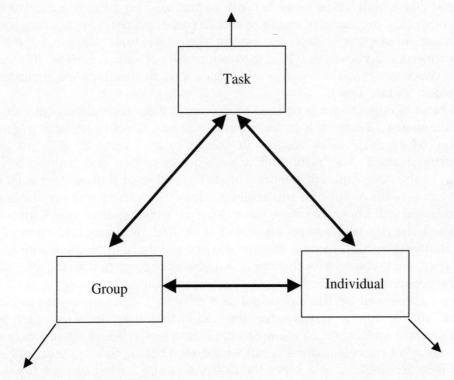

Source: adapted from Adair (1996)

Figure 3.9.1   Leadership as dynamic balancing

which I earlier set aside as a misleading and inadequate conception. Strategy must work upon the dimension of values, but not only upon that dimension. To take so narrow an approach would be to neglect the issues of process and power that also shape the way people act in their organizational settings. Equally, those who view the question of setting direction and leading a department towards it as simply a matter of instruction – or incentive, or constraint – make the corresponding mistake of ignoring the question of shared values. And both overlook the ways in which processes and values interact to support or subvert one another.

The model of managed change that I favour is one which I have used both as an analytic tool (in research) and as a diagnostic tool (in management). It focuses on the interaction of these two dimensions of values and power. Consider first the department in its institutional setting. The processes, formal and informal, that prevail may make for 'tight' or 'loose' organization. Where tight, procedures will be highly prescriptive, and an array of sanctions and incentives may exist to control and shape the behaviour of the individual academic. The powers of heads of department and deans may be extensive, as in the post-1992 universities, where a tradition of professionalized management has long existed.

Where it is loose – and this is recognizably the case in the old university sector – senior positions may be partly or wholly elected, seen as representative as much as executive, as in the case of many deans. Pro-vice-chancellors may be essentially amateurs, taking some time out of their departments, but typically continuing to teach and publish, practitioner-managers rather than professionals. Results have usually been achieved through custom and practice, or through regulations and ordinances that do more to guarantee the position of the individual academic than to provide for managerial direction. Procedures are often permissive either by design or by the realities of blind eye management. Sanctions may be almost unknown, and incentives hard to discern. These are two extreme states in what might be termed the organizational context of decision.

'Tight' and 'loose' in this sense are matters of degree, not binary values. The same is true of the quite separate dimensions of values and beliefs, that complex of subjective and inter-subjective factors for which we really have no satisfactory terminology, but which I like to term the appreciative context of decision in homage to the late Sir Geoffrey Vickers. Vickers' concern was with how we appreciate the situations in which we find ourselves: view them, construe them, respond to them, evaluate them (Vickers, 1968, 1983). These appreciations may be commonly held and consensual, or differ widely, as is generally the case given the whole gamut of actors in a university, ranging from vice-chancellor to post-doctoral researcher. So, again, a continuum, ranging from a concordance of the single-minded and compliant, to a Tower of Babel of the obstreperous, challenging and simply disengaged.

When an object has to be achieved – take, for example, the policy aim of raising a department's standing in research – the prospects of achievement depend on how the particular situation in that place and time is configured in terms of these two dimensions of power and values – or, if preferred, process and culture. And they interact in interesting ways. The attempt to employ direction in a situation where there are few real levers to pull and where views diverge markedly is scarcely likely to ripple the surface. It can be ignored, and the outcome will be a continuing variability in the way in which people conduct themselves and deploy their efforts. Where there is organizational muscle to be flexed, and leverage over individuals can be exerted, through (say) setting individual targets for publications, research grants, consultancy or the attraction of research students and backing them by sanctions and incentives, the outcome will depend crucially on the 'cultural' factors. Exerting power to this extent in situations of divergent values is likely to result in evasion, demotivation, even resistance. Only where such power is

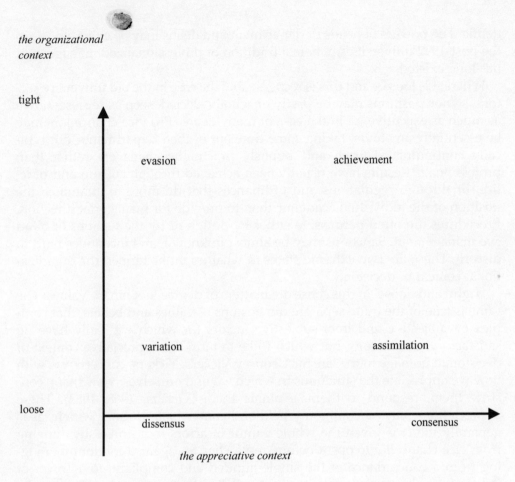

Figure 3.9.2 Context and outcomes

exerted in situations where there is a common and supportive appreciation of the issue is it likely to have any effect. But it is the combination of process and culture that produces results that neither alone can do. Hence the position, argued above, that exhortations to 'manage the culture' are as likely to be recipes for failure as the application of directive techniques. Both fail due to their one-dimensionality.

Figure 3.9.2 shows how these relationships might be conceptualized and mapped. The three outcomes discussed – of variability, evasion and actual achievement – are shown, as is the fourth possibility that a culture of valuing research pre-exists, and is of such strength that the desired outcome of enhanced performance is achieved without the exertion of power – indeed, can be achieved spontaneously through a process of assimilation. Again, the need for skill in reading organizations will be apparent, for the degree and means of intervention (perhaps requiring enhanced powers to be given) indicated are matters for accurate diagnostic judgement. It will also be obvious, given the very limited powers available to heads of department, that achieving change at that level requires the support of the institution in respect of both process and values. Strategy is a process, not a product.

THINKING STRATEGICALLY AT THE INSTITUTIONAL LEVEL

In comparison with the subtlety of the task of leading a department, setting strategic direction at the institutional level seems relatively straightforward. That is because it is primarily a policy role, requiring insight and judgement certainly, but placing less of a premium on sensitivity and skill in the reading of situations and the management of people within them. In those respects, the role of the head of department is, managerially speaking, the most challenging in the university system.

That said, leading a university in its research mission requires considerable analytical investment. Achieving change in the dual context of organizational and appreciative factors outlined above requires the ability to understand – conceptually – the nature of the problem, to assess the extent to which the norms and values across the institution favour change, and to identify the ways in which organizational processes can be employed to support it. A lot of listening is required, as well as the development of new procedures and requirements that 'tighten' the organizational context of research strategy. Fortunately, working in favour of those leading research at this level is the tendency of the organizational and appreciative contexts of intervention to work together in a benign fashion. New processes and procedures need not just stand alone, but can be used as vehicles to carry the message about where the institution should be, and so become to some extent self-justifying. The declaration of goals, the assignment of targets, and the prescription of the means by which they are to be delivered and monitored can be used to persuasive effect. Control for its own sake, either as an intention or as a perception of that intention is, on the other hand, more likely to have malign effects, undermine support, and induce a climate of resentment.

All of these comments refer of course to the means of achieving a given end, and assume that those who lead research strategy at the institutional level can define a feasible goal. Typically, this is done in terms of a global target, for example bringing all departments up to at least grade 4 in an old university, or achieving a given proportion of staff selected for submission as research active in a new institution. The problem with broad targets of particularly the first type is that they have generally not been subjected to any kind of feasibility analysis. The fact is that universities are highly stratified in terms of their research capabilities. Members of the Russell group are distinguished by high rankings across the board and by substantial flows of research grant and contract funding. Other old universities tend to have areas of strength and areas of weakness. New universities tend to have the occasional area of strength, and a narrower base of research activity.

This distribution of rankings tells us very little, however. The most important strategic goal is to build up staff numbers in areas of comparative advantage, and minimize them in areas of comparative weakness. Take the example of two similar institutions in the pre-1992 sector. The range of disciplines is comparable, though not identical, as is the broad distribution of rankings within those units of assessment (UoA). The first, however, has won high grades for its larger departments, while the lower-ranked departments tend to be small. In the second, the highest-ranked departments are mostly small, while staff numbers are concentrated in departments with only moderate research rankings. In terms of grade profile, the two are comparable. In terms of actual research strength, the first is more firmly located.

It is also necessary to consider the distribution of grades within any relevant UoA nationally in order to determine comparative advantage. In 1996, a high ranking in (say) English distinguished the university from others in the field, as the distribution of gradings was heavily skewed towards the lower end of the range. In other fields, a high grade may be both vulnerable to small shifts in comparative rankings and a generator of relatively modest sums of money if the grade distribution in that UoA is skewed towards the higher end of the scale. It may also be prudent to take into account corrections to any marked skew that a future panel might wish to make. Some departments in some universities will benefit from a reordering of grades next time round without any improvement in their performance. Others will find that the 'research unit of resource' for their subject has been dramatically diminished due to that same redistribution.

In management terms, the room for manoeuvre is actually quite small. Even where a strategic decision is taken to build up to critical mass by creating additional posts in a particular discipline, it will prove difficult to recruit to those posts unless there is a conviction abroad that the goal of grade enhancement can be realized. At the other end of the scale, and in old universities in particular, the mechanisms scarcely exist to adapt to the market by downsizing in a particular discipline. The institution's fate is settled more by external contingencies than the rhetoric of academic management suggests. It is all the more important, then, to proceed via careful appraisal and analysis of the sort suggested above.

One area of exception relates to the research postgraduate component of a university's operation. Although the choice of areas to develop is bound to be shaped by considerations of comparative advantage, it lies wholly within a university's competence to build up its graduate school. Not, of course, by relying on success in the intense competitions for research council or AHRB studentships, but by investing heavily – some £30,000 each, with fees foregone – in the creation of research student bursaries. Even a department of moderate reputation can expect to recruit successfully if there is money on offer.

Getting the students in place is one thing. Supporting and encouraging their performance is quite another. The organizational and appreciative contexts of doctoral research may or may not support research achievement, defined in terms of timely completion of important theses. Procedures for close and careful monitoring of progress may be in place or may be virtually absent. Processes for ensuring that sound judgements are made about potential at both initial admission and the crucial upgrading stage may be well developed, or non-existent. Weak procedures and inadequate compliance risk poor completion rates. Expectation of what constitutes a standard for doctoral studies varies between disciplines, but needs to be clearly defined. All of these are areas in which practice has moved ahead considerably since the first moves to tighten up in the 1980s, and Taylor's chapter (7) in this volume deals with good practice in today's world.

One particular type of initiative in postgraduate education merits further comment: the establishment of graduate schools. An overriding reason for setting up a graduate school is often the need to achieve a higher profile in the marketplace. Setting that aside, it is clear that providing some common services to research postgraduates and creating space within which their own collegiality can develop have real value in terms of research strategy. The limits, though, are set by the need to pitch provision to meet the commonalities of interest. The need for a place to work with access to a computer and the Internet is universal. Take-up of training on such generic topics as, for example, intellectual property could be near-universal. Interest in a particular form of technical training is likely to be discipline-specific. Further along the continuum are needs that are specific to the candidate and his or her topic, and have to be met on an individual basis. Unless the graduate school is also a significant budget centre, capable of commissioning provision, its impact is likely to be limited to the generic level. And at that level, the potential for developing research critical mass and collegiality is not great. Graduate schools, then, need to be serious operations if they are to feature in the research strategy.

OVERVIEW

The cliché that 'not changing is not an option' contains an important truth, for the RAE in particular has proved a relentless change driver. As managerialism gains a foothold in the universities, the danger arises of utilitarian and mechanistic approaches being applied to the pursuit of change. They are doomed to fail. 'Human systems are different', wrote Sir Geoffrey Vickers (1983), in what might be a fitting epitaph for this paper. Nevertheless, accepting the need for a more humanistic approach to change is not without its own risks, in particular that of adopting uncritically the vacuous slogans of cultural management.

A strategic approach to the promotion of research is possible, but it has to be based on a sensible appreciation of the academic marketplace, on a realistic estimation of feasible futures, and on a sensitive balancing of the unstable tensions that characterize an academic community. Above all, it must be based on an understanding of how process and values, power and culture interact to produce outcomes that, if skilfully handled, amount to real enhancements not just of research standing, but of levels of mutual and self-respect among colleagues. There is, of course, no formula for success. Developing the culture and processes that sustain a research-led university or department is an intellectual, and not a 'mere' managerial challenge. Those who can address it with insight and concern have little to dread in the coming research assessment exercise.

REFERENCES

Adair, J (1996) *Effective Leadership*, Pan, London

Barker, RA (1994) Relative utility of culture and climate analysis to an organizational change agent: an analysis of General Dynamics Electronics Division, *International Journal of Organisational Analysis*, **2**(1), January, pp 68–87

Handy, C (1978) *Gods of Management*, Pan, London

Henkel, M (2000) *Academic Identities and Policy Change in Higher Education*, Jessica Kingsley, London

Peters, TJ and Waterman, RH (1982) *In Search of Excellence*, Harper and Row, New York

Power, M (1994) *The Audit Explosion*, Demos, London

Taguiri, R (1968) The concept of organisational climate, in *Organisational Climate: Explorations of a Concept*, ed R Taguiri and OH Litwin, Harvard University Press, Boston

Vickers, G (1968) *Value Systems and Social Process*, Tavistock, London

Vickers, G (1983) *Human Systems are Different*, Harper and Row, London

Young, K (1997) Beyond policy and politics: contingencies of employment equity', *Policy and Politics*, **25**(4), pp 361–74

Young, K, Fogarty, M and MacRae, S (1986) *The Management of Doctoral Studies in the Social Sciences*, Policy Studies Institute, London

Part 4
At the Digital
Chalk-Face

Introduction

The Editors with Keith Trigwell

Part 4 focuses on teaching and learning. The title reflects the perception of the editors that teaching is the 'sharp end' of university life and that electronic intervention in the learning and teaching process is probably the single most important contemporary development in teaching. Electronic intervention is transforming learning and teaching, in both conduct and conceptualization.

Teaching takes place within a much wider context than the confines of classroom or laboratory. Teaching requires discipline-specific knowledge. Organization of teaching also requires understanding of policy and context. Other parts of this book allude to these broader contexts, for example national and institutional policy on widening participation, learning and teaching strategies, training for teaching, and the subject centres of the learning and teaching network (see Chapter 2). This part, however, focuses on four aspects of the learning and teaching process, taking an approach likely to be useful to those with responsibilities beyond delivery of their own teaching. It does not attempt to 'cover the ground' of how students learn, teaching methods, modes of assessment and so on. (For this see, for example, *A Handbook for Teaching and Learning in Higher Education,* Fry, Ketteridge and Marshall, 1999.)

The first chapter of the part, by Heather Fry and Stephanie Marshall, sets out some of the major influences on curricula and how they can be addressed in curriculum development. George Gordon then draws out the lessons for teaching from national teaching quality assessment activities. Alan Hurst, in Chapter 12, emphasizes the importance of considering the needs of *all* students, and building these into course design and institutional arrangements. Finally, Su White and Hugh Davis take up the theme of incorporating communications and information technology into learning and teaching.

Keith Trigwell, Principal Research Fellow at the Institute for the Advancement of University Teaching, University of Oxford, describes his development and use of a 'lens' (the student focus) through which to view, inform and transform teaching. He suggests that readers may find this lens helpful in considering the digital chalk-face.

> ## Student-Focused Learning – A Personal Perspective
> ## by Keith Trigwell

From a research project on learning, I learnt what I now consider to be the most important thing I know about teaching. Over a four-year period in the 1990s, together with five colleagues, I planned and conducted a large-scale study of university learning environments. In one area of the study, the outcomes were not what we had expected.

The research project was designed using an adaptation of the Biggs (1993) systems version of the 3P (presage–process–product) model of student learning (Figure 4.0.1).

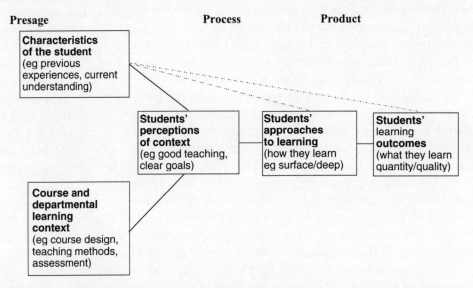

Fig 4.0.1   An adaptation of Biggs' (1993) model of student learning

One of the hypotheses of the project was that in qualitatively different learning environments (bottom left box) students with similar backgrounds (top left box) would have qualitatively different learning outcomes (right box). For example, we thought that in what was being called a student-centred environment, such as a well-implemented problem-based learning programme, students were likely to experience better quality learning than in one that had less student-centredness, all else being (roughly) equal.

At the time it seemed to be a reasonable hypothesis. If it was not reasonable, it would seem to cast considerable doubt on the idea of improving learning through changes to the learning context. Given that teaching was thought to be a part of that context, a vast amount of educational and teacher development practice would be rendered meaningless if such an hypothesis was not reasonable. What would be the point of teachers adopting a student-centred approach to teaching if it made no difference to student learning?

With two academic colleagues I spent nearly a year planning the study which, following peer review, was supported by the Australian Research Council. We, and our reviewers, were satisfied that the project was viable. Once the funding was agreed, we recruited three research assistants and began the process of collecting data.

My two senior research colleagues had previously taught university biology and physics courses and it was in the first year of study of those two disciplines that we sought our contexts for comparison. We collected data on four different departments of physics and five of biology. We interviewed the academic staff involved in teaching the first year in those departments, collected literature on their programmes, analysed their course documentation in detail and scrutinized their assessment practices. We found that within a discipline, all the programmes had similar aims, but we also found what we described as qualitative variation in the student-centredness of the environments established to achieve those aims. We selected for study the two biology contexts that differed most from each other, and the two physics contexts that differed most.

There was no doubt in our minds, in the minds of the research assistants and of the staff teaching the four courses, that there were qualitative differences between them. For example, we found that in Biology Context A the teaching appeared to be oriented towards the students' needs in such a way that they might see it as being directed at them personally. In Context B there were mechanisms separate from the teaching to support student needs, but the range of planned teaching ideas did not appear to form a coherent package, and could have given mixed messages. In assessment, Context A contained a range of assessment types including some emphasizing qualitative responses, whereas in Context B all assessment was in the form of multiple-choice questions.

If we had conducted an external review of the four programmes based on the course information we had collected, we would rate one biology course and one physics course in a qualitatively different category to the other two. We would (and did) describe one course in each pair as student-centred and the other as significantly (and qualitatively) less so. We would suggest that, thus, Context A was more likely to encourage desired learning approaches and outcomes than Context B.

You may by now see where this story is heading. When we collected and analysed the students' perceptions of their learning context, we found that students in Context A *did not perceive their environment to be significantly different* to that described by students in Context B.

There is now a considerable literature describing the relations between students' perceptions of their learning environment (including the teaching they receive) and the quality of their learning outcome. Indeed the project described here has contributed to that literature (Prosser and Trigwell, 1999). It shows that where students perceive their environment to be supportive of learning approaches aimed at developing understanding, they are more likely to develop a greater understanding.

So the *result* from our study suggested that Context A was unlikely to lead to learning that was any better than that in Context B, despite its appearing to be more student-centred. The indicators of learning outcomes confirmed that this was the case. Student-centred teaching may be good, but as an offering to students it may not be good enough.

The lesson I learnt from the study is that what we as teachers set up for students to learn (no matter how closely aligned it might be to existing best practice) may not be perceived in a similar way by students. If it is not perceived in a similar way, much of our effort may be in vain.

Following this study we coined the term student-*focused* teaching to indicate that we thought teaching had to go beyond the student-centred teaching idea (of consideration for and of the student). Teaching was more likely to support learning if it captured how students perceived their context. Student-*focused* teaching is student-centred, but it is more than that. It also builds on how students perceive that which has been designed to help them learn, in a way that aligns teachers' aims and students' perceptions.

Let me illustrate, with an example from lecturing, a difference between teacher-centred teaching, student-centred teaching and student-focused teaching.

Teacher-focused teacher: I prepare a coherent development of the content of the lecture and deliver it in a clear and concise way.
Student-centred teacher: I prepare the lecture content with material that I believe will be coherent and relevant to students and, in delivery, help them to engage with it.
Student-focused teacher: I prepare the content with an awareness of what is relevant to students, check how they engage with it and how their response might relate to the quality of their learning.

In all three cases it is possible that students will not perceive the content as being clearly delivered or coherent or relevant. Only in the case of student-focused teaching will the teacher be fully aware of this.

So is student-focused teaching just the use of evaluation with student-centred teaching? (This matter is not unrelated to issues raised by Chapter 11 in this part.) The answer is 'maybe', depending on the nature of the evaluation, but there are very few evaluative studies conducted that aim at gathering information (a) about students' perceptions of the purpose of what is taught, and (b) the type of learning resulting from (a). Most evaluations do not go beyond a focus on strategy (areas covered, quality of planning, how questions were handled and so on) and on students' degree of satisfaction or happiness.

What I have described here is a personal lesson, and I may be later than many in coming to these conclusions. But if this story also has significance for you, you may want to use this idea in looking at the subsequent chapters on aspects of teaching and learning that follow. When doing so, ask: 'In preparing to develop my teaching by harnessing IT, by preparing a more inclusive learning environment, or in devising an innovative curriculum, what do I know about how students perceive the purpose of the changed context, and how can I find out about those perceptions?'

REFERENCES

Biggs, JB (1993) From theory to practice: a cognitive systems approach, *Higher Education Research and Development*, **12**, pp 73–85

Fry, H, Ketteridge, S and Marshall, S (1999) *A Handbook for Teaching and Learning in Higher Education: Enhancing academic practice*, Kogan Page, London

Prosser, M and Trigwell, K (1999) *Understanding Learning and Teaching: The experience in higher education*, SRHE/Open University Press, Buckingham

10 Revitalizing and Renewing the Curriculum

Heather Fry and Stephanie Marshall

INTRODUCTION

The term 'curriculum' is used here to include content, outcomes, teaching methods, learning processes and assessment. Much excellent and recent literature provides a guide to course design in higher education (eg Toohey, 1999) and to the practicalities of specifying outcomes (D'Andrea, 1999); these aspects are not repeated here.

This chapter presents an overview of the major contemporary influences on curricula in British higher education. It then discusses in more detail seven themes important in contemporary pedagogy. The themes are illustrated by case studies of exemplary practice which show how some academics have addressed the themes and incorporated them into curriculum design. A number of ways in which those with responsibility for curriculum design and curriculum management may accommodate, exploit and ameliorate the themes, so as to revitalize and renew curricula, are suggested.

> ### Enhancing Practice
>
> Taking the whole of the period since you started to teach in higher education, or since you were first a student at a university:
>
> - Pick out three changes that come to mind on the types of things curricula include or how they are organized and constructed.
> - Similarly, pick out three changes in the way in which teaching is now conducted.

- Which three changes in the way in which students are now encouraged to learn, or in how their learning is supported, do you consider most important?

Responses to the above questions will typically include things such as modularization, external requirements of various types (such as programme specifications), 'learning to learn', subject review, the 'outcomes movement', information technology, larger class sizes and the taking of deep approaches to learning. Twenty years, perhaps even a decade ago, responses would have been very different. Despite the somewhat fitful shifts of policy and their impact on curricula, the most fundamental change of recent years has been, arguably, a shift of emphasis from teaching to learning. Gibbs (2000) provides a masterful overview of such changes and their relationship with improving student learning through a more strategic approach. How can this fast-changing scene be 'captured', understood, and responded to?

A CONCEPT MAP OF CONTEMPORARY BRITISH HIGHER EDUCATION CURRICULA

Many models of teaching and learning and their context in higher education and the education of adults have been proposed, including Marton and Saljo (1976), Dahloff (1991), Ramsden (1992), Biggs (1993), Entwistle (1994) and Jarvis (1995), to name a few. Prosser and Trigwell have recently added to this list (1999). Toohey (1999: 21–29) offers models of the design process. Squires' (1990) wide-ranging consideration of curricula draws attention, among other things, to the idea that curricula are the product of knowledge, culture and the needs of the individual.

Figure 4.10.1 (page 184) is akin to a concept map of curriculum formation in higher education. The inner circle denotes the importance of the shift in emphasis from teaching to learning. The large band of square boxes shows the main areas having influence or input into the shape of curricula. Individual factors are assigned to one of the seven areas, according to 'best choice', rather than being listed several times. The two-way arrows denote that virtually every area, and the individual factors within it, influences other areas and factors, and that the nature of the relationship is imprecise. The curriculum is represented as the outer, encompassing band. Chapter 2 makes considerable reference to factors in the three areas in the upper half of Figure 4.10.1 (external, internal and cross-level). This half of the figure could be considered to be that exerting most pressure within the diagram.

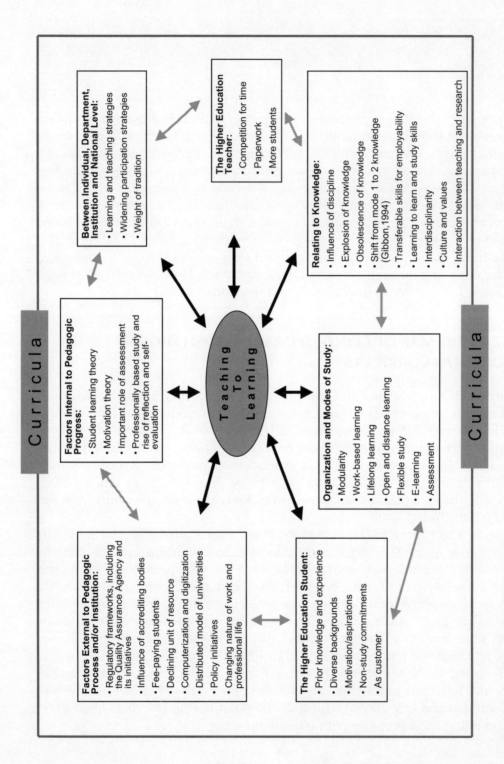

Figure 4.10.1 Contributory factors to the shape and form of higher education curricula

Curricula

Curricula

Between Individual, Department, Institution and National Level:
- Learning and teaching strategies
- Widening participation strategies
- Weight of tradition

The Higher Education Teacher:
- Competition for time
- Paperwork
- More students

Relating to Knowledge:
- Influence of discipline
- Explosion of knowledge
- Obsolescence of knowledge
- Shift from mode 1 to 2 knowledge (Gibbon, 1994)
- Transferable skills for employability
- Learning to learn and study skills
- Interdisciplinarity
- Culture and values
- Interaction between teaching and research

Factors Internal to Pedagogic Progress:
- Student learning theory
- Motivation theory
- Important role of assessment
- Professionally based study and rise of reflection and self-evaluation

Teaching To Learning

Organization and Modes of Study:
- Modularity
- Work-based learning
- Lifelong learning
- Open and distance learning
- Flexible study
- E-learning
- Assessment

Factors External to Pedagogic Process and/or Institution:
- Regulatory frameworks, including the Quality Assurance Agency and its initiatives
- Influence of accrediting bodies
- Fee-paying students
- Declining unit of resource
- Computerization and digitization
- Distributed model of universities
- Policy initiatives
- Changing nature of work and professional life

The Higher Education Student:
- Prior knowledge and experience
- Diverse backgrounds
- Motivation/aspirations
- Non-study commitments
- As customer

Frequently curriculum *design* is not undertaken in full or with acknowledged consideration of this broad context, and the rationale is often not made explicit; moreover there is usually a lengthy time lag before changes are reflected in the curriculum (Fry *et al* 1997). We suggest curricula need to be constructed with greater awareness of circumstances, needs, ideals and purposes if they are to attract and retain students and staff, and be fit for their intended purpose.

STRATEGIES TO ADDRESS CONTEMPORARY CURRICULUM DEVELOPMENT

Seven themes of importance in designing contemporary curricula have been selected with the intention of setting out strategies designed to cope with/promote them. Some themes appear in Figure 4.10.1, either as wholes or parts of factors. The themes are:

- understanding the starting point of students;
- overloaded curricula;
- moving students to higher-order conceptual levels;
- teaching diverse students;
- enhancing flexibility;
- achieving individual attention for learners in a mass system;
- employability.

Understanding the starting point of students

Views of the development of learning that incorporate the construction of schemata which are amended and added to, highlight the importance of understanding the starting point of students. This is recognized as crucial to enable students to adopt and adapt new learning into their existing repertoire of knowledge, skills and understanding. Kolb's (1984) learning cycle is based on the idea that learning is an incremental, adaptive experience. New learning requires moving on, to assimilate ideas new to the learner, apply these ideas, and then reconceptualize the way in which the world is viewed. Rogers (1983), coming from a psychotherapist perspective and based on his work with adults, stresses the importance of moving away from instruction and teacher-led education to facilitation and student-centred learning. This builds on the shared understanding of the learner's world, the facilitator having taken time to empathize with the starting point of the learner. (Use of these perspectives in understanding learning does not have to indicate a constructivist view of knowledge.)

Students come into higher education with an understanding (perhaps inadequate or flawed) of knowledge, skills and attitudes that higher education seeks to activate, improve, add to and amend. They are also likely to arrive with preconceived notions, experiences and preferences for the way they approach their learning and for particular styles of learning. (For an overview of these, see Fry, Ketteridge and Marshall (1999) and Brown, Fry and Marshall (1999).)

The crucial question is how the starting point of students can be ascertained, acknowledged and built upon. A possible approach is, firstly, to consider some form of audit of pre-existing knowledge, moving on, secondly, to use of learning style inventories. The notion of mind mapping has gained great popularity over recent years, particularly in its encouragement of lateral as opposed to linear thinking, and as a useful tool in generating 'thinking outside the box' (see, for example, Buzan (1998)). Through its use of hubs and nodes, this technique is a means of assessing students' thought processes through examination of the connectivity and interrelatedness of different factors deemed to be important enough to commit to paper. Further to individual mind mapping, a group work exercise, asking students to compare approaches and understanding, can help students reach a common level of knowledge and understanding. Thus the teacher is assisted in gaining an appreciation of the collective starting point of the group.

Teachers need to be aware of the approaches to teaching that will assist their students to move forward in developmental terms. Given the likely variety of student experience and preference that will influence students' approaches and styles of learning, the use of a range of techniques (as long as they are not used in a confusing way) is helpful. Over-reliance on one or two methods implies a 'one size fits all approach'. The sections below on taking account of diversity and flexible learning, as well as the case studies, contain further concrete examples of techniques that might be used.

Taking Account of the Starting Point of Students in a Large Group of Learners with Varied Backgrounds and Experience by Maggie Nicol

The School of Nursing and Midwifery at City University, London has excellent clinical skills facilities. During initial nurse education, most practical nursing skills are introduced with a lead lecture to the whole cohort (approximately 200 students), followed by practical demonstrations and supervised practice in groups of 20–24 learners. Opportunities for practice under the supervision of a lecturer are thus fairly limited, and nursing students are expected to practice independently in the skills centre.

When practising practical skills it is crucial that students obtain feedback to avoid 'bad habits' becoming ingrained. In nursing, failure to eradicate such habits could ultimately lead to unsafe patient care. However, the provision of lecturer supervision during all practice is not an option.

We wished to move from this model of unsupervized practice *after* tutor contact, towards one that could help students develop knowledge, skills and attitudes *in preparation for* tutor contact. We considered that harnessing information technology might provide a solution, despite the potential problems of layers of simulation in skills training. Through use of a 'virtual tutor' students will learn the relevant theory and be able to perform the skill(s) with reasonable dexterity *before* contact with the tutor. Such an approach has a number of advantages:

- Students can study at their own pace, at a time and place convenient to them, and use their preferred learning style.
- Using quality, interactive materials, learning will be more active and hopefully more effective.
- Anecdotal evidence suggests that students who fail to grasp essential principles in large lecture halls often feel discouraged and demotivated. Working at their own pace or with a small group of friends should enhance understanding and motivation.
- Contact with the 'human tutor' *after* learning the underlying theory will enable students to seek clarification of aspects they do not understand.
- Performing a skill in front of the 'human tutor' *after* learning the rudiments will enable feedback and expert coaching. Doing this as a group activity will provide peer support and promote the sharing of tips for successful performance.
- Making the content of the programme more flexible will help meet the needs of mature students and should also reduce demand for classrooms.
- Students will be able to take more responsibility for their own learning. Those who have previous healthcare experience will not be required to attend classes to learn skills they already possess. They will be able to concentrate on the theory, but performing the skill in front of the 'human tutor' will ensure their techniques are sound.

The award of a £50,000 National Teaching Fellowship has enabled me to focus on two projects. The first is the production of an interactive CD ROM for developing the knowledge and skills required to use safely a range of intravenous infusion devices. The second is to develop distance learning materials (initially workbooks and videos, but later computer and Web-based) to enable students to develop knowledge, understanding and dexterity in a range of fundamental nursing skills prior to their first clinical placement. Piloting took place prior to full implementation in April 2002. Evaluation research is planned into the project, and will feed into ongoing and future development.

Overloaded curricula

One of the most common complaints of staff and students is that of overloaded curricula. It may be a phenomenon that is especially obvious in science and technical subjects where there has been a 'knowledge explosion', but the tendency of subject experts is to add, not cut (eg see GMC, 1993). Another contributor to overload is simple addition of things such as study skills and career planning. Anecdotal evidence also suggests that modularization and larger numbers of students reduce 'teaching and study time'. Overloaded curricula are likely to be relatively incompatible with deep approaches to learning. The pressure to 'cover the ground' influences teaching methods towards the didactic end of the scale, and summative assessment towards testing little more than factual recall.

Different disciplines and contexts require different approaches to reducing overload. Suggestions for reduction, to be used discriminatingly, include:

- Take approaches to teaching and assessment compatible with promoting deep approaches to learning; avoid mere reciting of facts that are in turn regurgitated. Focus rather on underlying concepts and theories, some examples, the overview.
- Next make sure learners know how to find out more about topics from sources other than the tutor, such as books and the Internet. Learning how to learn, and where from, is vital, even though it 'steals' curriculum time.
- Sequence learning optimally, so as to avoid repetition and long gaps between linked topics. If the latter is unavoidable (or desirable for other reasons), make sure students are warned of the prior reference points and alerted to the need (and provided opportunity) to revise them. (Check where they are starting from.) The more students have sought to 'make meaning' from their learning, the more previous material and ideas are likely to be at their fingertips.

- Adopt techniques to 'prune' curricula. There are many different ways of doing this, including constructing concept maps of key concepts and content, and then removing the periphery. The programme specifications of the Quality Assurance Agency (QAA) may help to map curriculum content and highlight unnecessary repetitions. Define a 'core', for example as in curricula constructed around problem-based learning (PBL) where key or typifying situations, contexts, applications, theories or themes constitute the spine of the course. Another approach is to retain the key building blocks of a discipline; another is to take what is likely to be important for understanding a discipline or profession in the future. Toohey (1999: 88) suggests further ways of delineating a core. A core enables 'options' to be created, provided resources allow, which means that for any individual student the overall content burden may be lessened.
- A further aspect of reducing content should be the realization that more learners now proceed to further study. Some specialized areas that might once have been part of undergraduate degrees may need to be studied at postgraduate level because they do not fall within the definitions of core or of being a building block.

A key aspect when addressing curriculum overload is to consider the balance between breadth and depth within the curriculum.

Moving students to higher-order conceptual levels

Attempts have been made in each major domain of learning to construct a 'hierarchy of achievement'. The best known is that for the cognitive domain (see Bloom, 1956), which places acquisition of knowledge at the base of the hierachy, succeeded by comprehension, application, analysis, synthesis and finally evaluation. Learning outcomes for higher education spell out the intended achievement of learners. Designing teaching, learning and assessment to encourage achievement of the lower levels of the each hierarchy is easier than for higher levels. Table 4.10.1 (page 190) makes suggestions for promoting higher-order learning, although not all suggestions apply to every subject or discipline.

Most higher-order achievements involve interaction with and/or reflection between learner and material (whether concepts, people or skills), rather than copying or regurgitation. Higher-order achievement in the affective and psychomotor domains is the hardest to teach for and to assess. Curricula that feature few of the techniques mentioned in Table 4.10.1 and yet seek degree-level outcomes are likely to struggle in assisting attainment by all but the most able learners.

Table 4.10.1 Promoting higher order learning

Techniques/methods	Cognitive	Psychomotor	Affective	Interpersonal
Discursive writing (eg essays)	✓		✓	✓
Actual and vicarious experience/ practice (work-based, role-play, laboratory, field work, learning sets)	✓	✓?	✓	✓
Exploratory, discursive talking (tutorial, seminar, PBL discussion group, role-play, learning sets)	✓		✓?	✓
Reading	✓		✓?	
Intensive immersion (eg language courses, placements)	✓	✓	✓	✓
Spiral curriculum ('revisiting topics' at higher levels of complexity)	✓	✓	✓	✓
Interaction with tutor	✓		✓	✓
Formative assessment focusing on upper ends of the hierarchies and emphasizing feedback	✓	✓	✓	✓
Summative assessment focusing on upper ends of the hierarchies (eg essays, extended matching questions, observation of practice)	✓	✓	✓	✓
Projects	✓	✓	✓	✓

Teaching diverse students

Student diversity is of many different types. It may relate to cultural or national differences, to differences stemming from preparation by previous education, age differences, the needs of part-time students, place of study, disability (see Chapter 12) or the individuality of learners. Each element raises different aspects and may need different solutions. Many solutions relate to providing and encouraging more flexible contexts and structures (see below). For example, modular degrees are far more flexible and allow for interrupted or spread-out study in ways not possible in more traditional courses. Having available supplementary materials designed to take the most able or interested beyond where many may wish to go, can work well. Similarly, for those who need to refresh or acquire new basic skills or foundation knowledge, the use of Web-based self-study material, books, additional lectures, buddy schemes and so on may be useful. (See the nursing and peer learning case studies.) For example, building in a longer time for dyslexic students to take written examinations, allowing the help of assistants, or enabling the use of computers, are helpful. In some instances learners with different needs may need to be supported differently; in others the very diversity of needs and experience means that much can be learnt within the whole group, if it is not too large. All these factors will impact on curriculum design.

> ## Recognizing Diversity and Coping with Large Numbers of Students During Fieldwork by Mick Healey and Alan Jenkins

Fieldwork is a structured experience that takes place outside the classroom, where the object of study is also the place of study. It is particularly important for students taking field-based disciplines, such as geography, geology, anthropology, ecology, marine biology and archaeology. Taking large groups of students into the field is a challenge.

A large class is potentially not a group but a crowd. Sociologists tell us that crowds have no fixed members and feel little responsibility for each other. A crowd on a field course is likely to learn little, and potentially can do much harm to itself and others. In seeking to maximize potential student learning we need to turn a potential crowd into responsible learners (see Jenkins, 1997). Ways to achieve this include:

- *Break the crowd into groups and individuals.* Devise activities that require students to work in groups and be responsible for supporting each other's learning. This may also assist in promoting the key skill of teamwork and could be identified as such. Selectively use fieldwork trails to enable students as individuals or small groups to be in the landscape and not the crowd.
- *Recognize diversity within the student group.* Devising a range of different learning opportunities and ways of assessment, and building flexibility and choice into the field programme, help to address the issue of diversity. Providing appropriate learning support for disabled

students is also an important part of the design process (Healey *et al*, 2001).

- *Attend to assessment*. Assessment is the key to shaping student behaviour and learning; students need to see fieldwork as central to degree classification. This might mean cutting staff time assessing non-field based courses. It certainly means using assessments that are valid but limit staff time, such as group assessments; posters that are assessed on the field course (and use self- and peer-assessment); and perhaps ensuring that other course assessments require students to develop the learning done in the field. The attention given to assessing fieldwork is one way to show students how much it is valued, and ensure that crowd behaviour destroys neither the physical nor the learning environment of the course.
- *Establish clear rules of conduct and rigorously consider safety issues.* This may seem authoritarian, but clear boundaries of behaviour can ensure effective learning. Working with students to establish them can make them more effective.
- *Target fieldwork and (resources) to where they will have most impact.* Consider staff and student time in the field as valued but costly resources, and ensure that they have the greatest potential impact. This might mean targeting fieldwork at students who specialize in your discipline, or focusing on courses that enable limited time in the field to be supported by extensive pre- and post-fieldwork activities/learning.

Enhancing flexibility

Because of changes in policy (highlighted in Chapter 2 and Figure 10.1), higher education institutions have had to explore alternative means of delivering an expanding curriculum to appeal to new markets – that is, a larger and wider group of students. A more diverse intake (see section above) requires greater flexibility (and/or more differentiation between institutions). Since Derek Rowntree (1994) wrote his influential book *Preparing Materials for Open, Distance and Flexible Learning*, open and distance learning, resource-based learning, group project work and distributed learning have all become more commonplace practice, greatly aided by the advances in technology, particularly use of the Web (see Chapter 13). These features enable students with a variety of needs to 'study anytime, anywhere'.

Little research has been undertaken to determine the extent to which the pressures of the Research Assessment Exercise and resource shortage have been responsible for the current keen interest in student-centred learning, and the associated modes of curriculum delivery which place the student at the centre of learning. Irrespective of the drivers of such interest, QAA overview reports suggest that many teachers are embracing notions of student-centredness incorporating such practices as:

- self-directed study;
- directed study, done either in groups or by individuals through some form of tutorless coaching;
- work-based learning;
- modularity;
- use of learning centres;
- open and distance learning;
- part-time study, often involving non-traditional or no contact hours;
- computer mediated communication (eg e-mail, WebCT, COSE, Merlin);
- mixed mode study and teaching.

Communications and information technology (C&IT) in particular is transforming the ways in which staff–student and student–student interactions can take place.

Further to the QAA's requirement for programme specifications as part of Academic Review, higher education institutions are forced to consider an outcomes-based approach to teaching and learning, with the inevitable need to determine precisely which strategies are best suited to delivering the desired outcomes. Such a move may promote more or less flexibility, and do more or less to meet the needs of diverse student groups.

As new fields of study come into higher education (such as nursing) and as greater awareness of pedagogy comes into being, there is increased understanding of the need to select appropriate curriculum design and, in this sense, for curricula across an institution to be more variable. The Learning and Teaching Support Network, through the subject centres (see Chapter 2), may enhance this aspect of flexibility (for contact details see www.ltsn.ac.uk).

Achieving individual attention for learners in a mass system

It is an apparent paradox that as attention has shifted to learner from teacher it is becoming harder to provide individual attention to/for the learner. This is a major consequence for pedagogy of massification (Scott, 1995). Gibbs and Jenkins (1992) provide much guidance and good sense about coping with large classes; see also above. It could, however, be argued that the emphasis now placed on the role of the learner in bringing about his or her own learning is compatible with reduced contact between learner and teacher. How can the individual still receive support and attention in a mass system? Some options are:

- *Student to student rather than student to teacher interaction* (see case study 3). Part of the motivation for using buzz groups, discussion groups, peer tutoring, project work, online discussion, study groups and action-learning sets is to provide opportunities for student discussion. This is perceived as especially important when teacher-led tutorials and seminars are not feasible, or of ever-increasing size. Self- and peer-assessment may also be considered as ways of compensating for individualized feedback from the tutor.

- *Production of standard material that can provoke non-standard responses in learners.* Things such as the personal development through using a progress file, PBL, portfolios and resource-based learning generate work that can be privately reflected on or discussed in a group. Such materials enable the scarce tutor to 'provoke' individual learning in a large number of students.

- *The use of reflection.* Reflection is a multi-meaning term. It is key in turning experience into learning (Kolb, 1984). It is also key in processing knowledge and understanding, to take ownership of it and engage in a deep approach to learning. It could be argued that one-to-one and small group situations of the past often played the part of probing and extending, in other words of 'orchestrating' or provoking thought and reflection, which now has to be supported in other ways. In a similar manner to the second point above, standard formats, such as those for recording a critical incident, may assist the learner to become reflective and self-evaluative (Boud, 1995). Peer tutoring could be seen as another method used as a teacher substitute.

- *Support for learners* is now provided in ways other than through one to one tutorials. Help with study skills is a routine part of courses (through study books, Web materials or interactive lectures), and pools or teams of personal, pastoral or academic tutors, rather than assigned individuals with frequent meetings, are often used. For an example of peer-led team learning, see the case study below.

Many of these techniques can also have other positive benefits, such as increasing ability to self-evaluate, to learn independently, to take responsibility for one's own learning, and to develop habits likely to promote and be compatible with lifelong learning.

Peer-Led Team Learning by Ellen Goldstein and Vicki Roth

The peer-led team learning (PLTL) project was piloted in 1991 at City College of New York, United States, through a problem-solving workshop in chemistry. In 1995 it was selected by the National Science Foundation (NSF) as one of the five systemic national initiatives to change chemistry teaching and learning at higher educational institutions. It grew to involve more than 30 colleges and universities. In the fall of 1999, the NSF selected the project for a national dissemination grant to extend the model to other disciplines. Today PLTL is practised in over 45 colleges and universities, has its own quarterly newsletter and five publications. The materials and leader training formats have been developed through the active cooperation of learning specialists and faculty in biology, biochemistry, chemistry, computer science and physics. (More information, including how to join the project, is available at: http://www.pltl.org.)

The PLTL workshop model addresses the following issues:

- overall improvement of student learning, increased internal motivation for learning the material and changes of attitudes for the better;
- student performance and retention in large, lecture-based introductory science/mathematics courses;
- leadership preparation for the business and academic professional environment;
- encouragement to consider teaching as a career in secondary or higher education.

At the core of the model is an interactive, collaborative learning team which meets each week to work collaboratively in solving sets of rigorous problems. Teams meet under the guidance of skilled undergraduate and graduate student facilitators who receive training both before and during their workshop duties.

In our experience, the following elements have been found critical to success:

- Workshops are integral components of the course, well incorporated with the course lecture, laboratory and homework exercises.
- Faculty members are closely associated with workshop activities and the student leaders.
- Student leaders are carefully chosen and well trained by faculty and learning specialists in the course content, group dynamics, the basics of learning theory and diversity issues.
- Workshop materials are challenging and promote group problem-solving approaches.
- Logistical arrangements (rooms, lighting, schedules) are supportive of the workshop format.
- There is administrative endorsement for the workshop (for example, from department chairs and deans).

- Ongoing formative assessment shapes the practice of workshop faculty, learning specialists and student leaders and serves to garner support from key administrators.

Employability

In 1998, the Committee of Vice-Chancellors and Principals, the Council for Industry in Higher Education, and the Confederation of British Industry suggested that the development of employability skills presented a major challenge to 'make more explicit the development of attributes that have long been implicit and to help students appreciate the importance of such attributes and better articulate them, especially to employers' (CVCP, CIHE, CBI, 1998: 6). These concerns sum up well the mood of a number of government, national, regional and local pronouncements of the 1990s (see also Chapter 2). Graduate unemployment was said to be the result of higher education's lack of concern for the development of knowledge, skills and attitudes other than academic.

The personal transferable, core, or key skills deemed to be essential for employability have been rehearsed in a number of articles and documents. Fallows and Steven (2000) is useful in this regard and has many suggestions about enhancing skills learning. Such skills include learning to learn, literacy and numeracy, understanding others, working in teams, problem solving, use of information technology, personal mastery and effective communication. The QAA has perhaps been the greatest 'stick' for ensuring that key skills are integrated into the curriculum, as opposed to being considered a bolt-on to existing provision. Such skills are 'looked for' by QAA reviewers and required in programme specifications, which ask for 'clear information about the extent to which a programme will equip [students] to progress in their intended careers' (www.qaa.ac.uk). Progress Files will also add to these elements in the curriculum (eg see Fry *et al*, forthcoming).

Many key skills are promoted within existing curricula, but they have often not been identified as such by academics, not been formally/summatively assessed nor made explicit for students and employers in the ways now required. Thus project work, PBL, study skills, oral presentation, group work of various forms (especially if it requires team work), assignments requiring use of knowledge to solve problems, peer tutoring and assessment, essay and report writing and so on all promote one key skill or another.

Alongside this embedded approach, it is possible to offer accredited programmes that demonstrate, via portfolios or learning logs, student involvement in career management skills. The York Award (see case study below) is one such approach that has been regularly commended in QAA Review Reports.

The York Award by Robert Partridge

The University of York launched the York Award programme in 1997/8. The aim was to provide an integrated framework to enable students to draw together the variety of personal development opportunities afforded by the university experience. Three broad categories of opportunity were defined: the academic curriculum (transferable skills such as analysis and problem solving, team working and communication); outside the formal curriculum (supplementary training opportunities such as those provided by the foreign languages and information literacy programmes); and work experience and extra-curricular interests.

The programme is intended to:

- offer a modular programme of student skills training;
- be accessible to all students, regardless of experience and disciplinary background;
- offer a developmental structure, designed to encourage and motivate;
- provide recognition, in the form of a certificate of the university, of student achievement in respect of personal development.

The university has implemented and developed this approach in partnership with North Yorkshire Training and Enterprise Council (1997–2000) and a variety of public, private and voluntary sector organizations. The programme has been well received by students and employers alike, evidenced by a high level of student interest (approximately 15 per cent of the undergraduate population joined in 2001/02), and increasing employer involvement.

When the programme was first introduced, its underlying philosophy contrasted significantly with conventional thinking on skills provision in higher education, but this thinking has moved on and a growing number of institutions are now establishing similar programmes.

ASSESSMENT

Assessment is a key part of curriculum design and should be fully integrated from the start of the planning process. It is also, as already mentioned, probably the most dominant factor in directing and shaping student learning. All too frequently, modes of assessment incompatible with curriculum intentions are used because of economy, failure to understand the impact and limitations of different assessment modes, institutional or disciplinary norms, and assessing what is easy rather than what is important. It is no accident that assessment has received frequent mention and consideration in the themes and case studies in this chapter. Most subjects and courses are increasingly becoming aware of the desirability of taking a more systematic and sophisticated approach to assessment.

Enhancing Practice

Jot down any ideas or suggestions this chapter has given rise to that you could implement/apply to curricula for which you have responsibility.

CONCLUSION AND OVERVIEW

While the seven themes explored within this chapter have very different roots, some primarily in learning theory and others, for example, stemming from government policy, it can be seen that there is considerable overlap and coincidence in the 'solutions' that are in use to address them. That the 'solutions' are frequently dismissed as fashionable baubles is partly a reflection of these mixed antecedents. Another reason for dismissal includes the difficulty of providing incontrovertible evidence of the efficacy in all circumstances of any given approach in education. It is important to understand that the contemporary circumstances and contexts that are skeletally indicated by Figure 4.10.1 pose challenges for curricula. Discriminating, evidence-based where available, and appropriate use of a tool kit of techniques and approaches (such as those suggested in this chapter and its case studies) is important if the challenges are to be met and matched in a satisfactory manner.

REFERENCES

Biggs, J (1993) From theory to practice: a cognitive systems approach, *Higher Education Research and Development*, **12**, pp 73–85

Bloom, B (1956) *Taxonomy of Educational Objectives Handbook 1: Cognitive domain*, McGraw Hill, New York

Boud, D (1995) *Enhancing Learning Through Self Assessment*, Kogan Page, London

Brown, M, Fry, H and Marshall, S (1999) Reflective practice, in *A Handbook for Teaching and Learning in Higher Education: Enhancing academic practice*, ed H Fry, S Ketteridge and S Marshall, pp 207–19, Kogan Page, London

Buzan, T (1998) *Use Your Head*, BBC Consumer Publishing, London

Committee of Vice-Chancellors and Principals (CVCP) (now Universities UK), Council for Industry in Higher Education (CIHE), Confederation of British Industry (CBI) (1998) *Helping Students toward Success at Work: An intent being fulfilled*, CVCP, London

Dahloff, U (1991) Towards a new model for the evaluation of teaching: an interactive-process centred approach, in *Dimensions of Evaluation*, ed U Dahloff, J Harris, M Shattock, A Staropoli and R Veld, pp 101–15, Jessica Kingsley, London

D'Andrea, V (1999) Organising teaching and learning: outcomes-based planning, in *A Handbook for Teaching and Learning in Higher Education*: *Enhancing academic practice*, ed H Fry, S Ketteridge and S Marshall, pp 41–57, Kogan Page, London

Entwistle, N (1994) *Teaching and the Quality of Learning*, Committee of Vice-Chancellors and Principals (CVCP)/Society for Research into Higher Education (SRHE), London

Fallows, S and Steven, C (2000) *Integrating Key Skills in Higher Education*, Kogan Page, London

Fry, H, Davenport, E, Woodman, T and Pee, B (forthcoming) Developing progress files: a case study, *Teaching in Higher Education*

Fry, H, Jones, A, Davenport, E and Brook, A (1997) Changing curricula: an evaluation from dentistry, *Medical Teacher*, **19**(2), pp 108–13

General Medical Council (GMC) (1993) *Tomorrow's Doctors*, GMC, London

Gibbon, M, Limoges, C, Nowotny, H, Schwatzman, S, Scott, P and Trow, M (1994) *The New Production of Knowledge*, Sage, London

Gibbs, G (2000) A strategy for improving student learning on a national scale, paper at Improving Student Learning Symposium, 2000

Gibbs, G and Jenkins, A (eds) (1992) *Teaching Large Classes: Maintaining quality with reduced resources*, London, Kogan Page

Healey, M, Jenkins, A, Leach, J and Roberts, C (2001) Issues in providing learning support for disabled students undertaking fieldwork, Geography Discipline Network, Cheltenham, Cheltenham and Gloucester College of Higher Education

Jarvis, P (1995) *Adult and Continuing Education, Theory and practice*, Routledge, London

Jenkins, A (1997) *Fieldwork with More Students*, Oxford Centre for Staff and Learning Development, Oxford

Kolb, D A (1984) *Experiential Learning*, Prentice-Hall, Englewood Cliffs, New Jersey

Marton, F and Saljo, R (1976) On qualitative differences in learning: 1, outcome and process, *British Journal of Educational Psychology*, **46**, pp 4–11

Prosser, M and Trigwell, K (1999) *Understanding Learning and Teaching*, SRHE/Open University Press, Buckingham

Ramsden, P (1992) *Learning to Teach in Higher Education*, Routledge, London

Rogers, C (1983) *Freedom to Learn in the 80s*, Houghton-Mifflin, Boston

Rowntree, D (1994) *Preparing Materials for Open, Distance and Flexible Learning*, Kogan Page, London

Scott, P (1995) *The Meanings of Mass Higher Education*, SRHE/Open University Press, Buckingham

Squires, G (1990) *First Degree: The undergraduate curriculum*, SRHE/Open University Press, Buckingham

Toohey, S (1999) *Designing Courses for Higher Education*, SRHE/Open University Press, Buckingham

FURTHER READING

Fry, H, Ketteridge, S and Marshall, S (1999) Understanding student learning, pp 21–40 in *A Handbook for Teaching and Learning in Higher Education, Enhancing academic practice*, ed H Fry, S Ketteridge and S Marshall, Kogan Page, London

USEFUL URLs

www.niss.ac.uk/education/hefce/qar/overview.html
www.qaa.ac.uk
www.ltsn.ac.uk

11 | Learning from Quality Assessment

George Gordon

INTRODUCTION

In many countries one of the distinctive aspects of change in higher education in the 1990s was that of increased demands for public accountability. In essence these pressures were a manifestation of significant changes in the relationships between higher education and the state. (For a thorough analysis see Henkel and Little (1999).) The reasons are manifold and complex, but in large measure they involved the complex interplay of a shift to mass higher education, expanding costs associated with this shift, changes in the nature of employment, the knowledge explosion and the rise of what Pollitt (1992) terms the 'new public management' (involving surrogates for markets and explicit expectations about detailed accountability for expenditure and performance). National, regional and/or professional assessment and accreditation of such provision are now established, if evolving, features of such accountability. This chapter sets out to explore a by-product of this accountability, the learning derived from quality assessment, by:

- summarizing the main characteristics of the various types of approaches;
- considering the learning expectations of key parties, especially the designers and operators of the systems;
- examining the evidence of effective learning outcomes;
- discussing barriers which may impede success and how these can be avoided or removed;
- revisiting effective learning in the context of the new climate of quality assurance in the UK;
- offering possible pointers to ways of achieving effective learning outcomes and experiences for individual academics, programmes/departments, subjects and institutions.

VALUES AND PURPOSES

Brennan (1999: 233–34), drawing on case-studies from 15 OECD countries, proposed a fourfold typology based upon values underpinning systems of quality assessment:

- academic;
- managerial;
- pedagogic;
- employment/professional.

Actual systems may rarely fit solely into one type, for Brennan is focusing upon different primary loci of authority. Thus an approach emphasizing managerial values expects clear and consistent procedures which are reliably applied across an institution, whereas Brennan's academic category would be typified by sensitivity to differences between disciplines and would encourage professional control. The pedagogic model might be typified by the classroom assessment approach in the USA and elsewhere, which encourages effective classroom practice and active learning. An emphasis upon outcomes and responsiveness to the views of employers and professions serves to capture the essence of the fourth type.

Part of the dilemma for practitioners is that the systems operative in the UK are underpinned by the expectations that embrace Brennan's four types. That may be understandable, in terms of recognizing the views of different stakeholders, but it instantly introduces the probability of tensions, and even of conflict, because each stems from different bases of authority and value systems. Part of the challenge, then, for effective learning from quality assessment, audit, subject and institutional review is to either reconcile these tensions or use them creatively and constructively. Given the foregoing complexities, effective learning from quality assessment is a demanding task. Such a task is likely to be fostered or endangered by the quality of, and commitment to, the methodology, the understandings of it, widespread acceptance of responsibilities, active leadership and high levels of trust and mutual respect. The broadening and extending range of purposes of quality assessment further complicates the situation.

Brennan and Shah (2000: 31–32), in their study of 12 quality agencies, identified the 10 principal purposes for the evaluations, as:

- ensuring accountability;
- improving the quality of provision;
- informing funding decisions;
- providing information for students and employers;

- stimulating competition;
- checking quality;
- benchmarking provision nationally and comparing providers;
- enabling international comparisons;
- accommodating student mobility;
- displaying how institutions deliver their devolved responsibilities.

While individual systems vary considerably in detail, generally they are united by four common features:

- systematic oversight and coordination;
- the use of critical self-evaluations from providers;
- a predominance of academic peers as assessors;
- formal reporting structured by the criteria specified in the assessment methodology.

SOME APPROACHES TO QUALITY ASSESSMENT

Validation/accreditation by professional bodies, and in former polytechnics and colleges of higher education by the Council for National Academic Awards (CNAA), predate systems introduced in the UK in the 1990s for the audit and assessment of the quality of educational provision. These earlier systems predating the Quality Assurance Agency (QAA) made judgements but they had a strong developmental ethos and were generally conducted in the spirit of co-professionals seeking to recognize and applaud achievements and to foster good practice and encourage innovation and experimentation within a sound framework of quality assurance. Subsequent developments sought to build upon that culture and experience. However, as Brennan and Shah (2000) illustrated, the span of purposes which the processes are explicitly expected to inform has grown substantially, thereby introducing additional tensions.

It is important to remember that differences in the approaches of the differing funding councils existed throughout most of the 1990s. For example, it was only in the last year of quality assessment that the Scottish Higher Education Funding Council (SHEFC) adopted a version of the 24 points (six criteria each rated 1 to 4) system which the Higher Education Funding Council for England (HEFCE) had operated for several years.

In essence, all of the approaches in the UK involved a clear articulation of the scope of, and criteria to be used in, the methodology, and agreed timetables for audit/assessment. Teams of auditors/assessors were recruited and trained, and these peers undertook the visits (generally of three to five days duration). In advance these teams received documentation from the institution/provider, including a structured critical self-evaluation. Assessors/auditors could, and invariably did, request additional documentation prior to the visit. They also often sought further evidence during the visit. Both processes involved interviews with relevant staff and students. Assessment observed teaching and samples of student work. Audit trailed processes and procedures to check upon the robustness of the quality assurance systems, the efficacy of policies and the ways in which these were articulated, monitored, reviewed and revised. Institutions/providers received draft reports for checks on factual accuracy. Within the appropriate agencies (the funding councils, HEQC, or QAA) the process of report writing was overseen and monitored, and reports were approved by the designated authority prior to publication. These agencies also sought to distil broader messages from sequences of reports, as well as requiring institutions/providers to produce to specified timescales short post-report statements of actions.

LEARNING EXPECTATIONS

In the Foreword to the 1992/93 SHEFC *Annual Report on Quality Assessment* (1993), John Sizer, the Chief Executive, wrote:

> Quality assessment yields many benefits. The published reports on provision in named institutions are a source of reliable and independent information for potential students and their advisers, and employers of graduates. They also serve to inform the funding decisions of the Council itself. The process of preparing quality assessment has been acknowledged by many of those involved to have been a most valuable experience: it has obliged them to think carefully about their teaching and learning objectives, environment, student experience, and outputs and outcomes. This experience is enhanced by the visits by assessors to institutions.

Introducing the final SHEFC Quality Assessment Annual Report for 1997/98 (SHEFC, 1998), the chief executive, Dr Paul Clark, noted that the council had completed 315 assessments during the cycle which commenced in 1992. He stressed consultation and collaboration with the sector as a constant feature of the approach adopted by the council, and observed that:

> I believe the reports of individual assessments, together with the overview reports, will provide a valuable resource for students, staff and others who wish to obtain a current picture of the quality of provision in Scottish higher education institutions.

These are two perspectives of the same process. Many of the apparent differences are probably explained by historical context, for Clark was making a valedictory report, whereas Sizer was setting the scene for a new process. Both expected and hoped that the process would serve many beneficiaries.

A review of quality audit concluded that audit had produced many benefits for higher education institutions. It also referred to 'increased assurance about the seriousness with which institutions take their quality control' (Coopers and Lybrand, 1993: 12).

In the case study below, Brennan offers a different perspective.

Divorce, Bereavement and Quality Assurance
by John Brennan

With the above words, a head of department at one of Britain's largest and most prestigious universities sought to convey the nature of his department's experience of external quality assurance. He was not alone in his view of quality assurance as one of the most traumatic experiences of his professional life. Other departmental heads at the same institution reported high levels of stress and physical illness brought on by quality assurance experiences; one had resigned (Brennan, Frederiks and Shah, 1997).

Most academics have in recent years encountered new forms of externally- or institutionally-imposed quality assurance. For more senior academic staff especially, the time devoted to quality assurance activities can be considerable. Is the gain worth the pain (to quote a vice-chancellor from another large university)?

The Centre for Higher Education Research and Information has undertaken several projects in recent years into the effects upon institutions of new forms of quality assurance. We have worked with universities in the United Kingdom and many other parts of the world to investigate how quality assurance activities are affecting the inner lives of academic institutions and, in particular, the role which they can play in helping to drive wider processes of institutional change.

Generalizations are difficult. Not only do quality assurance methods differ but so do national and institutional contexts. Indeed, one of the conclusions we reached in a book on the subject (Brennan and Shah, 2000) was that contextual factors mattered rather more than the methods used. At national levels, forms of relationship between higher education and the state, and at institutional levels, factors such as status, character and decision-making style, shaped fundamentally the institutional reaction to and experience of quality assurance activity. Because context is so important, it is as well to beware of all-purpose recipes from quality assurance gurus.

However, there is one fundamental decision which all departmental heads and others faced with a quality assurance initiative must take: whether to respond actively or passively. The passive response is to do all that is necessary to satisfy the quality assurance agent, external or institutional. The sole consideration is to obtain a positive result in terms of whatever criteria are being used in the quality assurance process. A lot of time will probably need to be devoted to preparing documents and briefing (possibly rehearsing) staff, to interrogating colleagues from other departments who have already experienced the quality assurance process, to reading the small print of quality handbooks, guidelines, codes of practice and so on in order to attempt to discover exactly what is required. But after the quality assurance event has taken place, quality can be safely forgotten about – at least until the next time.

An active response to quality assurance starts from the assumption that change – in the department or in a particular course – might be desirable, that perfection has not yet been attained. In fact, many – probably most – of the institutions we have worked with over the last few years have been convinced, not necessarily that change was desirable, but that it was inevitable, was happening already, was in some cases dramatic, and what was desperately needed was a means to control the change process, to drive it for institutional purposes rather than the purposes of outside interests. For some within institutions, quality assurance processes provided just such a means of controlling change.

Thus, an active response to quality assurance will use the evidence collected, the debate and analysis undertaken, and the judgements reached during the quality assurance processes to make changes and secure agreement for them. There is likely to be conflict and opposition from those affected by the changes. But clever use of quality assurance will exploit the opportunities provided by quality assurance for collective debate enriched by external expertise and experience, to confront vested interests and drive forward change.

Both active and passive approaches to quality assurance are likely to be time-consuming, and for some individuals quite possibly traumatic. Which to adopt? A senior officer of the Quality Assurance Agency once said to me that good institutional quality assurance required just two things: trust and humility. Commodities in short supply? With them, quality assurance can achieve many positive outcomes for all involved. Without them, damage limitation is probably the safest course of action!

LEARNING BENEFITS

Gordon and Partington (1995) stated that there was good reason to suggest that audit and assessment had resulted in various inter- and intra-institutional developments. They cited the benefits which accrued from stocktaking in advance of external quality processes. Benefits can also accrue during the actual visitation. These may be fostered by the adoption and cultivation of a formative, developmental culture within the team of assessors/auditors. Equally, sternly inspectorial stances might cause the erection of invisible barriers to dialogue and learning. If an examination approach is adopted by a provider/programme/department or institution, the focus of attention on receipt of the report may be directed primarily towards the grades and the categorization of the recommendations, rather than some of the subtle and rich learning points that may be embodied in the text. Of course, if the text of reports is neither subtle nor rich the expectations for learning from that source could be diminished. In the reviews which led to the establishment of the new QAA procedures, there were external pressures for brief, crisply written reports. Generally the broad preference within the academy is for rich, subtly-written, balanced documents.

Just as it is widely recognized that academics can learn of interesting work while acting as external examiners, so it is broadly accepted that those performing the roles of auditors and assessors, through undertaking several audits/assessments, gain fascinating opportunities to understand a number of institutions, departments or programmes, to learn from the strengths, practices and policies, and to have an informed means of reflecting upon and benchmarking their own experiences.

Those involved in faculty and/or university-wide quality assurance and audit roles also accumulated substantial experiences from the processes. In effect many of them became a new group of experts, well voiced in the language and nuances of the external processes, avid readers of the documentation and of reports and uniquely knowledgeable of the strengths and weaknesses of their own institutions, in relation to policies and practices. Inevitably boundaries were crossed as institutional 'experts' were recruited as auditors and assessors and vice versa.

Most institutions learnt how to utilize these various experiences and insights of processes and practices to benefit forthcoming submissions and assessments. Some did so with extraordinary effectiveness, if assessment outcome grades/scores were used as an indicator. However, these tactics may not necessarily promote longer-term embedding of developmental approaches to quality assurance and enhancement, although they have been shown to result in score enhancement and significant benefits for morale (especially of departments/programme teams).

Brennan, Frederiks and Shah (1997) conducted an evaluation for HEFCE of the impact of quality assessment on institutions. They concluded that:

> There is little doubt that quality assessment has had an impact upon institutions of higher education in England. On the down side, it has used up a lot of time and resources and caused some stress. More positively, it has provided an impetus for institutions to give more attention to the quality of their teaching.
>
> *(Brennan, Frederiks and Shah, 1997: 74)*

Senior American writers such as Dill (2000) tend to favour audit as a more appropriate and flexible means of combining capacity building with the demands for public accountability.

BARRIERS AND SOLUTIONS

Formulating positive steps further to assessment reports can take time, particularly if one is to create understandings and achieve commitment. In contrast external agencies (and public perceptions) often expect brisk, clear and speedy leadership and managerial actions and remedies. An issue which needs debating is whether we are dealing with crisis management (the programme failed) or change management (the programme needs extensive enhancement). If the latter, then perhaps more attention should be paid to the relevant research literature about effective approaches to change.

In the case study below, Brown discusses some of the paradoxes that confront effective learning from quality assessment.

Learning from Quality Assessment by Roger Brown

One of the many paradoxes of higher education is that those engaged in delivering courses rarely apply to their own learning the same precepts that they apply to that of their students. Quality assessment is a case in point. UK universities and colleges have now had quality assessment of teaching for nearly a decade, yet the evidence that it is having a serious impact on the quality of teaching and learning remains patchy. Why is this? What can be done to improve matters? What is it that prevents quality assessment – both process and outcomes – from being an effective means of professional learning for academic staff?

These are complex and difficult questions. Answering them is not easy, not least because we lack not only micro studies of the impact of quality assessment (and indeed of other forms of external quality assurance such as institutional audit and professional body accreditation) but also because micro studies of local experiences are comparatively rare. Nevertheless it may be feasible to suggest some possible reasons and to put forward some tentative solutions.

There are, it seems to the writer, two main things that prevent the benefits of quality assessment, in terms of improving academic practice, from being fully realized.

The first is the 'distance' between the process of assessment and the actual day-to-day practices and experiences of academics. This distance can be expressed in various ways, from the fact that the proponents and managers of the process are usually external to the unit, individuals and work being assessed, to the unfamiliar and technicist language in which the content of the process is couched: 'units of assessment', 'subject providers', 'aims', 'objectives', even 'learning outcomes'. This means that there is very little prospect of real ownership of assessment by lecturers or groups of lecturers.

The second factor lies in the way in which academic staff develop and are developed professionally. Although individual institutions have development schemes, and although the Institute for Learning and Teaching has begun to develop a model of professional development, it remains the case that there is no real agreement on what it means to be a professional academic, or what processes of formation are appropriate to the various roles which professional academics now perform. Professional development, in short, is haphazard, and total quality assessment (TQA) makes at best a haphazard contribution to it.

How can these difficulties be overcome? The distance issue is probably insuperable as long as assessment is essentially an external process which leads to graded outcomes and which serves, at least in the eyes of many academics, an essentially external agenda for higher education: key skills, employability, learning outcomes and so on. Some progress might be possible if assessment were to involve not the direct scrutiny of learning and teaching, but the ways in which academic staff themselves protect the quality of their teaching: in other words, building on rather than challenging what currently passes for academic professionalism. But although the QAA has expressed the hope and intention that it will in future rely more heavily on institutions' internal processes, there is so far little sign of this happening.

The professional learning issue may be a little easier to tackle, if only because of the shift in the focus of assessment, so far little noticed, away from teaching and learning processes to outcomes and standards. So long as assessment was mainly about generic teaching and learning issues, distance was maintained. If it now begins to enter the academic heartland, through direct scrutiny of standards, the position may change. Is it too much to hope this may stimulate a more systematic process of reflection and review, or will the ownership issue still prevail? Only time will tell.

Brennan, Frederiks and Shah (1997) identified two bundles of factors mediating impact. The first revolved around the way the process was acted out in practice. Clearly if staff in the area being assessed feel uncomfortable with the assessors or the process, that is likely to influence their views about the outcome and outputs. Secondly, as Brown has suggested, internal forces and issues can sometimes exercise a profound influence, especially during periods of considerable turbulence. There is also the issue of the largely unquantified influences of the complexity, pace, and even of the primary causes of, change. Brennan, Frederiks and Shah (1997) reported that many interviewees considered many changes would have happened anyway.

Brennan, Frederiks and Shah (1997: 76–77) listed eight principal lessons for institutions:

- Staff groups who took quality assessment seriously generally did better at it.
- Taking it seriously could lead to other benefits, such as for staff morale and cohesion.
- There were dangers of over-bureaucratization and undermining of staff professionalism and trust.
- Most institutions needed to improve their mechanisms to deal with institution-level issues (as opposed to departmental issues).
- There was a need for more effective integration of quality assessment with internal quality assurance (but not seeing the latter solely as preparation for the former).
- Institutions could benefit from better institutional monitoring of the actions taken as a result of quality assessment.
- Institutions were more likely to achieve good results from quality assessment if they monitored their own experiences of quality assessment and disseminated the lessons learnt across the whole institution.
- Quality assessment was sometimes used as a 'management tool' to steer broader institutional change.

Fears of the dangers of a culture of compliance and issues of drivers, ownership and motivation lie behind several of the lessons listed above and other writings on quality assessment. There is a broad consensus, especially among senior academics and managers, that there should be an emphasis upon the provision of effective and stimulating opportunities for learning and that institutions, programmes and departments should be accountable for their attainment of those goals.

Likewise few would challenge the need to learn from others, for disseminating good practice and benchmarking practice. Moreover the funding councils, most notably through HEFCE's Teaching Quality Enhancement Fund, have provided substantial resources to lubricate quality enhancement and the dissemination of good practice, attributes which quality assessment reports have invariably sought to encourage. The greatest potential barrier to widespread dissemination is the perceived need for tailoring and contextualization. Many projects of the Fund for the Development of Teaching and Learning (FDTL) have sought to develop ways of inventively addressing this challenge at various scales, and much is being learnt in the process. These lessons suggest that proactive dialogue and involvement are essential ingredients for progress. If that deduction is soundly based it casts some doubts about the universality of any presumption that reading and reflecting upon assessment reports and overviews provides a rich and effective source for speedily disseminating good practice. Indeed the fact that HEFCE specifically set the terms so that FDTL projects arose from good practices and practitioners identified through quality assessment highlights a significant shift in strategy towards the means and locus of dissemination of effective learning. Similarly the implementation of the requirement by HEFCE that institutions submit a learning and teaching strategy prior to the release of enhancement funding can also be viewed, at least in part, as a means of sharpening and encouraging institutional commitment, practices and approaches.

THE NEW PARADIGM

After two phases of piloting, the QAA launched subject reviews in Scotland in the academic session 2000/01. In the rest of the UK the process will commence during the following academic year. Over a six-year cycle (2000–06) over 40 subjects will be reviewed. Within that period each institution will also be reviewed.

The broad structure of the new paradigm arose from recommendations in the Dearing Report (NCIHE, 1997). The QAA has service agreements with each funding council to conduct subject reviews that will satisfy the statutory purposes of assessment, which the QAA (2000: 1) describes as:

- to secure value from public investment, by ensuring that all education for which funding is provided is of approved quality, and by encouraging speedy rectification of major shortcomings in the quality of education, and

to enable judgements to inform funding should the funding council so decide;
- to encourage improvements in the quality of education through the publication of subject review reports and subject overview reports, and through the sharing of best practice;
- to provide, through the publication of reports, effective and accessible public information on the quality of HE.

The QAA propose to do this through three areas of activity:

- reporting on programme outcome standards;
- reporting on the quality of learning opportunities;
- reporting on institutional management of standards and quality.

In part the cumulative profile of subject reviews contains information on institutional management which will inform, and be tested, in institutional review. Several items frame and inform the new paradigm. These include:

- a national benchmark statement for each subject;
- two national qualifications frameworks;
- a programme specification for each programme;
- a self-evaluation document for each area under review;
- an extensive code of practice with some 200 precepts.

The new paradigm covers all award-bearing provision in higher education. The standard is ascertained by reference to the national benchmark, the programme specification and the evidence of attained, intended outcomes. The judgements on the quality of learning opportunities address three aspects:

- teaching and learning;
- student progression;
- effective utilization of learning resources.

Reviews may span several months. Teams are staffed in proportion to the size and complexity of the provision, and led by a review coordinator who will normally not be a peer from that discipline. The other members of the team will be academic and/or professional peers. The process leads to a published report with specified categories of outcome, which are still the subject of debate and negotiation between Universities UK and QAA. Full details of the process can be downloaded from the QAA Web site (www.qaa.ac.uk). The handbook for academic review is a useful starting point, especially Annex E, an aide-memoire for subject review.

At this early juncture many institutions and individual academics are unsure about the way in which the new paradigm will translate into operation and the outcomes which will accrue. They are wary of potential dangers and unintended problems, and remain to be convinced that the burdens will lessen and the benefits increase. The QAA argues that both can, indeed should be, achieved, since institutions have in place robust systems for quality assurance and virtuous cycles of enhancement. For an established institution to gainsay that assertion is to admit to not only 'game-playing' but also less than whole-hearted commitment to quality assurance and enhancement. We may have to revisit questions of purposes, drivers and ownership, especially since there is a growing belief that the Dearing compact between higher education and government has not been fulfilled.

POINTERS TO EFFECTIVE PRACTICE

Bowden and Marton (1998) persuasively argue, in their volume *The University of Learning*, that everything should be shaped by the kind of learning we want to engender. Their exploration of several crucial questions merits widespread consideration and reflection. For example, what are the purposes and nature of better learning? What does it take to learn? How is learning related to meaning and to context? What should be learnt? How can we foster learning effectively? Central to the achievement of their vision of a University of Learning is the development of collective consciousness within a networked organization. They argue:

> In a networked organization... there are many links between units in the organization and the communication is content-related, i.e. it is about work people carry out together with mutual support. Such contacts are likely to enrich the shared understanding of the object of communication.

(Bowden and Marton, 1998: 274)

Another supportive component occurs when ownership is connected by multi-centred leadership (Gordon, 2000), which respects diversity and enables flexibility, yet seeks shared understandings and the articulation of common guiding educational principles and purposes. Many potential tensions confront and challenge these visions. Most involve the issues of individual academic autonomy and collective approaches, principles, goals and understandings. External quality assessment focuses upon programmes/departments as the critical link in the chain of assurance and enhancement, of design, evaluation and review, of the setting of standards and the testing of attainment. But it is essential that there are effective connections to individual academics working on the programme and that all of the activities occur within wider shared institutional (and professional) understandings and principles.

Various key stakeholders have been active in endeavouring to foster reflection and effective learning. For example, the several strands of the Teaching Quality Enhancement Fund of HEFCE are specifically designed to promote inter- and intra-institutional sharing of good practice, to raise the prominence of policy debates about effective learning, and to encourage reflective practice, benchmarking and the scholarship of teaching. Ideally information from quality assessment, benchmarking of practice, feedback from peers, students, employers and professional bodies and inputs from research continuously inform the practice of individuals, programme teams, faculties/schools and institutions, with multi-centred leadership guiding agendas for debate and action, addressing lacunae and fostering a climate of creativity and innovation within a culture of reflective and deep learning.

Similarly the Institute for Learning and Teaching has both set standards for effective practice as criteria for membership and acts as an additional source of debate and dissemination of effective learning and the scholarship of teaching. The recently formed Learning and Teaching Support Network (LTSN) is also actively developing a role through the network of 24 subject centres and the Generic Learning and Teaching Centre, which includes drawing on the best practice and pedagogic issues as raised in QAA Subject Overview Reports.

Discussions between QAA and ILT and various professional bodies provide further opportunities for connectivity and dovetailing, with localized contextualization achieved through the institutional learning and teaching strategies that will soon become a universal feature of UK higher education.

Central to successful progress lie the twin challenges of achieving effective connections between autonomy (individual, subject, institutional) and ownership (purpose, principles, meanings, understandings) and of resolving the potential tensions generated by the pace and scale of change, especially in knowledge formation, management and dissemination. The emerging structures need to be sufficiently flexible and dynamic to accommodate these tensions, yet sufficiently focused to genuinely cultivate sharing, reflection, benchmarking and an evolving collective consciousness about learning.

OVERVIEW

The councils and those responsible for external assessment of quality expect individuals, teams and institutions to learn from assessment and to operate within a climate and culture of enhancement informed by reflection, monitoring and benchmarking of practice. The survey for HEFCE by Brennan,

Frederiks and Shah (1997) reported that learning from assessment had occurred. That study also identified impediments, lacunae and areas for improvement.

Additionally numerous developmental projects have taken place, some funded by institutions, some by external agencies. Attention has been paid to connecting different policies and linking policy to practice. Within institutions, learning and teaching strategies offer an important opportunity and vehicle for such work. At the pan-institutional level, HEFCE has sought both interconnections between initiatives with the Teaching Quality Enhancement portfolio and linkages between these, quality assessments and institutional strategies, policies, practices and innovations.

It can sometimes appear frustrating that conflicts and tensions persist. After all, if everyone is committed to better learning, why is it not possible to unite effectively the views of the different stakeholders? It may be salutary to pose the question, why should individuals, teams and institutions want to learn effectively from quality assessments? Betterment or improvement apparently provides a unifying bond, but it may be interpreted differently by the various constituencies. An individual teacher may view improvement in several particular ways. One is to remedy weaknesses. There is nothing more powerful than feeling that a lecture or a tutorial or a laboratory class did not work, to stimulate the teacher to do something about it. And that could embrace a wide range of feedback, such as on a module or on methods of assessment or on the detailed balance of content. But practitioners are influenced by other factors such as their professional desire to do a good job, concerns about the view which students and peers hold of them, personal intellectual curiosity to learn new things and explore new ideas and practices, and so forth. Each individual in a course team will hold personal opinions and values and respond to particular drivers and motivators. There can be many common items amongst the team and yet there can still be significant detailed differences in priorities and values. The point made by Brennan, Frederiks and Shah (1997) about the broad correlation between the seriousness with which teams approached quality assessment and the outcomes, may also reflect the ability to achieve what Bowden and Marton (1998) termed 'collective consciousness'.

At the level of the department or course team, effective learning and enhancement involves welding together individual commitment, professionalism, expertise and creativity in a coherent and explicit manner, which can be communicated effectively to students (actual and prospective), assessors, external assessors, internal reviewers and other interested parties.

At the institutional level, reputation often appears to be a powerful driver. One challenge is to seek to do better in the external test as a by-product of improved practices and policies for effective learning rather than as the reason for it. Creating the appropriate culture takes time and careful and thoughtful nurturing, in which a lot of attention has to be paid to meanings and understandings, and sharing and benchmarking good practice. Aligning different perceptions, perspectives and viewpoints demands considerable sensitivity lest it becomes compliance. Yet there are significant dangers if fragmentation or insularity of perspective or of responsibility for action characterize the climate of supposedly effective learning. Thus there is a need for effective leadership, committed to ways of developing a culture of collective consciousness characterized by shared ownership and fuelled by a spirit of curiosity to learn and thereby to improve.

REFERENCES

Bowden, J and Marton, F (1998) *The University of Learning*, Kogan Page, London

Brennan, J (1999) Evaluation of Higher Education in Europe in *Changing Relationships Between Higher Education and the State*, ed M Henkel and B Little, pp 219–35, Jessica Kingsley, London

Brennan, J, de Vries, P and Williams, R (1997) *Standards and Quality in Higher Education*, Jessica Kingsley, London

Brennan, J, Frederiks, F and Shah, T (1997) *Improving the Quality of Education: The impact of quality assessment on institutions*, Report to HEFCE, Quality Support Centre

Brennan, J and Shah, T (2000) *Managing Quality in Higher Education*, Society for Research into Higher Education (SRHE)/Open University Press, Buckingham

Coopers and Lybrand (1993) *Review of Quality Audit*, HEQC, London

Dill, DD (2000) *Capacity Building Through Academic Audits: Improving 'quality work' in the UK, New Zealand, Sweden and Hong Kong*, paper presented to EAIR Conference, Berlin

Entwistle, N and Ramsden, P (1983) *Understanding Student Learning*, Croom Helm, London

Gordon, G (2000) *The roles of leadership and ownership in building an effective quality culture*, paper presented at New Millennium: Quality and Innovations in Higher Education Conference, organized by the Chinese Higher Education Evaluation Research Society and the Hong Kong Council for Academic Accreditation, Hong Kong, December

Gordon, G and Partington, P (1995) The impact of national developments on the quality of teaching, in *Teaching Improvement Practices*, ed W A Wright and Associates, pp 369-392, Anker, Bolton, Mass.

Henkel, M and Little, B (eds) (1999) *Changing Relationships between Higher Education and the State*, Jessica Kingsley, London

National Committee of Inquiry into Higher Education (NCIHE) (1997) *Higher Education in the Learning Society (Dearing Report)*, HMSO, London

Pollitt, C (1992) Justification by works or by faith? Evaluating the new public management, *Evaluation*, 1(2), pp 133–35

Quality Assurance Agency (QAA) (2000) *Handbook for Academic Review*, QAA, Gloucester

Scottish Higher Education Funding Council (SHEFC) (1993) Foreword to *Annual Report on Quality Assessment 1992/93*, SHEFC, Edinburgh

SHEFC (1998) *Introduction (pp 2–3) to Quality Assessment Annual Report 1997–8*, SHEFC, Edinburgh

FURTHER READING

Hanson, M *et al* (2001) Trial by ordeal, *Guardian Education*, pp 12–13, 30 January

Marton, F, Hounsell, D and Entwistle, N (1997) *The Experience of Learning*, Scottish Academic Press, Edinburgh

Ramsden, P (1992) *Learning to Teach in Higher Education*, Routledge, London

Times Higher Education Supplement (*THES*) (2001) QAA is accused of meddling in universities' autonomy, *THES*, 23 February, p 3

12 Teaching for Diversity and Retention: The Example of Students with Disabilities

Alan Hurst

INTRODUCTION

Since about 1980 considerable attention has been given to widening participation in higher education. Many initiatives have been sponsored to investigate the under-representation of particular groups: for example the work undertaken by Sir Christopher Ball in his report *More Means Different* (1990). Most of these reports neglected students with disabilities. Progress for this group of students has come more recently, and in order to understand how the needs of such students can be addressed, it is necessary to provide some background information and to set what follows in its wider educational context. This chapter is aimed at those staff with responsibilities for the delivery of curricula, and will review ways in which students with disabilities can be included in teaching and learning programmes, drawing upon experience and good practice from across the higher education sector.

BACKGROUND

One of the key issues faced by those with disabilities wishing to study was the additional expense incurred. In 1990, the government introduced top-up loans for students, and to demonstrate its concern for students with disabilities, modified the system of additional allowances available for such students.

Since then, the disabled students allowances have comprised three parts: a general allowance paid for each year of the recognized course to cover additional costs incurred resulting from being impaired, an allowance also paid for each year to cover the costs of non-medical personal assistance, for example British Sign Language interpreters working with deaf students, and a single payment to buy study-related special equipment. Maximum amounts have increased annually to keep pace with inflation. The original system had shortcomings but in the ten years since its introduction, some of these have been addressed. Most significant have been the abolition of the means test and the extension to include many postgraduate students and part-time students, the latter being welcomed especially by the Open University, which has always recruited successfully large numbers of students declaring disabilities.

Many institutions claimed that they could not develop policy and provision for disabled students because of the additional costs incurred. This issue has been tackled following the Further and Higher Education Act (1992) and the establishing of the national funding councils. Each of these has given additional money to support students with disabilities. In England there has been a series of special initiatives funding particular projects, with institutions having to make bids for consideration by the Higher Education Funding Council for England (HEFCE) Advisory Group on Students with Learning Difficulties and Disabilities. Attempts have been made to coordinate developments, firstly through the establishing of the 'EquIP' team (Enhancing Quality in Provision) and since 1999 through the HEFCE-funded National Disability Team (URL: www.natdisteam.ac.uk). For the academic year 1999 to 2000 an element of core funding was introduced, giving an additional premium based on the number of students with disabilities recruited by institution. In Wales, following some special initiatives, attention has been given to improving aspects of infrastructure in institutions. In Scotland, a national coordinator was appointed and currently the SHEFC is funding three national projects, one of which, the *Teachability* project, is of key significance to this chapter and will be described in some detail below.

MOVING FORWARD

Unquestionably progress has been made, but there is no room for complacency. Many students with disabilities seeking entry to higher education still meet obstructions. Some stem from physical access to buildings. Many institutions rely upon older buildings, some of which are of historical and architectural interest and have protected status. However, lack of access to buildings must not become an easy justification for not considering how students with disabilities can participate. Lack of access to buildings does not create a barrier for students with impairments which are not related to mobility. Sometimes flexible timetabling means classes can be taught in more accessible locations. This willingness to think flexibly is a sign that positive attitudes prevail. Other barriers are created when staff have negative attitudes and retain prejudices and stereotyped views of 'the disabled'. Many institutions have organized programmes to make staff aware of how their courses can be made more inclusive.

The best of these awareness-raising programmes stress two points. Firstly, approaches to inclusion have been based upon applying the social/educational model of disability as opposed to the individual/medical/deficit model. The latter locates difficulties associated with participation in the individual, whilst the former accepts people as they are and considers what has to be done to allow them to participate as fully and actively as their non-disabled peers. Secondly, whilst it has been said so often that it seems to have become a truism, it does remain the case that approaches to learning, teaching and assessment which are appropriate for students with disabilities are also appropriate for non-disabled students. For example, if overhead projector transparencies are being used in a class in which there are blind students, reading out the content will not only improve access for these students, it will ensure that all others are clear about what is on the screen. Putting this slightly differently and adapting slightly the words of the proposed revised Code of Practice to be used in schools, 'we are all teachers of learners with special educational needs' (DfEE, 2000).

DEVELOPING HIGH QUALITY LEARNING FOR STUDENTS WITH DISABILITIES

In 1999 the Quality Assurance Agency for Higher Education (QAA) issued its *Code of Practice: Students with disabilities*. While this covers all stages of a student's career in higher education from initial contact to entering employment after qualifying, there is a section concerned specifically with curriculum. As with other QAA codes, there are precepts followed by suggested guidelines. For example, Precept 10 says:

> The delivery of programmes should take into account the needs of disabled people or, where appropriate, be adapted to accommodate their individual requirements.

> Institutions should consider making arrangement which ensure that all academic and technical staff:

> 1. plan and employ teaching and learning strategies which make the delivery of the programme as inclusive as is reasonably possible;

2. know and understand the learning implications of the students whom they teach, and are responsive to feedback;

3. make individual adaptations to delivery that are appropriate for particular students, which might include providing handouts in advance and /or in different formats (Braille, disk), short breaks for interpreters to rest, or using radio microphone systems, or flexible/interrupted study for students with mental health difficulties.

This extract draws attention to the QAA code and notes that it becomes legitimate during Subject Review visits for institutions/departments to be questioned about the progress made towards implementing the precepts. Certainly this would be the case for institutions subject to the regular Continuation Audit visits. As part of the Subject Review methodology, it has been possible to consider provision for students with disabilities under the six different aspects of provision. A significant change in the Academic Review process, the successor to subject review, will be in relation to provision for students with disabilities. In addition to its own self-assessment document, a department's aims and objectives should now be evaluated against a number of external criteria: the subject benchmarks, the National Qualifications Framework and the QAA codes of practice of which the code on Students with Disabilities is a part. This does present the opportunity to ensure that students with disabilities are not neglected in curricular provision.

Enhancing Practice

- Is the learning and teaching strategy for your department or discipline flexible enough to accommodate students with disabilities?
- How accessible are your courses at both undergraduate and postgraduate levels to students with disabilities? Can anything else be done to widen access and participation?
- Are strategies for including students with disabilities discussed routinely as part of quality assurance when new courses are validated and current courses reviewed?
- What opportunities are there for continuing professional development of all staff relating to support for students with disabilities?

WORKING WITH STUDENTS WITH DISABILITIES IN THE CLASSROOM: SOME PERCEIVED BARRIERS

Experience from staff development work suggests that academic staff have many questions about students with disabilities. Since we are not an especially inclusive society, for some academics meeting a student with a disability might be their first experience of disability, and because of this lack of personal knowledge, they rely on information derived from other sources. The kinds of image of disabled people promoted by the mass media may be unhelpful. Some portray disabled people as 'sick' and seeking a 'cure' for their impairment. Others emphasize the lack of independence and suggest that what for non-disabled people is routine, for those with disabilities is unusual – often described as 'triumph over tragedy'. (See, for example, Pointon and Davies (1997) for more about this.) To counter this lack of knowledge, an effective programme of disability-awareness-raising staff development is helpful. This might also introduce academics to the different specialist equipment available to support students with a range of impairments. For example, many people make use of Microsoft to meet their IT needs. This is often linked to using programmes such as Windows and Word, which rely on manipulating a cursor between icons on the screen. Some could expect this to be a problem for students who are blind. The problem becomes much less significant when the availability of voice-activated alternatives is identified. Another source of concern stems from inflexibility in various dimensions. Sometimes this originates within the institution's and department's own systems, structures and procedures. An example here might be the ways in which health and safety requirements are imposed. Additionally, sometimes inflexibility may be attributed to the interests of professional bodies who require, for example, periods of work experience.

A further source of concern might be described as personal. Academics are under increasing pressure to teach effectively, to produce good research, to generate income and so on, and the result of all these factors may be a feeling of lack of time. For example, to prepare materials in advance of teaching a class can be a problem if the materials need to be ready to be transferred into different formats. Academics like to make use of up-to-the-minute materials (eg articles from newspapers, publications and recent video recordings) and it may be argued that there is insufficient time to ensure that these are accessible to all students. Coupled with the lack of time is the higher priority accorded to other activities, and the continuing low status of working with students with disabilities.

There are a number of miscellaneous concerns relating to students with particular impairments. For example, in providing appropriate learning support for students with learning difficulties, questions have been raised about the potential negative impact on academic standards. Working with students with serious mental health difficulties highlights the potential impact on the effective learning and progress of other students in the group.

From this miscellany of items, it is necessary to adopt a more systematic approach to identifying barriers to inclusive learning. Perhaps it would be useful to make some distinctions. Firstly, there are barriers that are intrinsic to the nature of the subject and make it impossible for some people to access certain subjects. Thus, questions might be asked about the possibilities of people who are blind studying dentistry with a view to becoming professional practitioners. Secondly, there are barriers created as a consequence of the curriculum delivery strategies chosen by some academic departments. Thus, in introducing students to underpinning theoretical knowledge, students begin first with some practical activities. Thirdly, there are the barriers resulting from the inadvertent use of learning and teaching approaches such as using video playbacks lacking subtitles and thereby excluding deaf students.

WORKING WITH STUDENTS WITH DISABILITIES IN CLASSROOMS: POSSIBLE ROUTES TO PROGRESS

In suggesting ways in which academic staff can meet the needs of students with a diverse range of impairments and provide them with an educational experience which is of high quality and therefore likely to ensure that they do not withdraw from the course, close reference will be made to the SHEFC-sponsored *Teachability* project currently being delivered in Scotland and led by Anne Simpson and Graham Charters of the University of Strathclyde (SHEFC, 2000). The *Teachability* booklet, designed to be used by individual departments, provides a structured framework for looking at current practices in terms of both learning and teaching, and departmental systems and procedures. The main part of the booklet comprises a questions and resources section in which 'curriculum' is broken into smaller items (eg pre-course information, visits and placements) and for each a conception of 'inclusive' practice suggested. The questions are for self-review only and are not intended for audit purposes. The basic premise is that academic staff design and deliver courses, so they are in the best position to develop inclusive practices. What *Teachability* involves is working through a programme of questions systematically. There are five overarching questions:

- How accessible is the curriculum of the department for students with a range of impairments?
- How might it be made more accessible for students with a range of impairments?
- What steps need to be taken to implement the strategies identified to enhance access?
- What barriers are there to achieving the changes identified?
- How can the ways in which the curriculum is particularly accessible or inaccessible be made known to potential students with a range of impairments?

In putting into practice *Teachability*, a key question is the identification of what is core to the subject/course. In sessions so far, some colleagues have had difficulty answering this question, although reference to subject benchmarking and programme specifications might be of value in this process. *Teachability* covers eight aspects and considers each in the order in which it is likely to be encountered. Some further details follow.

Pre-entry information

Pre-entry information needs to make reference to course structure, syllabus content, sample learning materials including booklists which identify essential reading, requisite prior knowledge/experience/skills, methods of learning, teaching and assessment, modes of study and progression opportunities, and – importantly – the name of someone to contact for further information. The above constitutes a standard requirement to meet the needs of all prospective students. It is also necessary to ensure that this information is available in different formats such as Braille or on tape or in large print. Today more and more information is available on Web sites, but experience indicates that guidance is needed in producing accessible sites. Sometimes the information provided adopts a taken-for-granted approach, but it is one which cannot be seen in this way by some potential students. For example, departments do not think too much about where the course is taught, having taught the course in the same location successfully for many cohorts – until they get an application from a wheelchair user.

Some useful examples of information about courses and their accessibility have been provided by the Open University. For example, information relating to Module A206, The Enlightenment, states:

> Printed course materials are available on audio-cassette and in comb-binding, and there are transcripts of the audio-visual materials. Four weeks of the course are devoted to music and three weeks to art history. Alternative questions are provided when assignments depend on visual or aural material.

Note here that the decision whether an individual with a disability can participate fully in the module is left to the individual. This is in keeping with a fundamental principle of social life, namely that people have choices and are able to take decisions for themselves about their own lives.

Attendance requirements

A further aspect discussed in the *Teachability* project is the programme of study. A major dimension of this is the degree of flexibility in attendance at classes and in modes of study. This is important for many students with disabilities because although they are not sick (and indeed a major aim of this chapter is to move away from the medical model of disability), their impairment can mean that there are times when they feel unable to participate fully in classes. Sometimes intense timetabling exacerbates their difficulties. Again it might be suggested that while this is unhelpful for students with disabilities, it might also contribute to ineffective learning for their non-disabled peers.

Induction for students

Considering the important issue of induction, the concerns here are about providing information on the roles and responsibilities of staff and students, and indicating where staff are located. Often initial meetings between staff and students act as ice breakers and can build a strong foundation on which to base future progression. Sometimes during their first days on the course, students are introduced to unfamiliar strategies of learning and teaching with which they can experiment. Students with disabilities will benefit from this, but at this stage in their academic career they might value a little more time with individual tutors. Equally tutors might benefit from talking with students to find out how they can meet their needs, for example, when using audiovisual materials with blind or with deaf students. If the students use special equipment or need personal assistance, tutors will wish to ensure that this is in place for the start of their course.

Learning in lectures

Assuming that students have the basic information about when and where lectures take place, the question arises how students are presented with and retain the information being transmitted. More conventional methods of lecture notes are being superseded by placing materials on Web pages or in tutors' mailboxes. Again, this is helpful for all students, including those whose impairments might create barriers to collecting information during the session (for example, if they find it difficult to take notes). Experience also suggests that all students can benefit from advice about how to take or make notes. Students who use wheelchairs or have other kinds of impaired mobility need to be able to get into the lecture room, but once inside their choice of position might be limited. Sometimes this can result in isolation and drawing attention to their presence, or indeed absence!

There are some important issues for the lecturer to bear in mind. If a lecture is cancelled and information to this effect is put on an appropriate notice board, will this be within reading distance for someone using a wheelchair? How will blind students find out about this change to the programme? How will blind students have access to any visual materials such as tables, maps, diagrams or charts used in the lecture? Will they be able to access this at the same time as their peers? If they have to wait, what consequences might there be for their study patterns? Some blind students use cassette recorders to tape lectures but this is not always a success since it is sometimes difficult to index the content for easy access later.

The effective transmission of information in lectures is a crucial issue for students who are deaf or hard-of-hearing. For the former, staff will need to be aware of some of the potential barriers to communication when working with sign language interpreters. Many of these can be resolved if the lecturer can meet with the interpreter beforehand or at least supply a copy of the text. This gives the interpreter time to consider how to translate technical terms. Interpreting is an intense activity, and interpreters and the deaf students value regular breaks, say after 30 minutes. Such breaks might also benefit all students, since authors (such as Bligh, 1998) have noted the short attention span of students in lectures. If the student is hard-of-hearing and is relying on lip-reading for communication, the lecturer needs to remember to speak clearly and to face the listeners at all times. Turning round to use a board and continuing with the presentation destroys communication. Special efforts might also need to be made to ensure that the lighting conditions in the lecture room are appropriate, for instance when using overhead projectors or in cases of adverse natural daylight.

Learning in small groups

Other learning and teaching may commonly take place in seminars and tutorials, in which there should be a supportive atmosphere, and where the contributions from all students are valued. Academics use seminars and tutorials for a range of different purposes, but the general feature common to all is that the number of students involved is smaller than in a lecture. This should allow for staff and students to get to know more about each other as individuals. Clearly this opportunity should be useful for students with additional needs. Some of the factors impinging on lectures are also found in the smaller groups: for example the desirability of, and the strategies available for, retaining information. When deaf or hard-of-hearing students are present, it can be confusing if more than one person speaks at the same time. Designing and adhering to a system for speaking in turn again helps all members of the group. Tutors also need to remember that the translation and processing of information takes a little time, so there will be a short time space between deaf students getting the information and their feeling that they need to ask a question. Blind members of the group will find it useful if there are brief introductions at the start of each meeting and also if people say who they are before they start to speak. If printed materials are to be used, they should have been made available in time to be put into the format preferred by the student. This is yet a further example where all students might benefit from the need to prepare and distribute teaching materials in advance of the class. In situations such as tutorials or seminars, where students are expected to speak, there might be particular barriers for students with speech impairments. If tutors are aware of this, in discussion with the student, it might be possible to agree on strategies to allow the student to make a contribution to the discussion.

Enhancing Practice

- In your department what experience have you of working with students with different impairments?
- What small group learning strategies do you use, and how far might these facilitate/inhibit inclusive learning for students with impairments?
- What does your institution's disability statement, and what does your own course information, say about inclusive learning?

Learning in laboratories, studios and workshops

Other learning occurs during sessions in laboratories, studios and workshops. These are usually intended to allow students to develop a range of practical skills. The extent to which students with a range of impairments can be included fully in these activities depends upon how far the skills to be developed are seen as core, and how far there is flexibility to allow students to demonstrate their acquisition in other ways. Developments in technology now allow for simulations and for virtual realities, and these might facilitate inclusive learning. Many of the barriers to inclusion in laboratories have been overcome using very simple solutions. The work of Professor Alun Jones, formerly of the Nottingham Trent University, has demonstrated how students can participate full in laboratory-based activities without infringing considerations of health and safety. For example, Jones has devised ways to ensure that the layout and equipment is accessible to wheelchair users, while the use of sound-based communication can assist blind students carrying out experiments in the sciences (Hopkins and Jones, 1998).

Other types of learning activities

Some courses require students to complete work placements, to undertake field trips or study overseas. Many barriers which might be perceived initially can be overcome with good careful assessment of potential risks and advance planning. This demonstrates the need to ensure that students with disabilities have this requirement made known to them at the earliest opportunity.

The range of associated questions is considerable. How can students prepare? Are additional costs involved, and if so who pays? Is any special preparation necessary? Is the experience assessed? Is there an alternative which allows students to acquire and demonstrate the skills/competences the experience aims to produce? If work placements, field trips and study overseas involves students with disabilities, the first stage must be to discuss with each individual student what challenges there might be and how these might be met. For wheelchair users there are issues relating to travel, access, accommodation and the availability of adapted facilities, such as bathrooms and lavatories. If students use special equipment, it might not be easy to transport it. There might be a need for additional equipment which then could raise issues about the use of the equipment part of the Disabled Students Allowance, especially if the student has already spent his/her full quota. Where work placements are required, there might be questions surrounding compliance with the Disability Discrimination Act 1995 which, while it applies to employees, might be less clear-cut when applied to students on placement. In the case of study overseas, there is a growing body of information available that identifies facilities in other countries and in universities abroad (Gagliano and Moore, 1997; Van Acker, 1996).

Access to information

This leads into the penultimate section of the *Teachability* project, which is about information and communication. Basically this is about ease of access to the main information sources available to all students: the library and electronic communication. There are several dimensions to this. Wheelchair users might be unable to access the book stack because the aisles between the shelves are too narrow and they are unable to reach high shelves. Access to print materials for students who are blind has improved in a number of ways. At a more general level, it is now common to find popular books available on cassette recordings, while other specialist texts can be accessed using scanners and speech outputs. Over time this equipment has become more compact and easier to transport. However, when asked to read in preparation for submitting an assignment, blind students might still be disadvantaged because of the difficulties they encounter in using book indexes and speed-reading texts. It helps them – and other students too – if academics whenever possible identify essential reading and key texts.

Assessment issues

Finally there is formal academic assessment, whether it be formative or summative, continuous or end-of-programme, written or oral. All students need precise information about how their progress will be assessed, at the point at which they start their programme of study. Different assessment methodologies carry different implications for students with impairments, and they find flexibility in approach helpful. The *Teachability* project suggests several ways in which assessment regimes might be modified. There are alternatives to the ways in which the assessment may be carried out. Some of these are obvious, such as providing materials in appropriate formats such as large print or Braille. Less obvious is the improved readability of an examination paper for some students if the colour of the paper and of the print is different from the usual black on white. Deaf students who use British Sign Language (BSL) as their method of communication might experience some difficulties with the questions, since the structure of BSL is not the same as standard English. In this instance, moderating the language of the questions prior to the examination could help. Students who have difficulties with writing might prefer to record their answers on cassette tape. Alternatively they might prefer to use a scribe and to dictate their responses. The last sentence in itself might be an example of how choosing to use certain terms can improve access and understanding. Would the point have been made as easily to all readers had the term 'amanuensis' been used instead of 'scribe'? There might be alternative timing of assessment. Thus it has become common to allow students with specific learning difficulties, for example dyslexia, additional time to complete the tasks. However, some students might prefer the additional time at the start of the examination because their reading time is slower than others.

A Brief Case History

Many of the points raised above can be demonstrated by exploring a simple hypothetical case history. Jenny has been totally blind since birth. Having had experience of both segregated and mainstream schools, she decided to take her A levels in a local college. She obtained passes in English Literature, French, and History, all at grade B. She chose to spend a year out of education before applying to enter university. She failed to find a satisfying steady job. However, she did acquire a guide dog to aid her mobility. She has decided that now she would like to try to obtain a place at university, for Joint Honours degree in French and History. Ultimately she would like to work using her foreign language skills.

Factors which need to be considered include the following:

- She has been blind since birth and so knows best her own needs, although some aspects of life in higher education might be new to her.
- Having been in mainstream further education, she will have some familiarity with the hurly-burly of being a student.

- The high standard of attainment in A level exams indicates her academic potential.
- Her work/life experience prior to entry should have brought other important skills such as interpersonal relationships.
- It is essential that information about courses/universities/specialist support is available in accessible/preferred formats, including anything that is Web-based. University Disability Statements should be useful as should the publications of Skill: The National Bureau for Students with Disabilities (URL: www.skill.org.uk).
- Other students and staff could benefit from disability awareness sessions prior to her arrival.
- The formal assessment of her support needs and the provision of assistive technology should be considered.
- She might need training for working with new equipment and on the maintenance of equipment.
- With regard to access to learning and the curriculum, Braille format/cassette recordings need to be available for use as soon as possible.
- There are challenges to be faced in academic assessment and examinations, for example changing script from Braille to traditional orthography.
- She is studying French and so a foreign placement might be required, which will necessitate long-term planning.
- If she chooses to live in university accommodation, attention has to be paid to meeting Jenny's needs and also those of her guide dog.
- Assuming that the higher education experience is about more than what happens in classrooms, she might need support to enjoy a full social life.
- Given her current imprecise ideas about future employment, careers advice is important, especially if it is offered by those with experience of working with students like Jenny.
- Financial support during the course and the availability of the Disabled Students Allowance is important.

This represents a relatively straightforward situation, and much of it would be replicated at a general level for students with impaired hearing or impaired mobility. Some of those working with students with disabilities encounter more complex challenges, for example in meeting the needs of students with multiple impairments and students experiencing mental ill-health.

OVERVIEW AND CLOSING COMMENTS

This account of how curricula might be made more accessible and more inclusive for students with disabilities is timely. In the opening sections of the chapter attention was drawn to the work of the QAA and the imperatives it is introducing. There is also a potentially stronger change imminent. In December 2000, the government outlined its plans to introduce legislation to end disability discrimination in education. The new law will expect institutions to plan in advance to meet the needs of students with disabilities, rather than taking the more reactive approach found currently in many institutions. In the past some have commented that there is no purpose in making their courses and facilities more inclusive since they receive no enquiries or applications from people with disabilities: hardly surprising if it is known that these institutions have nothing in place to support them. Institutions will also have to ensure that these students are not treated less favourably than others, and that 'reasonable adjustments' have been made, including 'adjustments' to the curriculum. To avoid becoming among the first of the test cases involving student complaints, institutions need to start looking now at their course provision and curricula to ensure that they are accessible and inclusive. In the past, the rallying cry was 'access for all'. While that challenge has not been met completely, sufficient progress has been made to suggest the cry now should be 'access to excellence for all'.

REFERENCES

Ball, Sir C (1990) *More Means Different: Widening access to higher education*, Royal Society of Arts, London

Bligh, D (1998) *What's the Use of Lectures?*, Intellect, Exeter

Department for Education and Employment (DfEE) (2000) *Draft Proposed Revised Code of Practice on the Identification and Assessment of Children with Special Educational Needs*, DfEE, London

Gagliano, G and Moore, N (1997) *Studying Abroad: A guide to accessible university programs and facilities for students with disabilities: USA and Canada*, University of New Orleans, New Orleans

Hopkins, C and Jones, A (1998) *Able Scientist, Technologist: Disabled person*, Nottingham Trent University, Nottingham

Pointon, A and Davies, C (eds) (1997) *Framed: Interrogating disability in the media*, British Film Institute, London

Quality Assurance Agency for Higher Education (QAA) (1999) *Code of Practice: Students with disabilities*, QAA, Gloucester (accessible through URL: www.QAA.ac.uk)

Scottish Higher Education Funding Council (SHEFC) (2000) *Teachability: Creating an accessible curriculum for students with disabilities*, University of Strathclyde, Glasgow (URL: www.ispn.gcal.ac.uk/teachability)

Van Acker, M (1996) *Studying Abroad: Checklist of needs for students with disabilities*, Katholik University of Leuven, Leuven

13 | Harnessing Information Technology for Learning

Su White and Hugh Davis

> There is nothing more difficult to plan, more doubtful of success, nor more dangerous to manage than the creation of a new system. For the initiator has the enmity of all who would profit by the preservation of the old system, and merely lukewarm defenders in those who should gain by the new one.
>
> *(Niccolo Machiavelli, 1513)*

INTRODUCTION

Machiavelli's statement is very apt for the context of introducing communications and information technology (C&IT) into learning and teaching in higher education.

This chapter suggests that the issues facing academics who are in a position to consider integrating C&IT, across a course or on a departmental-wide basis, are more complex than those associated with similar innovations made in the context of an individual's personal teaching commitment. (See White (1999) for suggestions about getting started in using C&IT in teaching in an individual context.) The remainder of this chapter presents an outline of processes that can be used to work through the change process in a systematic way, along with some tools which may help in this activity.

FRONT-LOADED CHANGE

While there may be a chance for long-term savings in time and energy through introducing widespread use of technology to support learning and teaching, change agents need to be especially sensitive to the 'front-loading' of academic effort required. Such effort is needed to plan, introduce and review the impact of technologically-oriented innovations. If large-scale changes are to be brought about effectively, there is a need to meet the often hidden costs that go alongside this loading. Large-scale changes necessarily mean the involvement of a (sometimes large) number of academics, and will impact on a wide cross-section of the student body. There are likely to be further demands on overstretched resources, especially the time of academics and support staff, never mind any needs for support and development to enable new systems to be brought into use effectively.

The plans and new methods will have to be supported by new equipment and perhaps additional staff to maintain and support the use of that equipment. There may be a need to specify, purchase and install new systems (computers, software printers, scanners, networks etc), or to work within the institution to champion the changes. Academics may have to make a business case for their proposals to secure funds and to win the hearts and minds of colleagues to work collectively to gain support for any additional investments required by the proposed changes. Budget planning will need to be incorporated into the process, and full costing undertaken.

Motivations for moving towards greater use of technology in learning and teaching will vary according to context. Some individuals will be the instigators of technology-oriented change. They may have reflected on the organization of their department or their programmes, and concluded that some kinds of innovation driven by the use of C&IT will enhance their current practices and performance.

Others may find they are to some extent being driven by external motivations, perhaps institutional or professional (see Chapters 1 and 2), and that neither they nor their colleagues are totally convinced that the changes they are set to embark upon are right or bound to succeed. Such reservations may well be encountered in a more concrete form along the way, when they may find themselves subjected to warnings in the form of those clichés which go hand in hand with the doubts, and foot dragging designed to slow change. It may be implied that while it is very noble to be considering such changes, they have of course been tried before. Colleagues may refer to a previous review 'that was done ten years ago' and resulted in changes which made no difference. They may warn that 'if it ain't broke don't fix it', pointing out that people are in danger of 'reinventing the wheel'.

In any of these circumstances, an approach which takes an ordered review of and subsequent attack on the issues should enable individuals to gain some control over their position and provide them with an individualized plan with which they can set about making change. They will also need to put together ad hoc teams of people committed to achieving the change, and willing to do the work necessary to counter the negative arguments that might be encountered on the way.

From the point of view of the programme, course or department, there will need to be some consideration of whether C&IT-based systems should or could be best used to improve the educational, pastoral or administrative aspects of the student experience (see Chapter 10). It is also worth considering to what extent it is possible easily to decouple these three aspects. There will be a need to decide which changes are most likely to have the most impact, what can be managed within the budget, and what can be achieved within a reasonable timescale.

It is important to remember that for individual academics the skills, knowledge and understanding that they have of teaching and supporting learning are probably their most powerful tools when it comes to integrating technology into learning and teaching. In a similar way the most effective tools available to academics setting about change in a course or department will be those which they can effectively harness in their existing practice (Geoghegan, 1994). Managing change related to technology is merely a special case of managing change, and they would be well advised to look both at the examples in the rest of this book, and at the existing and extensive literature (for example Kiesler and Sproull, 1987). They should also look to their own knowledge, skills and expertise as well as that possessed by their colleagues.

STARTING OFF

In order to identify the issues which need to be addressed, it may be helpful to examine the change process by way of asking a series of interrelated questions:

- What change do we need?
- How will we do it?
- When will we do it?
- How (and when) will we review it?

It is often useful to move through the questions successively, refining our ideas of what we want to do and how we are going to set about doing it. This is because when dealing with new approaches, concepts and ideas, our understanding will become increasingly more sophisticated as we gain familiarity with the issues. It may be helpful to consider the first question, from your own perspective, before reading further.

> ## Enhancing Practice
>
> Consider what types of change you think are needed to learning and teaching in the course for which you have responsibility/oversight. Remember to think around this area broadly, including information from evaluation of courses and things such as recruitment and student profile.

Once you have started to consider what/if change might be desirable, you will find it necessary to consult and to consider how, when and to what effect change might be introduced. It is also necessary, specifically, to consider the part C&IT may play in addressing the identified areas, whether it can bring further benefits not previously identified as 'needed change', and what role it plays generally in the institution. The questions suggested in Figures 4.13.1 and 4.13.2 provide some indication of the breadth and depth likely to be needed at this preparatory stage.

Figure 4.13.1 Questions and reflections on the current situation

Probably the first question we should ask ourselves is 'Where are we now?' The list below has been derived from some tools originally designed by the TALENT project (see Web resources at end of chapter) funded by the Teaching and Learning Technology Programme to collect knowledge and experience of using the Web for teaching and learning institution-wide.

Learning and teaching:

- What use is being made of C&IT (teaching, admin, student support)?
- What do we want to achieve through using C&IT?
- What are the predominant approaches to learning and teaching?

Infrastructure:

- What is the current C&IT provision for students?
- What is the current C&IT provision for staff?
- What is the level of technical support?

Stakeholders:

- Who are your key stakeholders?
- What are attitudes of academics to technology for learning and teaching?

- Who is providing the greatest driver for change?

Context:

- How is the balance between research and teaching/learning addressed?
- How does local organization impact on likely changes (eg academic focus, scale or unit, institutional model devolved/centralized)?
- What central support is available to support teaching and learning technology?
- What other factors may be particular to your context?
- What is already provided in your institution, in terms of teaching and learning technology support and strategic direction?
- Are there efforts in your computing service, central services, library or within departments to support teaching and learning technology?
- What relevant staff development support is there (for both academic staff and support staff)?
- Are any workshops or seminars on offer in your institution's staff development programme?
- Do you have links with other academic groups or outside initiatives in its efforts to implement teaching and learning technology?

Figure 4.13.2 Framework for an IT learning and teaching audit

---

The following questions are designed to be used as a basis for discussion/exploration:

Strategy and policy

- Does the department have a printed strategy on the development of the use of IT?
- Does the department have a printed strategy on the development of good practice in learning and teaching (L&T)?
- Does the department have a printed policy for the use of IT?
- Does the department have a printed policy on L&T?
- Does the department have a printed policy of the use of IT in L&T?
- Is there any policy of reward/recognition for innovations in L&T?
- How do these strategies and policies relate to the university's strategies and policies?
- How old is each of these?
- How often are they updated?
- To what extent are they being implemented?
- How are the documents available? Restricted circulation/departmental circulation/university-wide/circulation on paper/on the Web?
- If no strategies or policies exist, are there plans to develop any of the above?

Provision

- What is the balance between departmental provision and central provision?
- What use is made of other central provision for IT in L&T? Computing service/library/other learner support?
- What is the ratio of IT support staff per student?
- What is the ratio of IT support staff per staff member?

- Where do students/staff access departmental IT? (See also hardware/software.)
- What is the ratio of students to computers?
- What is the ratio of staff to computers?
- What kind of machines does the department use? Age, platform, software set-up?
- What is the level of IT literacy among department staff?
- What access to the network do students have? Centralized/cross-campus/24 hours/halls of residence/dial up?
- What proportion of students have e-mail?
- What IT support is there? Help desks/24 hour helpline/library support/L&T support?

Organization

- At what level of seniority does IT planning take place?
- What proportion of the total budget is for IT?
- Which academic in the department is responsible for IT in L&T?
- Does the department have a L&T centre/initiative?
- Are there any departmental/faculty/university/externally funded projects involved in IT and L&T?
- Are there any departmental/faculty/university/externally funded projects in good practice and L&T?
- What formal/informal networks of enthusiasts/champions exist?
- Who takes responsibility in the department for producing Web pages? Individuals/technical support/secretarial support staff/no one (in percentages)?
- Who takes responsibility for finding and installing external software for departmental use? Individual academics/technical support/some team/committee (identify composition)/no one?
- Who is responsible for producing new interactive L&T resources? Individual academics/technical support/ team/committee (identify composition)/no one?

Practice

- How does the management team make use of IT?
- How do the support staff make use of IT?
- How do the academic staff make use of IT?

In each case is use limited, individual, integrated, extensive?

- Does the department make use of IT for internal communications? Limited/extensive/sporadic?
- What percentage of all staff and of each set of staff has IT connectivity?
- Is there a programme to develop IT skills for staff?
- Does the department benchmark its efforts and success in using IT for L&T?

It may be necessary to ask the following as an overview and for each course:

- How much is IT integrated into the curriculum?
- How often do students use IT in learning?
- How often do students use IT in assignments?
- How often are students required to use IT in assignments?

- Is there a programme of IT skills for students?
- Do students have access to e-mail?
- Do students have access to the Internet?
- What is the level of use of the Internet for L&T?
- How in the teaching programme is IT generally used? Administration, information, tutorial?
- What strategies are employed for supporting student learning with IT?
- Does the department have any special initiatives that relate to IT in L&T or good practice in teaching? Internal/external funded?

Much needed or wanted change can be identified and achieved through curriculum and administrative review followed by the adoption of a strategic approach to learning and teaching innovation. We would all relish the opportunity to make better use of academic time and to enhance the student experience. Whether we are taking forward a personal plan, or have been instructed to make the changes as part of a department or institution-wide initiative, making such changes is no small matter.

Change at a programme, course or departmental level can be most effectively implemented when it is driven from both the top down and the bottom up. This means that alongside a strategic approach to changing practice, activity needs to be cultivated that will provide examples of good practice. This will help to build confidence throughout the community that change will work.

Sometimes the starting point for making a large-scale change to the use of technology-supported learning and teaching comes from a product point of view. It may be expressed as a thought, intent, formal decision or a policy to make use of a particular product, for example a virtual learning environment, an automated assessment tool, a student information system or a range of courseware. If we are to make effective and strategic use of technology we need to first ask the question, 'What changes do we want to make?'

The consideration of products may be very useful in helping us clarify our ideas of what can be possible with new technology. (See also the next section of the chapter.) It is important to perform an analysis and consult with colleagues to determine needs, and to check that we are driven by agreed needs rather than product wants. Over-emphasis on what the products can do and under-emphasis on learning and teaching needs and benefits do not make a good basis for successful use of C&IT.

From the top down it is important to conduct a needs analysis, asking questions such as, 'What do we do already? What works? What could be improved? What changes might we want to introduce?' Meet, consult and discuss with colleagues to find out their views, what they want and what they think the organization needs. Find out what peers do both in your own institution, and in comparator and competitor institutions/faculties/ departments. As well as using your own network of contacts to find this information, the Learning and Teaching Support Network may be able to assist you in this area. (See the 'Resources' section below.)

Seek out good practice. Go with colleagues to visit other departments and institutions, and gently also research bad practice: find out what failed, why it failed. Conferences can be a good source of investigating and discussing possible ways forward. As well as the support networks, various sources of information from both the UK and United States may help at this stage. Details of some of these can be found at the end of the chapter under 'Resources'.

One additional consideration is whether you will have to harmonize your technology-based innovations with existing institution-wide systems. For example, you might be restricted to particular software, or need to use a system that can interface with your existing student information system. In this case you may well need to broaden the range of colleagues with whom you collaborate in working through your needs analysis.

Enhancing Practice

You may find it helpful to distil from the above up to 10 major steps that you are likely to need to take in the course of introducing/extending the power of C&IT in teaching and learning in your department/institution. You may wish to order these steps so as to create your own flow diagram or route map of the process. (Each of the major steps may then require its own sub-parts.)

WHAT CAN C&IT DO?

At a more detailed level, it may be helpful to contemplate what area of focus will be most suitable for introducing change. Changes can fall into three broad areas: learning, course administration, and learning and pastoral support. Each of these areas to some extent overlaps with the others.

Learning innovations can encompass replacing existing teaching, designing new courses and enhancing existing courses. It covers the introduction of distance learning courses, and flexible (mixed-mode) learning and teaching. At its most overarching extent it covers important-sounding projects such as virtual universities and e-learning projects. At a lower level of detail it can cover the introduction or integration of courseware, automated assessment, virtual learning environments, Web-based learning, video conferencing, Web-based conferencing, portals, virtual libraries and self-access learning resources.

Course administration innovations can encompass electronic coursework submission, electronic file exchange, learner progress tracking, online publication of course handbooks and staff support materials (eg quality guidelines, learning and teaching strategies). Pastoral/learner support can be provided by many of the computer applications mentioned above.

Particular applications can be provided through means such as customized information systems, e-mail, online tutorials, answer gardens and online key skills courses. Table 4.13.1 defines these terms.

Table 4.13.1   Types of technology-based learning and teaching

Answer gardens	A means of providing and growing a set of answers which relate to an area of study, information that may be key to the course of study, or in associated areas. Answers are held on a database with a system in place for seeking new answers to questions not already in the database.
Automated assessment	For self-test, formative tests, and summative tests. Results from tests can be fed back into a student information database. If the system is to be used for summative testing, issues of unique student identification and encryption of responses have to be addressed.
Courseware	Computer system devised specifically to teach a particular academic topic.
e-learning projects	Individual initiatives which make use of learning technologies to enable the provision of electronic (remote or local) learning resources.
Electronic coursework submission	A system for accepting, monitoring and tracking student submission of coursework, usually implemented via a Web-based system.
Electronic file exchange	Methods for providing and receiving information.
Learner progress tracking	Provides information for a student information database indicating progress through the course. Sophisticated systems may alert learners or tutors of unexpected levels of progress.
Portals	A Web page or set of pages which provides a broad range of links to information sources with additional services such as customized search engines.
Self-access learning resources	Structured texts: effectively digital versions of traditional paper-based course materials.
Video conferencing	Use of video via a computer system which can be used to enable face-to-face activities between learners and instructors at a distance. Uses include individual tutorials, master classes and remote lecturing.

Web-based conferencing	Use of computer system to enable collaborative working at a distance. Uses include integration of live discussion boards, working on shared applications (word processing, drawings), visual sketchpad via a 'whiteboard'.
Web-based learning	Used to cover a range of applications from simple publishing of lecture notes on Web pages through to more comprehensive offerings such as those outlined in the virtual learning environments definition.
Virtual learning environments	Systems that incorporate a range of facilities such as Web authoring, conferencing, e-mail, assessment and learner tracking. Designed to be more accessible for academics to create an onine course, and to provide the learners with all the different activities through a single viewpoint.
	An integrated set of tools in a consistent format, giving us a single multi-function environment.
Virtual universities	Integrated use of learning technologies with electronic administrative systems to enable entire university courses to be followed electronically from registration through to graduation.

HOW IT CAN BE DONE

Once you have identified the changes that you believe you need to make, you may find it helpful to draw up a list of drivers and barriers for change. Once again this activity may be undertaken individually or with colleagues in some form of consultation process. Decisions will have to be made as to how far barriers (eg financial) will compromise the desired change and its possible outcomes.

Enhancing Practice

- Identify drivers and barriers to change.
- When you have completed your first attempt, take the list of the various drivers and barriers and see if you can cluster any of the components. Rank the different factors in order of their strength and then identify the three most important drivers and the three most important barriers.

Setting the drivers and the barriers alongside the needs analysis will give you a framework from which you can move forward to devise a strategy to bring about the changes you need.

The next step will be to work with your colleagues to make a first attempt at defining your strategy for the changes you wish to make.

Although the changes proposed may not be institution-wide, a useful reference source, details of which can be extrapolated to the smaller-scale context, is the set of institutional learning and teaching strategies and their associated case studies collected by the national co-ordination team for the Higher Education Funding Council for England (HEFCE)'s Teaching Quality Enhancement Fund. (See the 'Resources' section below.)

Organizing an out-of-office working day to review and develop these ideas after their initial drafting, perhaps with an external facilitator, may be a very productive approach to working through this part of the process. If you are going to make major changes which impact on the curriculum you may need to ring-fence some time for a team of individuals to work together planning the detail of the changes and their implementation. You may identify shortages in the skills of existing staff as a major barrier to change. In this case you may have to decide between developing the skills of existing staff and making new appointments to fulfil your new objectives. You will also need to address how and from where monetary resource for change will be available.

Key issues to consider when introducing technology into learning and teaching are the ways in which it is to be integrated into existing activities. Technology-based activities which are simply bolted on to the existing programme are unlikely to make any impact. Similarly it is important to schedule a period of trialling and evaluation of the innovations, and to be prepared to modify the new practices in the light of feedback from both staff and students who are involved with the new system.

WHEN IT SHOULD BE DONE

Start as soon as possible, but not before you are happy with your planning process. Probably the most difficult aspect of making changes that relate to the use of learning technology is fitting the change with the tempo of the academic year and with institutional and departmental academic planning. Major changes that impact on the curriculum will probably need to go through the committee system in your institution. You will need to identify and free staff time to support this type of activity. If you need extra staff there will be institutional administration plus the need to schedule advertisements, shortlisting, recruitment and training.

HOW (AND WHEN) IT SHOULD BE REVIEWED

With a large-scale major innovation it may be wise to seek an external evaluator who can act as a critical friend to your project. If you are proposing major curriculum innovations you may wish to discuss them with your external examiner. You will also be able to analyse and reflect upon student feedback via your normal unit or programme evaluations. The Learning Technologies Dissemination Initiative produced a useful and extensive guide to evaluation, and a version of this book can be downloaded from the Web for printing. (See Harvey, 1998). You will probably also be interested to discover whether any proposed timesavings have been achieved, and it will be useful to perform a staff time audit. Having made the changes you may want to organize some kind of show and tell with colleagues to get their feedback, and to plan the next thing you are going to do.

Using WebCT at the University of North London
by David Andrew

I have used WebCT on a large HND module with about 300 students in the Business School. WebCT is supported by the University of North London as the virtual learning environment (VLE) of choice. Because of this, some of the issues about introducing technology (eg computing support) were taken care of. Other types of issue remained. I was neither a 'lone academic', nor directing a whole course team in their use of technology.

The positive reasons for choosing to use a VLE were:

- Lectures were not an effective way of getting across the information.
- I was finding the lectures difficult to control and not enjoyable.
- I wanted to encourage the students to use electronic communication for their group work.
- I wanted to try it out.

I introduced the use of WebCT in week 4 of the semester, in the context of discussing the problems of the lectures. This is perhaps not the best way to introduce the change but it meant I had an opportunity to explore the issues with the students. Some students were immediately keen, others clearly unhappy. Objections ranged from the fact that they would miss the contact with me, to wishing to keep the traditional way of doing things. One student said something like, 'We come, you put things on the OHP, we write them down and that's it!' We agreed that while I would put the lecture content onto WebCT I would still be in the lecture theatre for a discussion.

I found that:

- I enjoyed preparing the content and used a number of links to Web sites.
- I put up a crossword to check understanding of the text book and was surprised that it was the favourite page for quite a while.
- Tracking of students' activities was very useful, in terms of pages viewed and the activity of particular students.
- It was interesting to see a clear relationship between number of log-ins and marks for the module.
- I enjoyed the electronic communication with the students.

In evaluation of the modules:

- Students mostly enjoyed the experience of using the programme.
- Students enjoyed the electronic communication.
- Students still missed the contact. Interestingly the attendance at the discussions which took place instead of the lecture did not reflect this! Again at least two of the forms referred to one-to-one contact with the lecturer in lectures. So we may see it as one to 300, while students see it as one to one.
- Some felt I wasn't doing my job!

What was difficult about WebCT was the cumbersome process of adding files, which for someone who likes to change what they are doing is not easy. Tracking students is difficult if the system is not set up to enable sorting of students into seminar groups to make it manageable.

I have now passed the module on to a colleague who is still using the WebCT structure. The WebCT programme is now used to supplement a lecture programme and continues to be well used and popular with students.

I am not using WebCT at the moment. For general support for my modules I use a general Web site. I am using a knowledge management system (LiveLink) for one of my modules, which I find more flexible than WebCT, but it does not allow for student tracking in the same way. I would use WebCT where I wanted to track students closely and where the module is not in need of constant updating. The original experience of using technology has been invaluable in developing my own ideas and understanding, not only in the use of C&IT but about teaching and learning in general.

OVERVIEW

This chapter has presented the process of harnessing C&IT to support learning as a series of questions to which answers have to be sought. It has emphasized the large and 'up front' time and resource that is likely to be needed. It will have been evident that the route and process are likely to have involved compromise (for example, between cost and benefit). Harnessing C&IT in the context of a new course or department may be easier than when amending existing structures. The importance of understanding what the technology can do, and winning hearts and minds in the change process, have been emphasized. But the bottom line is that a largely pedagogical perspective should not be lost.

REFERENCES

Geoghegan, WH (1994) Whatever happened to instructional technology?, paper given at the 22nd Annual Conference of the International Business Schools Computing Association, IBM Baltimore, Md

Kiesler, S and Sproull, L (1987) *Computing and Change on Campus*, Cambridge University Press, Cambridge

White, S (1999) Using information technology for teaching and learning', in *A Handbook for Teaching and Learning in Higher Education: Enhancing academic practice*, ed H Fry, S Ketteridge and S Marshall, Kogan Page, London

FURTHER READING

Hall, W and White, S (1997) Teaching and learning technology: shifting the culture, in *Facing Up to Radical Change in Universities and Colleges*, ed BS Armstrong and G Thompson, Kogan Page, London

Harvey, J (1998) *LTDI Evaluation Cookbook*, ICBL Heriot Watt University, Edinburgh (*http://www.icbl.hw.ac.uk/ltdi/ltdi-pub.htm*)

Oblinger, DG and Verville, A-L (1999) Information technology as a change agent, *Educom Review*, January

Ramsden, P (1998) *Learning to Lead in Higher Education*, Routledge, London

White, S (1997) Shifting the culture: models of institutional change, *Technology in Teaching and Learning: Some senior management issues, Teaching and Learning Technology Programme*, vol 1, pp 10–11

Yorke, M, McCormack, D *et al* (1996) *HE2005+: Towards a sectoral strategy for teaching and learning in higher education*, Higher Education Funding Council for England, Bristol

RESOURCES

The TQEF national coordination team (*http://www.ncteam.ac.uk/*) is responsible for work in the area of learning and teaching strategies, and works with projects concerned with good practice and innovation in learning and teaching and learning technologies. For examples of institutional learning and teaching strategies see *http://www.ncteam.ac.uk/ilts/examples/index.html*. You will also find a range of case studies which may be of interest.

The Learning and Teaching Support Network (LTSN *http://www.ltsn.ac.uk/*) consists of 24 centres across the disciplines, a generic centre and a technologies centre, funded by the Joint Information Systems Committee (JISC) to investigate and develop new technologies in higher and further education.

The TALENT project (*http://www.le.ac.uk/TALENT/*) has designed resources to support managers in the introduction and use of technology in learning and teaching.

The TLT (*http://www.tltgroup.org*) group is part of the American Association for Higher Education. It offers resources, discussion round tables, and also hosts the Flashlight Project which is concerned with the evaluation of the use of learning technology.

The Joint Information Systems Committee (JISC *http://www.jisc.ac.uk/*) promotes the innovative application and use of information systems and information technology in higher and further education across the UK. It runs a number of services, runs information and dissemination events and provides a range of publications including a series of management briefing papers and guidance documents. It offers a support and advisory service via JISC ASSiST (*http://www.jisc.ac.uk/assist/index.html*). Updates on current JISC activities can be obtained through subscription to their mailing list *JISC-ANNOUNCE@JISCMAIL.AC.UK*.

The Universities and Colleges Information Services Association (UCISA, *http://www.ucisa.ac.uk/*) is a representative group for higher education with a special focus on information services/computing services departments. It has a number of activity areas of relevance and useful to learning and teaching technologies, notably the teaching, learning and information group: *http://www.ucisa.ac.uk/TLIG/*, and the staff development group, *http://www.ucisa.ac.uk/SDG/*

Part 5
The Harsh
Reality

Introduction

The Editors with Johanna Laybourn-Parry and Mervyn King

This part of the book examines the harsh reality of pursuing and benefiting from an academic career, in an increasingly pressurized environment. Academics have long been implicit lifelong learners in respect of their research activity, although many would not consider using the term in this way. Similarly, for research, the notion of continuing professional development has been implicit: either it happens, or one ceases to be a research leader. Academics who are also members of other professions (if being an academic is a profession) are also used to an externally-verifiable notion of continuing professional development. However, academics have generally not adopted a similar approach to other aspects of academic practice, namely teaching, management and career development. Continuing professional development is arguably a term not unrelated to lifelong learning. Both concepts are often poorly defined and subject to 'political' interpretation, with lifelong learning high on the government's agenda. These notions, coupled with the generally unsystematic, unplanned and ad hoc nature of most academic careers, form the backdrop to this part.

Chapter 14, written by Gus Pennington and Brenda Smith, attempts to define continuing professional development, and offers some models against which academics may wish to compare their own experiences. Chapter 15, 'Making Choices: Routes to Success', by the editors, considers changing views of academic life and academe as a career.

The 'personal perspective' of Professor Laybourn-Parry, Professor of Environmental Biology, University of Nottingham, shows how an initially unfocused approach changed to a highly successful, focused and strategic approach, primarily going down the research route. At the other end of the spectrum, other academics use their burgeoning academic career as the springboard into other walks of life, as highlighted in the 'personal perspective' of Mervyn King, former Professor of Economics at the London School of Economics (LSE) and now Deputy Governor of the Bank of England.

Setting the Scene – A Personal Perspective
by Johanna Laybourn-Parry

My brilliant career?

I grew up on a council estate in Swansea, failed the 11-plus and languished for four years in a very down-market secondary modern school. Repeated childhood illness prevented me from attending school until I was eight. I was virtually illiterate when I started school properly. I did not catch up the lost ground in time for the dreaded 11-plus, and was cast on the rubbish heap of the educational system. However, luck intervened, as it has done many times in my career. Swansea obviously had a director of education with vision who felt that all children should leave school with a certificate. All secondary modern pupils sat what was known as the Swansea Certificate. Those of us who excelled were offered the opportunity to attend a technical school to do O' levels. I stayed on to take A' levels and was one of only two girls in my year who went to university. The technical school was not an institution with high academic standards, but it was better than nothing, and it provided an entrée to another world. My parents were somewhat perplexed by the cuckoo in their nest, and were not altogether clear what a university was, but to their great credit they encouraged and supported me. Fortunately in the 1960s there were full grants for working-class kids like me. I tell this story because my childhood experiences and my unlikely start have shaped my character, which in turn has contributed to my career success. I learnt early that the key is to grasp the opportunities that chance your way, and fully exploit them.

When I went up to Reading University, I was so pleased with myself that I would have been content with a pass degree. However, I did moderately well, despite being significantly distracted by my future husband. Armed with an upper second, and encouraged by my tutor Elizabeth Johnson, I took myself off to University College North Wales to do a Master's degree with no particular object in mind. It was during that year that I developed a passion for research and discovered that I had a talent for it. Thus I stumbled into an academic career, a PhD and all the rest.

The profession was, and still is, dominated by men. In the 30 years I have worked in science, the culture has stayed much the same in the UK. There are few senior women in our universities. The fact that I am a polar scientist puts me into an even smaller minority. My first chair was in Australia where women fare much better than they do in the UK. I crashed through the glass ceiling. I was given challenging tasks, encouraged to develop new initiatives and learnt a great deal about management. Importantly, I gained a lot of confidence. In 1996 family circumstances forced my return to the UK. I was lucky in securing a chair at Nottingham University. However, without the Australian experience I would have found my new position less easy to cope with. My faculty had never had a female professor before. I was clearly expected to keep my mouth shut and do as I was told. I was disinclined to play that game. I am sure I have irritated a significant number of people in my five years at Nottingham, but apparently not the ones that matter, because I was made the head of a new school in 2000.

My observations indicate that effective women get on just as well as men do. The lack of senior women has little to do with discrimination and a lot to do with the difficulties of combining an academic career with child-rearing. The profession in the UK is not family friendly. The greatest loss of women from science occurs at the postdoctoral level. This is the point when they recognize the price they will have to pay for the glittering prizes. Many successful women in science and technology are childless, and very often single. I am childless (my choice – I was standing at the end of the queue when Mother Nature was dispensing the maternal instinct genes), and I am divorced. Despite being told by many younger women that I am a role model, I do not think that a woman who is childless, single and spends part of her time working in some of the most remote, God-awful places in the world is a good role model. This is a very unsuitable job for a woman. I have enjoyed science and academia, it has given me an exciting life. However, I have paid a price for it in terms of my private life. I pray that future generations of women may have an easier time, but there will have to be a radical change of employment culture before that happens.

My Career Path – A Personal Perspective by Mervyn King

Most of the turns in my career have been unexpected, and perhaps for that reason, rewarding. At school in Wolverhampton my interest was physics and mathematics. But, handicapped by a lack of natural ability in practical experiments, I decided to look for new outlets where mathematics might be valuable. My interests in cosmology were transferred to economics. At that time my school, in common with most, did not teach economics. So I was able to embark on a new subject full of enthusiasm. A key factor in my commitment to both economics and a career as an academic was the sense of excitement imparted by my teachers in Cambridge. The late 1960s was a good time to be embarking on a career in economics, and the atmosphere in Cambridge proved inspiring to a number of us who embarked on research careers at that time.

After a first degree and two years of postgraduate study in the Department of Applied Economics, I secured a Kennedy scholarship to visit Harvard for a year. That year was a turning point in my career. First, I learnt that research was truly international. To be successful in research one had not only to learn about what was happening elsewhere in the world, but to be ready to compete with academics from the United States and elsewhere. The international stage is the only one to play on if one is serious about a research career. Second, the different styles of economics in Cambridge Massachusetts and Cambridge England complemented each other well, and it was important to be trained in both. Third, I made friendships, both personal and professional, which have stood the test of time and were invaluable in my subsequent career both as an academic and later in the world of policy-making.

On returning to the UK after my stay at Harvard, I spent almost 20 years as an academic teaching in Cambridge, Birmingham and the London School of Economics. During that time I returned regularly to the United States and was a visiting professor at both Harvard and MIT. I did not spend more than about five years in any one place, and on reflection I think I have benefited from the fresh stimulus that new pastures offered.

I learnt also that, at the best universities, teaching and research were complements, not alternatives. Of course, an impossibly high teaching and/or administrative burden will undermine any research effort, but an ability to communicate ideas is crucial if those ideas are to have an impact on the way others think.

During my research career, my interests gradually evolved from a primary focus on public economics, especially taxation, towards a wider interest in public policy and its link with financial markets. Together with Charles Goodhart, I started a research centre at the LSE, the LSE Financial Markets Group, which not only provided a focus for the research interests of academics and students alike, but also offered a platform for our work on issues related to public policy. In 1990 I was offered the chance to become a non-executive director of the Bank of England, and later that year was offered the position of chief economist. I accepted it for a limited period, intending to return to the LSE. But, in one of those unexpected turns, in September 1992 sterling was ejected from the Exchange Rate Mechanism. A new framework for monetary policy was needed. At that point the contributions of economists became more important. The UK introduced an inflation target, and the Bank of England started publishing its *Inflation Report* – the first truly independent voice of the Bank of England on monetary policy for a very long time. Gradually, the work of the Bank became higher profile and well respected.

In 1997 the incoming Labour government granted independence in respect of monetary policy to the Bank, and created a new Monetary Policy Committee. I was made Deputy Governor. Several of my former academic friends and colleagues joined me on the Monetary Policy Committee. The new monetary policy framework in the UK has attracted a great deal of interest from around the world. One feature has been of particular interest to economists. The Monetary Policy Committee comprises nine members, and the majority of these are professional economists with a distinguished academic background. The committee probably has the longest publications record of any monetary policy decision-making body in the world! And the Bank of England recruits a large number of PhD and Masters students each year to form the analytical base for the work of the Bank. Policy making does require research of the highest calibre. At the Bank of England the standards of research are as high as in the academic world, although they are clearly rather narrowly focused on the needs of the Bank. There is a natural partnership between the Bank of England and the academic community of economists around the world.

This experience has led me to conclude that an academic career can open up many more options than is sometimes believed. First, research in itself is a truly international activity, and it is important to feel part of an international community. Second, much research nowadays requires teams which need to be managed. Management of research, in contrast to much of what has become known as university administration, offers real challenges and the opportunity to develop new skills. Third, many of the qualities required for success in academic life are, contrary to widely-held views, very useful in activities outside universities. When a new policy needs to be devised, the best minds come into their own. This is true not just in the UK, so academic friends and colleagues overseas may prove extremely useful contacts in other spheres. I have continually been surprised at how many former academic colleagues have moved into the economic policy world, where our earlier friendships have become extremely valuable in our new roles.

So the only advice I would offer is – keep hoping for the unexpected. And remember that the reason academics look young is because they keep on learning.

14 Career-Long Competence: Unattainable Ideal or Professional Requirement?

Gus Pennington and Brenda Smith

INTRODUCTION

> CPD is any process or activity that provides added value to the capability of the professional through the increase in knowledge, skills and personal qualities necessary for the appropriate execution of professional and technical duties. It is a life-long tool that benefits the professional, client, employer, colleagues, professional associations and society as a whole. CPD is a professional responsibility and an appropriate expectation placed on the professional by those likely to benefit from it. CPD is particularly relevant during periods of rapid technological and occupational change.
>
> *(PARN, 2000: 14)*

This chapter is based on an understanding that universities and other institutions of higher education are complex organizations operating in a challenging, dynamic and volatile environment. This being the case, institutional staff, whatever their age or specific expertise, need to engage with continuing professional development (CPD) to ensure they are competent to perform both their current roles (maintenance learning) and foreseeable future demands (anticipatory learning). A further assumption is that the responsibility to remain professionally competent throughout an individual's career is one that should properly be shared between the individual and his or her employer. This goal is only achievable, the authors maintain, if individuals, working groups and organizations are committed to dialogue, reflection and the use of formal mechanisms to identify, pursue and evaluate CPD activities. (See Mabey and Iles (1994).)

The chapter aims to:

- inform and help individuals in the early to mid-point of their careers to think about a range of issues central to effective engagement with CPD;
- highlight the need for a systematic, reflective and holistic approach to CPD which reconciles the interests of different parties;
- suggest practical ways in which individuals and institutions might tackle the process of engaging with appropriate activities.

A thread running throughout the chapter is that being knowledgeable about, committed to and competent to perform to the demands of one's role is the fundamental hallmark of any individual claiming professional status. It is recognized that sustaining professional competence throughout a career is challenging, particularly against a turbulent or fast-moving backcloth. To be effective and satisfying, CPD requires effort and perseverance from individuals and an institutional culture which prioritizes, values and manages work-based learning strategically.

Ideally, CPD should cover the *full* range of responsibilities and duties academics undertake in their role. Typically, this will involve a mix of administrative, research, teaching, management and other tasks which individuals are solely or jointly responsible for delivering and evaluating. Striking an appropriate balance of CPD across responsibilities is sometimes difficult, and it is not uncommon to find individuals committing more time to one or two favoured areas of work and ignoring or paying cursory attention to others. Staying competent and up to date across the range requires balance, planning and personal discipline.

WHAT IS MEANT BY CPD AND WHAT THE ISSUES ARE

According to the Institute of Personnel and Development (1997):

> CPD is systematic, ongoing, self-directed learning. It is an approach or process which should be a normal part of how you plan and manage your whole working life. CPD is *continuing* because learning never ceases, regardless of age or seniority. It is professional because it is focused on personal competence in a professional role. It is concerned with development because its goal is to improve personal performance and enhance career progression.

Activity which is both continuous and developmental implies engagement through time; a concern with the here and now *and* future states or contexts.

Herein lies a potential difficulty. While it is relatively easy to identify what might be required to maintain present levels of competence in a given context (maintenance activities), it is infinitely more difficult to anticipate future demands in an evolving and to some degree unknown environment. This is particularly true in the kind of networked society in which professions no longer enjoy complete control over their own affairs, and in which they are called to account by many legitimate interests (Nicholls, 2001). In networked societies, complexity reigns. For this reason it is inevitable that over the decades of a typical working life there will be peaks, troughs and plateaux in professional expertise. Individuals change, the roles they fulfil are transformed, they seek new roles, and the organizational environments in which they operate are subjected to a variety of pressures which impact on the character, processes and emphases of work.

Some changes in work contexts obviously arise from shifts in individual roles and personal career progression, but many emerge directly from the wider sociopolitical and policy-driven environment within and external to the higher education sector itself. (See also Chapters 1 and 2.)

For individuals thinking about their CPD, personal needs and career aspirations typically interact with professional and organizational imperatives. This creates a rich and extensive set of potential developmental activities in terms of subject updating, enhancement of teaching competence, new demands in scholarship and research, periodic curriculum redesign and support for a diverse range of individual learners. For a majority of academic staff these 'constants' of professional life are also surrounded by a nexus of more contingent activities associated with course administration, management, leadership and community-based responsibilities.

To stay up with the game (or even slightly ahead of it) is demanding of time, energy and commitment: the very ingredients in short supply in turbulent environments. Maintaining expertise in a changing world demands a clear reciprocity between personal investment and institutional resourcing, with the intention that continuous professional development becomes a key, but *normal requirement of all individuals*. In a sector marked by flux and complexity in which responsiveness and quality are central features, lack of appropriate CPD opportunities may lead to a dispirited, underperforming workforce, ill-equipped to meet current and future professional requirements. Job satisfaction rarely occurs under these conditions, and careers may become blighted through lack of professional nourishment.

This fact is increasingly being recognized by individuals, institutions, professional bodies, funding councils and government departments. In the UK a number of initiatives have been recently introduced to support the development of staff in a way hitherto unachievable (eg HEFCE, 2000). These developments are welcome, as a great deal of professional development in the past has relied on the goodwill, initiative and persistent endeavour of individuals and their immediate working groups. New times demand new practices (Boud and Solomon, 2001), not least a strategic commitment by institutions to the development of competence in all employees. This is not merely a matter of having appropriate policies and procedures, but of demonstrating enthusiasm, commitment and support for the development of people. Signalling the importance of CPD is part of managerial responsibility. As Dearing so aptly indicated, 'staff often perceive a lack of commitment towards and inadequate funding for their personal development. Whether or not the perception is accurate, it needs to be addressed by institutions' (NCIHE, 1997, para 14.24).

CPD: PUSHED BY THE PAST OR PULLED BY THE FUTURE?

Apart from a minority of individuals who seek explicitly to direct and manage their careers through a predetermined and time-bound plan, most academics' careers follow an indirect, and to some extent, unplanned, route (see Chapter 15). Career advancement rarely follows a simple linear progression from 'novice' to 'expert', and is generally marked by opportunity rather than strategic thinking. In retrospect it is often possible to describe early, mid and late phases to a working life, but frequently the overwhelming sense in reviewing where we have been and where we might be going is one of randomness. It is certainly true that some individuals are positively driven to move onwards and upwards and, equally, that their approach to CPD is strongly influenced by needs for status, recognition and reward.

Some individuals are less overtly ambitious to progress, and take on more organizational responsibilities by steady accretion over the years; yet others adopt a markedly 'interests-driven' approach based on personal satisfaction derived from research and teaching in their chosen discipline. All these approaches (and others involving deliberate avoidance of responsibility) can be found in any group of academic staff. Each approach has its own demands and concerns; each takes a different stance in relation to what are perceived to be worthwhile and necessary CPD activities.

Given that it is not possible for people to develop against their will, it is perfectly reasonable to accept many approaches to CPD based on differing personal goals. The only proviso here is that individuals remain competent to perform their main role and responsive to legitimate organizational requirements. Essentially, the issue is one of balance, fitness for purpose and personal agency. Even so, when reflecting on CPD needs, it is not uncommon for individuals to adopt a short-term here-and-now stance aimed at identifying an area of current 'deficit' requiring some form of 'remedial' action. A more balanced approach (see Candy, 1995) would involve identifying *'maintenance'* needs (that is, what do I need to do to ensure competence in *this* role?) and *'anticipatory'* needs (that is, what knowledge, skills, experiences do I need to move into another role and to manage a successful transition between the two?).

In reality, rational planning is not easy, and CPD too often becomes a bricolage of separate and often ephemeral activities lacking an overarching rationale and organizing framework. Typically, with few exceptions, little attempt is made to reconcile shorter and medium-term objectives, or to mediate between individual, group or corporate goals. A more systematic approach aimed at personal mastery of the kind proposed would involve:

- identifying needs in different domains across the totality of academic practice (for example, in relation to research and scholarship, teaching, assessment, curriculum development, subject updating, course administration, student support and guidance);
- identifying generic needs arising from working with others in an organizational context (for example, committee skills, team-working skills, organizing and planning skills, management and leadership competence);
- mapping specific and generic skills onto early, mid and late career responsibilities to ensure appropriateness of fit;
- establishing mechanisms for both individual review (appraisal) and the alignment of individual needs with departmental and organizational objectives (performance management);
- building a shared vision among stakeholders about the purposes and objectives of CPD, so that individuals across the organization engage in development activities within a coherent human resource development strategy;
- evaluating changes in work-based effectiveness after development activities, and incorporating this learning into subsequent activity (see Bramley, 1996; Guskey, 2000).

Viewing CPD in this way begins to acknowledge the complexity of professional development, the influences which shape it and the need for a multi-layered approach. It also acknowledges that there are a range of stakeholders with a legitimate, equal, but *different*, interest in ensuring that people are competent to undertake their work. Peers, co-professionals, students, senior managers and bodies external to institutions all have an interest in how well individuals and institutions are performing with respect to CPD. More significantly, this approach establishes that the entitlements, rights and responsibilities of different stakeholders need to be mediated, reconciled and managed through appropriate bilateral and multilateral mechanisms. If such mechanisms can be established, individuals and institutions could more accurately talk about *continuous* professional development rather than activities that are discontinuous, fragmentary and incoherent.

ESTABLISHING PRIORITIES AND IDENTIFYING NEEDS

If it is accepted that 1) we live in a complex professional world crammed with competing demands and 2) much of CPD provision presently lacks coherence, a key task becomes the identification and prioritization of individual and institutional CPD needs. Anything less means that CPD as a key component of organizational health, corporate learning, workforce motivation and individual satisfaction is damaged and undermined. In a world awash with competing demands and insufficient resources to service them all, choices have to be made about the relative value of:

- urgent needs versus important needs;
- shorter term needs versus medium/longer term needs;
- 'surface' learning versus 'deeper' learning;
- academic needs versus administrative, management and leadership needs;
- specific learning versus generic transferable learning;
- individual learning versus team learning needs;
- departmental needs versus institutional needs.

CPD activities rooted in organizational demands are often more explicitly, and thus more easily, identified than those relating to individual professional agendas. As Dearing noted:

> We recognize that many institutions have human resource development policies which serve them well. But, in view of the pace of change, the increasing range of demands being placed on staff, and the centrality of their contribution, (policies) will need to be kept under review, to ensure they support institutional priorities.

(NCIHE, 1997 para 14.25)

Just as institutionally-derived needs form part of a corporate agenda, at subject level, quality enhancement imperatives associated with programme review and external assessment (such as QAA academic review or professional body accreditation) generate a plethora of team or subject group CPD needs. The mark of a well-managed environment is that institutional and subject-related CPD needs are transparent, acknowledged and resourced.

Because individual CPD needs are more diffuse, implicit and idiosyncratic, it should not be assumed they are less well regarded or less frequently responded to. A great deal of evidence exists to suggest that significant numbers of academics are committed to evaluating their own performance and are strongly motivated to professional improvement through appropriate review and action. Evidence from different national contexts (Ballantyne *et al*, 1997; Webb and Murphy, 2000) indicates that individuals willingly take up opportunities to reflect on their practice and to join appropriate professional bodies committed to progressing their development needs. Such bodies include subject associations, learning and teaching support networks, learned societies and professional practice-based bodies such as the UK Institute for Learning and Teaching (ILT), the British Psychological Society (BPS) and the Institute of Personnel and Development (IPD: see IPD, 1997). These organizations (and a wide variety of similar ones) have developed guidelines and frameworks to support systematic engagement with CPD in their specialist areas.

There are a number of frameworks which serve the dual purposes of being diagnostic and also allowing individuals to demonstrate and test their competence against specific criteria. The case study below describes one such framework for research staff, for whom many academic heads will have responsibility

---

Electronic Data Collection and Analysis – The CPD Skills Matrix for Research Staff at Loughborough University

As a HEFCE-funded project Loughborough University has developed an easy-to-use electronic recording and planning tool for research staff which enables individuals to profile their skill levels across a comprehensive range of competence categories (for example communication skills, report writing, team working, winning funding, handling the media, managing change). Skills are organized into three groups:

- personal and professional skills;
- general research skills;
- research and additional skills (which includes more discipline-specific items).

These groupings are congruent with those identified by others for effective research activity (Harris, 1995; Webb, 1994).

The tool comes in the form of a self-extracting archive to use on screen or in paper form, and enables staff to collect, analyse and present evidence related to their CPD needs. Guidance notes take users through the matrix and encourage systematic reflection and planning on the basis of a self-assessment of current skill levels within the different groupings.

Descriptors of four levels of competence allow for differentiation on a gradient from 'basic' through 'intermediate' to 'advanced' and 'super'. This gradient also provides targets for progressive attainment. (The skills matrix can be found at http://www.lboro.ac.uk/service/std/skills_matrix.htm.)

Increasingly, CPD requirements – either for external or for quality assurance purposes – will need to be recorded. Given that some academics may have competing requirements made upon them (eg membership of ILT *and* the Royal College of Surgeons), care has to be taken that professional body and 'licence to practise' demands do not become disproportionate or in practical terms mutually exclusive. Nottingham Trent University has attempted to overcome this concern through its 'Individual Development Folder', described in the case study below.

Recording CPD – The Individual Development Folder at Nottingham Trent University

In order to encourage staff to record and draw together information about their training and development activities in a coherent format, Nottingham Trent University has developed a portfolio which is distributed to staff in an A4 ring binder. Organized into 10 sections, the portfolio provides a framework for:

- individual needs analysis and record keeping;
- institutional information related to in-house training and development providers;
- material to prompt reflection and planning.

Like other documents of this kind, the portfolio aims to strike a balance between flexibility and structure, and institutional and personal needs with regard to CPD.

A number of other universities in the UK and elsewhere have introduced CPD portfolios with a range of formats but similar purposes. (See, for example, Baume (1998), Seldin *et al* (1995), O'Neil and Wright (1994), Weeks (1996).) Although these portfolios differ in presentational formats, they share a common intention of stimulating analysis and reflection, and encouraging planning for future action on the basis of evidence collection and recording. The better portfolios also provide a platform for institutions to seriously progress teaching standards.

An equal concern when people reflect on or engage with developmental activities is whether the activities they undertake are appropriate for the outcomes desired. It is a truism that CPD comes in many forms with a variety of objectives. This makes it essential for all those engaged with CPD to identify its purposes and to know clearly what any given activity might achieve. For example:

- What kinds of CPD will ensure continuity of individuals' existing expertise?
  Objective: *Maintenance of competence*.
- What kinds of activities should be undertaken to increase individuals' current repertoire of knowledge and expertise?
  Objective: *Extension of competence*.
- Which elements in individuals' present repertoire of skills need to be improved in quality?
  Objective: *Enhancement of competence*.
- What additional expertise should individuals be acquiring alongside their current repertoire?
  Objective: *Anticipation of future competence*.
- What performances should individuals cease to do to improve their effectiveness?
  Objective: *Removal of negative features/substitution of more appropriate behaviours*.

While some CPD is aimed primarily at imparting new information, other activities seek to develop new attitudes and values; a proportion of activities also aim ambitiously to generate learning which leads to different behaviours and enhanced performances. Self-evidently, these differing kinds of outcome require different time-frames and present individuals with varying degrees of difficulty in terms of their achievement. (See Figure 5.14.1.)

From Figure 5.14.1 it can be appreciated that acquiring new information is relatively easy and normally does not take much time. Getting people to act in different ways, to enter into the idiom of new, complex behaviours or to rehearse performances in a semi-structured, safe environment is more difficult, however, and takes considerably longer. The key message here is that form (the nature of the learning) and function (the means for acquiring that learning) should be aligned. Thus CPD activities can range from the tactical 'quick fix' to more experiential-based approaches aimed at a shift in understandings, attitudes and behaviours. Adept staff developers and skilful individuals who know how to learn use the *whole* range of learning vehicles as circumstances dictate. The also pay particular attention to contextual features of learning by asking the following kinds of questions:

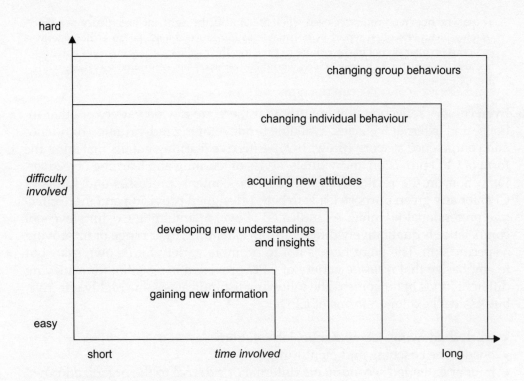

Source: after Hersey and Blanchard (1988)

Figure 5.14.1   Degrees of difficulty in CPD

- What is this learning opportunity intended to achieve?
- Are the learning outcomes appropriate for me/my team/the institution?
- Will I be in a better position actually to use the newly acquired information/skill?
- What ongoing support might be necessary to ensure my newly acquired expertise is effectively embedded?
- What other changes in the wider environment might be necessary to ensure embedding?
- How will the effectiveness of the learning be identified?

Moving beyond courses

While attendance at taught programmes, courses and workshops has a role to play in developing the capacity of individuals to perform more effectively in work contexts, they are not, and cannot be, the sole ingredients of effective CPD provision. Gibbs and Blackmore (1996: 54) capture their drawbacks neatly when they say:

> Those who do attend courses – even when the topic is the right one and even when the training is superb, often report being unable to introduce change because the generic solutions on offer do not fit the culture or practices their colleagues are engaged with, or because the structural changes which would be necessary are controlled by others who are not present.

Even cursory reflection will identify that there are a wide variety of other in-house and external 'vehicles' available for developing individuals' confidence and competence at work (Brew, 1995). Effective learning entails matching the form of CPD provision, individuals' styles of learning and learning objectives. Reflection on the relationship between the content, processes and forms of CPD for any given purpose leads to better-designed provision and more effective professional learning. As indicated above, maintaining existing levels of competence is qualitatively different from extending their range or improving a specific skill. The point here is not to promote variety for its own sake, but to emphasize that *requisite* variety of CPD provision is essential for achieving different kinds of outcomes. The following list indicates some highly effective, but less well exploited forms of CPD:

- work shadowing, job exchange, job rotation;
- one-to-one coaching and mentoring;
- mini or extended secondments (internal or external to the organization);
- preparation of competitive tenders and subsequent project management;
- succession planning, working in parallel, 'tapering' in and out of role;
- planned membership of committees, working parties, professional bodies;
- writing to individual or group publication;
- planned external examining; acting as an academic reviewer/professional body reviewer;
- membership of a facilitated action-learning group;
- leadership of preparation for accreditation or external review;
- three hundred and sixty degree feedback with subsequent action planning;
- structured 'fact finding' visits; study tours with a report;
- structured observation with feedback;
- use of psychometric tests with developmental feedback;
- leadership of a change initiative;
- course/module redesign with peer support and critique;
- 'master classes' with expert practitioners;
- acting as an in-house or external consultant.

Greater use of these kinds of opportunity for learning will move CPD beyond the course attendance mentality, promote greater relevance, facilitate transferability of learning, and of greatest significance, make CPD more satisfying to the individual. Moreover, widespread exploitation of such approaches should lead to greater institutional impact and help to manage and embed change more effectively. A learning culture will have been achieved when the majority of individuals in institutions engage with such activities as a normal part of their daily activities; and when individuals themselves make choices about *how* to engage with their CPD needs.

A related point is that learning can be triggered just as well by informal and accidental occurrences as it can through formal means. Everyone is surrounded by learning opportunities, but they only exist once they have been seen (see Garrick, 1998). Moreover, the opportunities for learning (and developing) tend to be self-sought and self-created. However, such an approach could have less successful outcomes if applied to, for example, financial management of a major research grant. In this situation everyone concerned might be more confident if an individual had received a formal introduction to effective, conventional systems for accounting. Striking the balance between formal and informal learning is partly determined by an individual's role and responsibilities. It is also linked to career progression and experience, in that individuals tend to benefit from formal CPD in the early stages of their career and less formal activities as they become more competent and confident.

CPD AND THE LEARNING ORGANIZATION

Experience confirms that CPD is more productive when individuals and groups engage with development activities in an institutional environment which is supportive of their needs and which encourages and recognizes commitment to improvement. Such 'learning organizations' create an infrastructure and culture which values and actively seeks out opportunities to enhance every employee's performance through a wide range of formal and informal mechanisms. The idea of the learning organization is relevant for CPD, as illustrated in the case study below.

The University as a Learning Organization

What does this mean in practice? According to the European Lifelong Learning Initiative (1994), a learning organization is any group, large or small, with a common bond, which:

- seeks to improve its performance through cooperative learning;
- invests in its own future through education and training;
- creates development opportunities and encourages all its people to fulfil their human potential;

- shares its vision of tomorrow with its people and stimulates them to challenge it, to change it and to contribute;
- integrates work and learning and inspires all its people to seek quality, excellence and continuous improvement;
- mobilizes all its human talent by emphasizing 'learning' rather than 'training';
- empowers everyone to broaden their horizons in harmony with their preferred styles of learning;
- uses open and flexible delivery technologies appropriately to create broader and more varied learning opportunities;
- responds proactively to the wider needs of the environment and encourages its people to do likewise;
- learns and relearns constantly in order to remain innovative, inventive, invigorating and in business.

Figure 5.14.2 represents diagrammatically the interrelationships that learning organizations establish between an analysis of different kinds of CPD and the personal and organizational activities necessary to ensure there is an appropriate institutional response at a variety of levels. Above all, everyone in a learning organization (individuals, managers, staff development professionals) must understand the need to:

- balance challenge in learning with security;
- distinguish between basic, additive, integrative and holistic competence (see Bowdon and Marton, 1998);
- ensure that some CPD learning outcomes are concerned with equipping individuals and groups with the capabilities for dealing with an unknown future, rather than simply preparing them better for their current professional role.

In its most effective form CPD ensures:

- *consolidation* and *updating* of existing skills;
- *extension* of core skills across the whole organization;
- *enhancement* of existing performances to deliver qualitative improvements and increased personal/organizational effectiveness;
- *preparation* for change at an individual, group and organizational level.

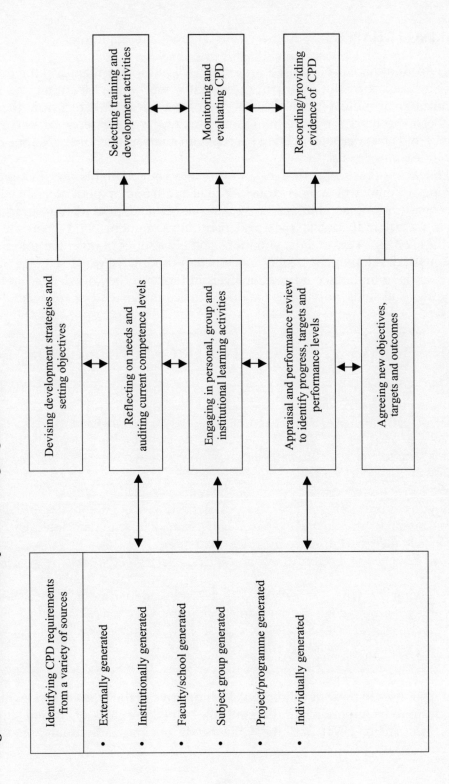

Figure 5.14.2 Interrelationships in learning organizations

MAKING IT HAPPEN

Thus far this chapter has raised a number of issues with regard to the ever-pressing need for CPD, the nature of effective work-based learning and the organizational context in which it might be best pursued. A recurrent theme has been the need for individual commitment, a strong sense of personal agency and clear decision making based on an analysis of choices. No one can do our learning for us!

'Enhancing practice' is designed to provoke your thoughts on CPD, highlighting a number of typical situations that academics experience. They are presented to stimulate thinking and to encourage readers to identify practical ways in which individuals, teams and institutions might respond. There are no 'off the shelf' answers to these situations, merely a series of potential solutions in terms of developing the people concerned. A productive way to engage with the cases is to undertake a needs analysis in terms of the knowledge, understandings and skills individuals may need to acquire, extend or enhance.

Enhancing Practice: Thinking About Different Approaches to CPD

Jenny is a new programme leader who is coordinating preparations for a forthcoming QAA subject review. She has been asked to prepare a schedule of activities over the next nine months to ensure this exercise is successful for all the 50 staff involved from two different departments. This schedule is to include all staff: academic, academic related and technical and support staff.

If you were Jenny, what kind of personal preparation should you make?

Lloyd is a contract researcher in a '3A' department as rated by the previous research assessment exercise. This team of researchers intends to improve their performance by at least one grade.

What developmental activities would you advise Lloyd and the team to engage in?

Following the long-term illness of her head of department, Carrie has been asked to manage the department in its move to a new location.

What skills would be required to ensure all staff feel comfortable and able to operate successfully in this new environment?

Your responses to these questions will be indicative of the types of CPD which you deem to be important for different roles. In taking stock of current situations (see Webb, 1994) and the CPD needs arising, individuals need to identify:

- key result areas (activities absolutely essential to effective performance);
- current levels of confidence and competence to perform well in these areas;
- areas of underperformance that need improvement;
- areas of strength to be built upon, extended or shared with others.

Although such a review focuses on the individual, subsequent collaborative reflection has been demonstrated to be an effective means of validating self-audit and encouraging individuals to move into developmental mode (see Martin and Double, 1998).

OVERVIEW

At one level of analysis, CPD can be seen as infinitely complex and the product of multiple-interacting factors from a variety of personal, organizational and systemic sources. At another level, what we call 'professional development' is much simpler; merely the external manifestation of individuals wanting to perform well, be recognized as professional and moving with the times. For most of us, reality probably lies somewhere between these two descriptions, with a pinch of self-interest and a wish for career advancement thrown in. Like most human endeavours it is frequently difficult to distinguish between 'wants' and 'needs', or between intrinsic and external motivations.

This chapter's central message is that individuals some years into their career need to recognize the necessity for regular updating, periodic retraining and further development with respect to their practice. To remain competent, such individuals should build appropriate development activities into their work on a regular, voluntary basis, knowing that this helps to ensure continuity of effectiveness and responsiveness to students and colleagues alike. In this sense, commitment to relevant forms of CPD represents not only an investment in one's own future career, but also an ethical duty of care for others. This being the case, the character, uptake, variety and volume of CPD taking place in our universities and higher education colleges at any given moment might be taken as an indicator of organizational and professional health. And like all forms of positive healthcare, prevention and self-regulation seem more appropriate and desirable than external prescription and invasive action.

REFERENCES

Ballantyne, R, Bain, J and Packer, J (1997) *Reflecting on University Teaching: Academics' stories*, DEET, Canberra, Australia

Baume, D (1998) *Portfolio Guide: Course H851*, Open University, Milton Keynes

Boud, D and Solomon, N (eds) (2001) *Work-based Learning; A new higher education?* Society for Research into Higher Education (SHRE)/Open University Press, Buckingham

Bowdon, I and Marton, F (1998) *The University of Learning: Beyond quality and competence in higher education*, Kogan Page, London

Bramley, P (1996) *Evaluating Training Effectiveness* (2nd edn), McGraw Hill, Maidenhead, Berks

Brew, A (1995) *Directions in Staff Development*, SHRE/Open University Press, Buckingham

Candy, PC (1995) Priorities for academic staff development in the nineties, *Australian Universities Review,* **38**(1), pp 16–20

Candy, PC (1996) Promoting lifelong learning: academic developers and the university as a learning organization, *International Journal for Academic Development,* **1**(1), pp 7–18

Dale, M (1994) Learning organizations, pp 23–33 in *Managing Learning,* ed C Mabey and P Iles, Routledge/Open University Press, London

European Lifelong Learning Initiative (1994) *Lifelong Learning: A survival concept for the 21st Century*, European Lifelong Learning Initiative, Brussels

Garrick, J (1998) *Informal Learning in the Workplace: Unmasking human resource development*, Routledge, London

Gibbs, G and Blackmore, P (1996) *Supporting Staff Development within Departments*, Oxford Centre for Staff Development, Oxford

Guskey, TR (2000) *Evaluating Professional Development*, Corwin Press, California

Harris, I (1995) Research related staff development – an approach, pp 102–16 in *Research, Teaching and Learning in Higher Education,* ed B Smith and S Brown, Kogan Page, London

Hersey, P and Blanchard, K (1988) *Management of Organisation Behaviour*, 5th edn, Prentice Hall, London

Higher Education Funding Council for England (HEFCE) (2000) *Rewarding and Developing Staff* Circular 00/56, HEFCE, Bristol

Institute of Personnel and Development (IPD) (1997) *The IPD policy and guidelines on CPD*,IPD, London

Mabey, C and Iles, P (eds) (1994) *Managing Learning*, Routledge/Open University Press, London

Margerison, CJ (1994) Action learning and excellence in management development, pp 109–17 in C Mabey and P Iles, *Managing Learning*, Routledge/Open University Press, London

Martin, G and Double, JM (1998) Developing higher education teaching skills through peer observation and collaborative reflection, *Innovations in Education and Training International,* **35**(2) (May), pp 161–70

National Committee of Inquiry into Higher Education (NCIHE) (1997) *Higher Education in the Learning Society (Dearing Report)*, HMSO, London

Nicholls, G (2001) *Professional Development in Higher Education*, Kogan Page, London

O'Neil, C and Wright, A (1994) *Recording Teaching Accomplishment: A Dalhousie guide to the teaching dossier*, 4th edn, Dalhousie University, Nova Scotia, Canada

Professional Associations Research Network (PARN) (2000) *Continuing Professional Development in the UK: Policies and programmes*, PARN, http://www.PARN.org.uk

Seldin, P, Annis, LF and Zubigarreta, J (1995) Using the teaching portfolio to improve instruction, pp 237–54 in *Teaching Improvement Practices,* ed A Wright and Associates, Anker, MASS

Webb, G (1994) *Making the Most of Appraisal: Career and professional development planning for lecturers*, Kogan Page, London

Webb, G and Murphy, D (2000) Organisational approaches to staff development to support teaching and learning, *Teacher Development,* **4**, pp 15–30

Weeks, PA (1996) The teaching portfolio: a professional development tool, *International Journal for Academic Development,* **1**(1), pp 70–74

FURTHER READING

McGill, I and Beaty, L (1992) *Action Learning: A practitioners' guide,* Kogan Page, London

Megginson, D and Clutterbuck, D (1995*) Mentoring in Action: A practical guide for managers,* Kogan Page, London

Pennington, RC (1996) Pursuing quality through work-based learning: the case for mentoring in higher education, *Management in Education,* **10**(2), pp 11–12

Wright, AW and associates (1995) *Teaching Improvement Practices: Successful strategies for higher education,* Anker, MASS

15 | Making Choices: Routes to Success

Steve Ketteridge, Stephanie Marshall
and Heather Fry

INTRODUCTION

This chapter presents some of the routes that academics have used to develop
their careers. It includes summaries of three recent research studies on aspects
of academic life, work and career development. Interwoven with the studies
are a snapshot of statistics of academic employment in the United Kingdom,
and a section on the use of career consultants, mentors and role models. The
intention is to provide a survey of the changing scene, to give insight into how
commentators view and make sense of it, and to highlight the diverse routes
to success. It is worth noting that 'success' to the academic is often a personal
construct, in that what is one person's success, could be another person's
imprisonment: for example, a teaching-only contract, freedom to do unre-
strained research, titles that provide status, flexible working hours and
performance indicator attainment. This chapter, therefore, is not designed as a
'how to do it guide', but instead takes on an exploratory role, highlighting
some key research findings alongside reference to a range of useful means of
gaining support to achieve whatever an individual academic might deem to
be 'success'. The chapter may also be a prompt for reflection on why a career
has gone in one direction rather than another, and provide ideas about possible routes for the future. For those seeking something more straightforward,
there are two potentially useful guides which readers of this volume, particularly in their own roles as mentors and advisers to younger academics, might
wish to recommend: Blaxter, Hughes and Tight (1998) and Royce Sadler
(1999).

CHANGING VIEWS OF ACADEMIC LIFE

In 1992 Halsey proclaimed that the academic profession had been subject to 'proletarianization', or deprofessionalization. He suggested it had perhaps been transformed into a 'professional bureaucracy' (1992: 124). He based this view on examination of the data from a survey of British academics conducted 20 years on from his first survey of academic life in Britain (Halsey and Trow, 1971). He defined the main characteristics of proletarianization as being firstly, a reduction in autonomy; secondly, insecurity of employment; and, thirdly, reduced chances for promotion (1992: 125). From this perspective, old-style professionalism was viewed as 'good', as it implied high status and a high degree of autonomy over work. Fulton (1996), for example, stresses that loss of autonomy is one of the characteristics of contemporary academic life. Cuthbert (1996) draws attention to another dimension of the debate, namely that for many academics 'professional' is (now?) a sobriquet with which they would rather not be tainted. For some academics, 'professional' carries overtones of being efficient and effective – an idea viewed favourably by some academics but with a degree of distaste by others. In the perception of the authors, views have not changed greatly since 1996.

There is much speculation and some hard information in the literature about the influence of discipline and institution on career pattern. Much of it stems from Becher's seminal work (1989) in which he described, discussed and analysed the influence of 'tribe' (discipline) on patterns of thought, work, career, teaching and research. Fulton drew on this work when suggesting 'the idea that there is a single, cohesive academic profession is both powerful and contested' (1996: 157). This is another theme of the literature: academia is so diverse that it does not constitute a single entity.

Another key feature often used in writing about academic careers (which owes much, at least in exposition, to Becher (1989)) is that of the evolution of an academic career, whereby the pursuit of research gives way over time to academic management and service. For some academics and commentators (eg Oakley, 1997, cited in Taylor, 1999), this facet is viewed as painful and undesirable. One way in which academics have sought to ameliorate this trend is through accepting management roles on a fixed-term basis of three to five years, and resisting the pressure to wholly 'go native'.

Taylor maintains that to help academics become 'players rather than pawns', they need to be aware of the process of change in universities (1999: back cover). He suggests that it is part of the tradition of universities to change, but the new feature of contemporary academe is the scale of change, which is now 'discontinuous rather than incremental' (1999: 2). There has been considerable discussion whether senior academics are relatively isolated from much of this change. For example, Altbach (1997, cited in Taylor) notes this to be the case in the United States, with Martin (1999) pointing out that this is certainly a view held by academic managers. Taylor, however, asserts that the 'academic underclass', the part-time and non-tenured or fixed term (see Table 5.15.1, page 278), are much more likely to be aware of change and multiple pressures.

The case study below is concerned with much of the same ground that the various commentators above have considered. It describes an empirical study which examined these areas from the perspective of staff in seven disciplines in 11 universities.

Academic Identities and Policy Change in Higher Education by Mary Henkel

---

The study summarized here (see Henkel, 2000 for a fuller version) was part of a comparative project in three countries. It was carried out by research teams from Brunel University, England, the University of Bergen, Norway, and the University of Gothenburg, Sweden. (See also Bauer *et al*, 1999; Bleiklie *et al*, 2000; Kogan and Hanney, 2000; Kogan *et al*, 2000).

Aims of the study

A key aim was to consider the implications of recent reforms for academic identities. The understanding of identity was drawn substantially from communitarian philosophy. This embodies an actor–structure perspective, within which it is possible to analyse the interplay in academic careers between the imperatives of distinctiveness and embeddedness in two communities, the discipline and the university. These communities shape individual identities, for example, in the myths and formative relationships that inform the language, academic agendas, values and self-perceptions of their members. At the same time, they provide the 'normative space' (Bleiklie, 1994) in which individuals make choices.

The study aimed to analyse how far policies changed the 'normative space' of academic identity development and what the implications were for academic values, agendas and self-esteem.

Methods

The main methods of inquiry were semi-structured interviews, questionnaires and documentary analysis. In England approximately 300 academics from seven disciplines (biochemistry, chemistry and physics, economics and sociology, history and English) were interviewed, based in 11 universities (seven pre-1992 and four post-1992).

The interviews were carried out in two stages. The first consisted of three case studies of quality assurance, research selectivity and the Enterprise in Higher Education initiative. In the second stage, interviews, supplemented by questionnaires, focused more directly on the implications of the whole raft of policy changes for academic identities.

Main findings

A key consequence of policy change was that universities assumed a higher profile in the dynamic between individual, discipline and institution. They had more power to shape the lives, practices and self-perceptions of academics. Departments and individuals were more open to scrutiny and intervention by senior academic managers and administrators. Academics lost power and status *vis-à-vis* other occupational groups in the university.

In this process institutions could become more distanced from their academic members. In effect, the discipline was reinforced as the dominant source of identity in academic lives. Departments and subject groups became more significant as teaching and research performance assumed more collective importance. Research assessment, together with a more competitive labour market, stimulated more publications, more conferences and more networks.

The structure of academic careers was changing. Graduate education was more structured. Post-doctoral experiences were more prolonged and uncertain. The established academic career was shorter. Inequalities of pay, security and sense of self-worth within and between institutions had increased, in a system where stratification had been reinforced rather than weakened by policy change.

Those whose identity had centred on teaching, particularly but not only in post-1992 universities, experienced loss of identity. Commitment to the research–teaching nexus remained strong in the humanities and the social sciences. Always weaker in the sciences, it was now under more pressure. As the imperatives of income generation hardened, scientists' research agendas required multiple networks and collaborations outside the institution, notably with industry.

Management was now a recognized component of academic career trajectories, although for managers, too, the discipline remained important to their identity.

Academic values remained robust, notably in the importance accorded academic autonomy, in concepts of higher education emphasizing personal and social development, and in curricula for developing intellectual rigour, critical judgement, depth of knowledge and understanding of a discipline.

Academics had, individually and collectively, developed a variety of more or less conscious strategies for conserving their identities in the face of competing values and agendas. Probably the most effective was that of accommodation. Individuals or departments, for example, accommodated into discipline-based curricula the aim of developing transferable skills within an economic instrumentalist educational agenda. Scientists accommodated industrial needs in their research agendas, while striving to sustain their own priorities.

Perhaps most important for the future was the resilience of younger academics. They were less likely than their seniors to have an exceptionalist view of their profession, in their expectations of society. They were, however, prepared to maintain individual and collective identities, in terms of chosen, largely traditional values. They were committed to their development as researchers and teachers, well embedded in their disciplines and focused on acquiring recognition within them.

QUALIFICATIONS TO WORK IN HIGHER EDUCATION

There is no national requirement for those teaching in higher education to possess a teaching or training qualification. The minimum qualification for academic staff is in practice a first degree, but usually most institutions will require a higher degree in the relevant discipline. In many cases, this will be a research degree which will appear as an essential, and virtually assumed, criterion for appointment. This reflects the fact that in making new appointments, many institutions are seeking to strengthen returns made in the research assessment exercise, and career progression often relates more to research output than educational or pedagogic knowledge.

For academic staff in disciplines where there is a requirement for a 'licence to practice', then clearly a professional qualification or a membership of a professional body will be an essential requirement for the post, and is usually the basic requirement for appointment.

Post-Dearing, across the sector, increasing attention has been given to the development of a threshold qualification in teaching and learning in higher education. The titles of awards vary from Postgraduate Certificates in Learning and Teaching in Higher Education or in Academic Practice (60 credits), to Postgraduate Diplomas (120 credits) to a full Masters qualification (180 credits). These are often validated by the individual institutions for their own staff, with an increasing number of programmes being externally accredited by the Institute for Learning and Teaching (ILT). Policy on these matters varies widely, and some institutions may make this a criterion for appointment, or may require new staff to complete an in-house programme leading to an award as part of their probationary period of employment. Some institutions allow accreditation of prior experiential learning (AP[E]L). Moving beyond these initial induction programmes, there is now concern to address both continuing professional development (CPD) and management development for succession planning. The former is being considered by the Institute for Learning and Teaching and is explored in detail in Chapter 14. The latter is a key issue highlighted in HEFCE 01/16 (2001), and explored in Chapter 6.

ACADEMIC STAFF WORKING IN HIGHER EDUCATION IN THE UK

The usual route for progression for the academic is from lecturer (including senior lecturer in the post-1992 universities) to the grade of senior lecturer (including principal lecturer in post-1992 universities) or reader. In the pre-1992 universities, the grade of senior lecturer may often be regarded as the 'career grade' for those staff who are competent in all areas of their academic practice, but make a particular contribution to two of the three key performance areas of research, teaching and learning, and administration. The same is true of principal lecturers in post-1992 institutions. The grade of reader is usually awarded to staff progressing along a research route, and universities set clear criteria on this basis. In the University of London, for example, for conferment of the title of reader the candidate will need to demonstrate 'standing and promise in the relevant subject or profession as established by important contributions to its advancement through publications, creative work or other appropriate forms of scholarship, and through teaching and administration' (University of London, 2000).

The title of professor may be achieved either through the senior (and principal) lecturer route, or more usually through the readership route. Again the criteria for appointment to professor vary from institution to institution, but in the University of London, for instance, these specify that in awarding this title 'regard shall be had to the person's national/international standing in the relevant subject or profession as established by outstanding contribution to its advancement through publications, creative work or through appropriate forms of scholarship, and through teaching and administration'.

Academic staff enter and leave the profession at various points along these career routes. Some of the more common reasons for movement include entry and re-entry to industry, commerce, the City and the professions, often driven by financial rewards.

The numbers of academic staff in UK institutions in different grades in the year 1998/99 are shown in Table 5.15.1. For this purpose the Higher Education

Statistics Agency (HESA) defines academic staff as those staff whose primary employment function is teaching only, teaching and research, or research only. This includes fixed-term staff, such as contract research staff working at different levels. The category of 'professors' includes heads of departments, professors, clinical professors and those senior research staff on similar salaries. 'Senior lecturers and researchers' include clinical senior lecturers and experienced research staff on similar salary scales.

Table 5.15.1 Numbers and distribution of academic staff in UK institutions in 1998/99

	Total	Full-time	Part-time
Numbers	131,136	112,374	18,762
Grade:			
	Total	Total	Total
Professors	8.2%	9.1%	3.3%
Senior lecturers and researchers	16.4%	17.7%	8.9%
Lecturers	38.2%	38.4%	36.9%
Researchers	26.7%	27.5%	21.2%
Other grades	10.5%	7.3%	29.7%
Primary function:			
Teaching/teaching and research	70.3%	69.2%	76.5%
Research only	29.7%	30.8%	23.5%
Clinical status:			
Non-clinical	94.6%	94.4%	95.8%
Clinical	5.4%	5.6%	4.2%
Gender:			
Female	34.8%	31.8%	52.8%
Male	65.2%	68.2%	47.2%

Adapted from Higher Education Statistics Agency, 2000

Some caution is needed when considering the proportions of academic staff that have reached the grade of professor. Because of differences in reporting to HESA by some pre-1992 universities, the numbers of professors may be undercounted.

What is striking from the figures in Table 5.15.1 is the gender imbalance. Men occupy slightly over two-thirds of full-time academic posts, and the majority of senior posts. In contrast women occupy slightly more than half of the part-time posts, and as their careers progress, remain 'locked' in the lower grades of posts.

The contrast in the types of post occupied by men and women has an impact on many other aspects of academic life. One notable area of difference is in research funding applications. A survey on research funding applications commissioned by the Wellcome Trust and the research councils, undertaken by the National Centre for Social Research (Blake and La Valle, 2000), showed that women were less likely than men to be eligible to apply for grants provided by the Wellcome Trust and all the research councils, except the Economic and Social Research Council. Such variations in terms of eligibility reflect the fact that women are over-represented among lower grades of academic staff and those with fixed-term contracts. Many grant schemes provided by the main funding bodies are not open to academic staff in these groups. However, when women applied for funding, they were as successful as their male colleagues in securing grants.

The case study below offers an interesting insight into the different routes to senior posts in higher education, and the accompanying training and development received for such roles.

New Managerialism and the Management of UK Universities by Rosemary Deem

---

Introduction

A multi-disciplinary project, New Managerialism and the Management of UK Universities, funded by the Economic and Social Research Council, was conducted by a team of researchers based at Lancaster University between October 1998 and November 2000. The remit of the project was to examine the extent to which 'new managerialism', a set of reforms of the management of publicly-funded services popular with many Western governments, was perceived to have permeated the management of UK universities. The study also explored the roles, practices, selection, learning and support of manager-academics. The first phase of the study comprised focus group discussions with learned societies from several disciplines, where respondents considered what was currently happening to the management of universities. The second phase involved interviews with 135 manager-academics (from head of department to vice-chancellor) and 29 senior administrators in 12 pre-1992 and post-1992 universities. The interviews explored the backgrounds, current management practices and perceptions of respondents. In phase 3, case studies of the cultures and management of four universities enabled comparison of the views of manager-academics with those of academics and support staff.

Academic managers' narratives and 'new managerialism'

The focus group data suggested that the UK higher education system was now highly managerial and bureaucratic, with declining trust and discretion. Higher workloads and long hours, finance-driven decisions, remote senior management teams and greater pressure for internal and external accountability were mentioned. Phase 2 interviewees noted changes to the environment (reduced funding, massification, research and teaching assessment) but were more positive about the effects. Respondents discussed their routes to management, emphasizing personal biographies, gender processes and identities defined by teaching, disciplinary commitment and research. Three typical routes into management were identified. Firstly, **'career track managers'** had had early and full acceptance of the management role but were a minority of interviewees in post-1992 universities, often in pursuit of higher salaries or fleeing dissatisfaction with teaching or research. The **'reluctant manager'** was found among fixed-term heads of department (HoDs) in pre-1992 institutions, and rejected the label 'manager'. Motivations included fear of the incompetence of others as manager-academics. Finally there was the **'good citizen'** route, often at a late-career stage and found in both pre-1992 and post-1992 institutions, motivated by repaying a perceived debt to the institution.

Analysis of the selection and training of academic managers

The study offers useful lessons about tenure and selection for management roles, as well as on manager-academics' learning. In post-1992 universities, a formal appointment process was common. Pre-1992 universities largely relied on colleague consultation with higher-level confirmation, or informally identifying suitable individuals. Informal selection mechanisms may exclude some eligible staff, including women. In the post-1992 sector most management roles were permanent, whereas temporary posts were common in the pre-1992 sector. The issue of temporary and permanent roles is complex. Permanent posts attract willing recruits with appropriate skills and knowledge, and no need to continue to pursue a research career. But incumbents are not always seen by 'managed' staff as accountable, and may become regarded as less effective after a while, with no route back to an academic career.

Temporary managers have a steep learning curve, but such posts allow academics to try out management roles with less risk to their academic careers, and can overcome initial reluctance by good candidates. Temporary manager-academics may also be perceived as more accountable by colleagues.

Only one-third of our sample had received any formal training, but most had engaged in important informal learning, including seeking out more experienced colleagues. This aspect of learning was often poorly supported. Interviewees related early management experiences to more onerous posts later; they drew on strengths, skills and knowledge involved in teaching and researching their own disciplines. Few felt that they received adequate feedback on their management role. In addition, many manager-academics felt overwhelmed by paperwork and e-mail, yet few universities studied had a management information strategy perceived to be effective.

APPROACHES TO CAREER DEVELOPMENT

Academics develop their careers in many different ways. Some have a very strategic and managed approach, others rely much more on serendipity, with most people mapping somewhere between these extremes.

Readers will recognize a number of different categories/styles of academic success amongst their colleagues. These include:

- the top class researcher;
- the good all-rounder;
- the political animal;
- the media star;
- the career teacher;
- the national authority on topics of the day;
- the committee person;
- the academic manager;
- the safe pair of hands;
- the competent administrator.

Many leading academics manage to combine a number of these traits. Some exceptional academics excel in a wide range of areas and set themselves onto a career for vice-chancellorship. In some of these models the way to succeed is explicit. The chances of a particular strategy leading to success will depend on many factors, not least the type of institution in which the academic works.

> ## Enhancing Practice
>
> - What factors were influential in leading you to your current position?
> - Do you have a clear vision of where you want your career to develop?
> - If you do, how are you going to get there?
> - Who or what is going to help and hinder you?

The *Times Higher Educational Supplement* has acknowledged the complex roles academics may assume by giving advice for the aspiring TV performer. Adrian Mourby, writing in the *Higher* (2001), offers some advice, perhaps tongue in cheek, for academics who want to give their careers a kick-start through some media exposure. He notes that radio and television are always looking for academic experts who can, given an issue, offer expert opinion in a given field without any axe to grind. A list of 10 dos and don'ts for aspiring TV dons (adapted from his article) includes:

- *General appearance*
  Important – be distinctive and keep in shape. Remember, 'the camera adds 10 lbs'.
- *Hair*
  Again, be distinctive and decisive. Some academic media staff like a splash of colour.
- *Clothes*
  You might get some advice on your wardrobe. Dress for the camera and be snappy.
- *Choose your subject*
  Something to capture the public's imagination.
- *Sound bites*
  You will have to be knowledgeable in a 30-second sound bite. There is no time for 'it all depends what you mean by…'
- *To err is maddening*
  Be fluent – retakes are expensive.
- *Gimmick*
  Find something that makes you distinctive that the public can remember.
- *Cultivate the press officer*
  University press officers are often asked by the media for an expert who can string a few words together.
- *Be prepared to be silly*
  You might need to be willing to bow to the producer's every whim.

- *Push yourself*
  Do you really think the current batch of academic media stars were sought out by producers and coaxed reluctantly in front of the camera?

Each career route requires different types of support systems, which may include networking, careers consultants, patronage and the use of role models and mentors. These systems can give help, advice, reassurance and confidence. Furthermore, they allow sharing of experiences and understanding of criteria for promotion and possible hidden agendas. A range of 'developmental' activities as distinct to training programmes has been uncovered in two surveys recently undertaken by the Higher Education Staff Development Agency (HESDA), and is outlined in the case study below.

Surveys on Current Practice in Higher Education Institutions (HEIs) on Management Development by Anne Sibbald

Bett (Independent Review of Higher Education Pay and Conditions, 1999, para 65) noted:

> The present provision of training and development for higher education staff is said to be generally insufficient either for enhancing the effectiveness of their contribution or for helping them realize their full potential. More HE institutions need to take the lifelong learning agenda seriously for their own staff... and there is a particular need for more and better training for those... who will assume senior management roles in the sector.

During 2000/2001, two surveys were undertaken by the Higher Education Staff Development Agency (HESDA), funded by the HEFCE 'Good Management Practice' fund. The first survey was an audit of baseline data with respect to the extent and range of management training and development activity in support of senior management staff. The term 'management development' was defined as the range of activities, including formal courses and informal developmental activities such as mentoring, work shadowing, away-days, appraisal systems and secondments. The second survey aimed to establish the current level of provision for staff who are in, or about to commence, the role of head of department (or equivalent).

Methodology

Both projects invited staff to complete an in-depth questionnaire, followed up with a number of interviews and focus groups.

Key findings

- Management development activity was more a concern for junior to middle managers only.
- Any training and/or development activity which was undertaken was ad hoc, individualized and relatively informal.
- A small number of institutions had mandatory formal programmes which drew on corporate objectives, and included an induction and continuing professional development (CPD), the former including psychometric profiling and the latter including mentoring, action-learning and case studies.

CAREER GUIDANCE AND SUPPORT

Mentoring

Mentoring is a professional relationship in which an experienced individual provides support and guidance to assist the career development of a more junior individual. Over the past two decades, mentoring has been used primarily as a means of inducting staff into a new role or institution and, increasingly, as a means of providing mentors as role models to encourage 'minorities' to aspire to more senior roles, or roles within areas traditionally deemed to be more appropriate for a particular gender or mindset – for example, girls into science and technology. The general objectives of mentoring include firstly, the provision of professional and personal support; secondly, assistance with the professional development of individuals; and, thirdly, to motivate and encourage 'mentees'. Generally, mentor and mentee set time-bound, realistic goals, and further to meetings, agree action points to be addressed in readiness for the next meeting's agenda, thus aiding the mentee to move forward toward the initial agreed goals (Field, 2001). Scanning the Internet reveals a burgeoning interest in mentoring, particularly for those aspiring to senior positions in management and leadership, with mentors and 'coaches' advertising their services online.

Of more recent interest, however, has been the use of action learning sets – peer groups of about four to seven people – to support the professional development of individuals seeking career development, most particularly in the area of management development. Action learning sets are designed to address the specific needs of the 'set', and require agreed action by the end of each meeting. Sets may or may not be facilitated, or may start with a facilitator and later become self-facilitating. Whichever the case, it is important for ground rules to be negotiated at the outset.

Action learning is based on the relationship between reflection and action, where the focus is on issues and problems as faced by individuals. The group reflects on these together, assisting with planning of future action further to structured attention and support of the group (Beaty and McGill, 2001). Action learning has proved popular in delivering results with a number of key national programmes in Britain, most particularly HESDA's Top Management Programme and the '94 Group's Best Practice for Senior Management Through Inter-Institution Collaboration. In both these programmes, action learning sets are instrumental in enhancing opportunities for participants firstly, not only to learn from each other, but to learn more about other institutions and institutional practices; secondly, to highlight immediate management issues which cannot easily be resolved through lectures and seminars; and, thirdly, to provide space in which participants can build relationships and networks which will provide mutual support well after the training programme.

Career development consultants

Some academics have found the services of professional career development consultants helpful at critical points in their career. Career development consultants can provide invaluable assistance when individuals realize that they are not on the career path that will provide them with what they need (eg financial or intellectual rewards), or at times of restructuring of organizations when offers of severance may be on the table. Indeed, some institutions may provide professional support to staff at times of organizational restructuring. Career consultants offer a range of services, and may help the client with an analysis of personal skills, knowledge, motivation, specialist knowledge, beliefs and opportunities for networking at different levels. This can be of help in formulating a personal development plan and/or assessing one's potential for an alternative career, either inside or outside higher education.

CONCLUSIONS

This chapter has provided a brief overview of what the authors perceive to be possible career routes and potential support for academics seeking 'success' in their careers. Four key themes emerge, which remain under-researched and underdeveloped.

Firstly, the issue of fixed-term versus time-bound managerial positions provides an interesting source of debate. The managerial route to success afforded by post-92 institutions is recognized by many as offering a clear and well-articulated career route, with a permanent hierarchical management structure.

Secondly, an attempt to offer a set of occupational standards and competences (as has been done in other public sector organizations) to guide academics as to what constitutes the skills and competences they will need to acquire to pursue different career routes in, for example, research management, media work, management generalist positions, has not been forthcoming.

Thirdly, it is interesting to note both the paucity and 'ad hocery' of well-planned and coherent training to underpin different career routes. Unlike the introduction of accredited programmes of teaching and learning or academic practice, which induct academics into their teaching and/or academic roles, there appears to be little in the way of coherent continuing professional development being planned, let alone offered, by the sector in support of other aspects of career development. To pursue a career route in academia still requires individuals to determine their own fate: determining individual goals, watching out for 'routes' which might deliver goals and ultimately success, and watching out for training and development activities or opportunities which might assist in delivering the desired success.

Finally, gender remains a key issue when examining routes to success. The factors contributing to the gender imbalance in senior positions in higher education still remain under-explored, despite a number of interesting studies (Eggins, 1997). Until these four issues are addressed, higher education will continue to reward those for whom the routes to success appear quite straightforward, while others attempt to fathom the terrain. Hopefully this chapter will have offered a few pointers to those in the latter category.

REFERENCES

Altbach, P (1997) An international crisis? The American professoriate in comparative perspective', *Daedalus*, **126**(4), pp 315–38

Bauer, M et al (1999) *Transforming Universities: Changing patterns of governance in Swedish higher education*, Jessica Kingsley, London

Beaty, E and McGill, I (2001) *Action Learning: A guide for professional, management and educational development*, Kogan Page, London

Becher, T (1989) *Academic Tribes and Territories: Intellectual enquiry and the culture of disciplines*, SRHE/Open University Press, Buckingham

Blake, M and La Valle, I (2000) *Who Applies for Research Funding? Key factors shaping funding application behaviour among women and men in British higher education institutions*, independent summary report for National Centre for Social Research, Wellcome Trust

Blaxter, L, Hughes, C and Tight, M (1998) *The Academic Career Handbook*, Open University Press, Buckingham

Bleiklie, I (1994) Justifying the evaluative state: new public management ideals in higher education, *European Journal of Education*, **33**(3), pp 299–316

Bleiklie, I et al (2000) *Policy and Practice in Higher Education: Norway*, Jessica Kingsley, London

Cuthbert, R (ed) (1996) *Working in Higher Education*, Society for Research into Higher Education(SRHE)/Open University Press, Buckingham

Eggins, H (ed) (1997) *Women as Leaders and Managers in Higher Education*, SRHE/Open University Press, Buckingham

Field, J (2001) *Learning Organisations and Higher Education Institutions*, Briefing paper 88, Higher Education Development Agency, Sheffield

Fulton, O (1996) Which academic profession are you in?, in *Working in Higher Education*, ed R Cuthbert, SRHE/Open University Press, Buckingham

Halsey, AH (1992) *Decline of Donnish Dominion: The British academic profession in the twentieth century*, Clarendon Press, Oxford

Halsey, AH and Trow, M (1971) *The British Academics*, Faber and Faber, London

Henkel, M (2000) *Academic Identities and Policy Change in Higher Education*, Jessica Kingsley, London

Higher Education Statistics Agency (2000) www.hesa.ac.uk

Higher Education Funding Council for England(HEFCE) (2000) *Rewarding and Developing Staff* (circular 00/056), www.hefce.ac.uk

HEFCE (2001) *Rewarding and Developing Staff in Higher Education*, 01/16, HEFCE, Bristol

Independent Review of Higher Education Pay and Conditions (1999) *Independent Review of Higher Education Pay and Conditions: Report of a committee chaired by Sir Michael Bett (the Bett Report)* The Stationery Office, London

Kogan, M and Hanney, S (2000) *Reforming Higher Education*, Jessica Kingsley, London

Kogan, M et al (2000*) Transforming Higher Education: A comparative study*, Jessica Kingsley, London

Martin, E (1999) *Changing Academic Work*, SRHE/Open University Press, Buckingham

Mourby, A (2001) You're smart, but are you 'box' clever?, *Times Higher Education Supplement* 1485, 4 May, pp 18–19

Oakley, F (1997) The elusive academic profession, *Daedalus*, **126**(4), pp 43–66

Royce Sadler, D (1999) *Managing Your Academic Career*, Allen and Unwin, St Leonards, Australia

Taylor, P (1999) *Making Sense of Academic Life*, SRHE/Open University Press, Buckingham

University of London (2000) University of London Ordinances: 1, September 2000: Ordinance 16 para 7 (www.lon.ac.uk/statutes-ordinances/)

INDEX

NB: numbers in italics indicate figures and tables
personal perspectives and reflections are indexed under case studies